The Elizabethan Theatre IX

The Elizabethan Theatre IX

Papers given at the Ninth International
Conference on Elizabethan Theatre held at
the University of Waterloo, in July 1981

Edited and with an introduction by
G. R. HIBBARD
Department of English
University of Waterloo

Published in collaboration with the
University of Waterloo

P. D. Meany

Canadian Cataloguing in Publication Data

International Conference on Elizabethan Theatre
(9th: 1981: University of Waterloo)
The Elizabethan theatre IX

"Published in collaboration with the University of Waterloo."
Includes bibliographical references and index.
ISBN 0-88835-018-X

1. Theater—England—History—16th century—
Congresses. 2. English drama—Early modern and
Elizabethan, 1500-1600—History and criticism—
Congresses. 3. Shakespeare, William, 1564-1616—
Dramatic production—Congresses. I. Hibbard, G. R.,
1915-.   II. Title.

PN2589.I52 1981   792'.0942   C86-094552-9

This book has been published with the help of a grant from the Canadian Federation for the Humanities, using funds provided by the Social Sciences and Humanities Research Council of Canada.

Printed and bound in Canada by
T. H. Best Printing Company Limited
Don Mills, Ontario
for
P. D. Meany Company Inc.
Box 534, Port Credit
Ontario, Canada L5G 4M2

Acknowledgments

Like its predecessors, the Ninth International Conference on Elizabethan Theatre, held at the University of Waterloo in July 1981, owed
its existence to the support it received from without the University as
well as from within. A generous grant from the Social Sciences and
Humanities Research Council of Canada was supplemented by
another from the Research Grant Subcommittee of the University
itself; and the English Department could always be relied on for
practical assistance of an unobtrusive yet indispensable kind. I am,
indeed, grateful to Bill Macnaughton, Chairman of the Department, to
Robin Banks, the Dean of Arts, and to J. F. Willms, the Assistant
Dean. I also owe much to Mrs. Diane Mew who did the work of copy-
editing this volume, and I am particularly indebted to three graduate
students, Gabrielle Bailey, Sheryl Loeffler, and John Greenwood, for
the tactful efficiency with which they organized the movements of
their flock of wayward, absorbed-in-argument academics.

One paper included here draws heavily on hitherto unpublished
material of various kinds. Proper acknowledgments of permissions
readily given are made in the appropriate places, but a special word of
thanks is due to the Society of Authors acting on behalf of the Estate
of George Bernard Shaw, to Penguin Books, and to the Governors of
the Royal Shakespeare Theatre at Stratford-upon-Avon.

This book has been published with the help of a grant from the
Canadian Federation for the Humanities, using funds provided by the
Social Sciences and Humanities Research Council of Canada.

G. R. H.

Contents

Introduction

The essays printed in this volume were originally given as papers at the Ninth Waterloo Conference on Elizabethan Theatre, held in July 1981. The theme of that conference was "The Staging of Plays in the Age of Shakespeare," a topic which still remains, after some two hundred years of patient labour on the one hand and impatient guessing on the other, almost as baffling and elusive as Ophelia finds the dumb show in *Hamlet*. We too have our troubles over this episode; but they are not hers. Unlike Ophelia, we know what the dumb show "means," in both senses of that word, because we have listened to the Ghost's revelations, and to the Prince's statement of his purpose in having the Players perform "The Murder of Gonzago." But if we are to see the dumb show as Ophelia sees it, there is much more we need to know or be sure of than any of the three earliest texts can tell us. Does the Player King sit "downe in an Arbor," as the reporter of Q1—influenced, perhaps, by his memories of *The Spanish Tragedy?*—assures us he should; or does he lie "downe vppon a bancke of flowers," as Q2 and F substantially agree that he should? The Ghost will not help us here, for all he tells us is that he was sleeping in his orchard when he was poisoned by his brother. How, moreover, does the arbour or bank of flowers, as the case may be, manage to outdo Birnam Wood by finding its way unaided on to the stage-upon-the-stage, and off again when the play-within-the-play is suddenly broken off and brought to its premature close? None of our three texts gives us so much as a hint about the practical solution to these necessary questions. Nor do they concur about what is to be done with the body of the dead Player King. Q1 simply ignores it, yet shows no hesitation whatever about requiring it to enter, in resurrected form, a minute later to play its part in "The Mousetrap." Q2, characteristically more considerate and generous, introduces "some three or foure" to carry the corpse away; while F, cheeseparing as usual, reduces that inexact number to an equally inexact "some two or three Mutes."

The questions the dumb show poses are not, of course, insoluble; but in order to answer them we have to make use of information derived from other parts of *Hamlet*—for example, "Let four captains/ Bear Hamlet like a soldier to the stage"—and from other plays. The same observation also holds good for the major issues of staging in general. These can, as Ronald Huebert concisely reminded members of the conference when he spoke about the staging of a specific play, conveniently take the form of three separate yet closely related questions. What was the design of the playing place where a play was first put on? What was the size, composition, and ability of the company that commissioned it? What were the particular demands, in the shape of properties and the like, that it made on the company's resources? By sheer good fortune, it was precisely these questions and others intimately connected to them that the contributors to this volume sought to answer.

D. F. Rowan, who has given so much to these conferences ever since they began in 1968, set the stage for what was to follow with a judicious survey of the theory that the public theatre had its origins in the inn-yard. The story he tells is one of rise, dominance, decline, and rise again. Starting with Malone's espousal of this hypothesis, Rowan shows how it hardened into orthodoxy in the nineteenth and early twentieth centures; was vigorously challenged in the 1960s by Glynne Wickham and others, who asserted the claims of other playing places, such as the great hall of the great house, the town hall, and, above all, the court; but has since been resuscitated by David Galloway and by O. J. Brownstein, who has discovered that plays were being performed at the Saracen's Head in Islington by 1557, and that playhouses were operating "in the precincts of the Bell Savage Inn" by the mid 1560s and at the Bell Inn by the early 1570s. Knowing far too much about Elizabethan playhouses to commit himself to any theory which suggests a common origin for all of them, Rowan concludes that the inn and the inn-yard did exert an influence on the design of some of them.

T. J. King, who gave a paper at the Third Conference in 1970, turns his attention to the second division of the overall theme with an account of "The King's Men on Stage: Actors and Their Parts, 1611-1632." Challenging T. W. Baldwin's belief that when Shakespeare wrote his plays "The play was regularly fitted to the company, not the company to the play," King uses surviving stage-plots from the 1590s to demonstrate how parts were divided at that time between the sharers in a company, the boys, and the hired men. He then goes on to apply the same kind of analysis to ten plays performed by the King's men over a period of some twenty years for which there is information about who played which role. The results are consistent and very illuminating. In these plays the leading actors usually played one major part apiece; so did the boys; while the hired men did a lot of doubling in minor roles. The most important of King's findings is that it was the length of a part, not its nature, that determined which actor should play it. The company took it for granted that a sharer would be versatile.

King's meticulous survey of the evidence leaves one in no doubt that the King's Men did indeed allot roles in the manner he suggests. Can one, then, assume that other companies pursued the same policy? Ronald Huebert's consideration of Shirley's *The Lady of Pleasure*, first performed by Queen Henrietta's Company at the Cockpit in Drury Lane in 1635, makes it plain that it would be unwise to do so. It is true that Richard Perkins, the company's leading player, was versatile enough; but there is much in the play, including parts which appear to have been written for the company's thin man, William Robbins, and its fat man, William Sherlock, that gives the impression of type-casting. Tailored to fit the players, *The Lady of Pleasure* also exploits the design of the theatre, the taste of its patrons, and their readiness to respond to the significance of "hand-held articles which not only contribute to the action but also reveal the social circumstances or personal inclinations" of the characters.

In its recognition that the language of the theatre is not confined to words alone Huebert's paper leads on naturally to Barbara A. Mowat's "The Getting Up of the Spectacle" which concerns itself with one aspect of the visual impact a play can make: the costuming. Her main point is that for an audience in Shakespeare's day, accustomed as it was to see in clothing a kind of language which told one much about an individual's social standing, the costuming of a play was no mere matter of show but could well become an important part of the meaning. In plays written prior to 1576, dress, she argues, had two distinct functions: it could be used for purely symbolic purposes, as it is in Redford's *Wyt and Science*; or simply for disguise, as it is in Gascoigne's *Supposes*. By the time of John Lyly, however, and especially in his *Gallathea*, the two functions coalesce. Once this has happened, there is no looking back. Clothing is used for ends that become ever more complex, until they find their culmination in such Jacobean masterpieces as *Macbeth*, *The Revengers Tragedy*, and *Volpone*.

Alan Dessen too is interested in non-verbal language, but of another sort. "Interpreting Stage Directions: Elizabethan Clues and Modern Detectives" illuminates the visual from a different angle. Drawing his material from a wide range of sources, he demonstrates that the stage directions in plays tend to fall into groups, and even, on occasions, to take the same form as one another. Beginning with the common formula "as from dinner" and what it implies—crumbs, napkins, and the like—he goes on to explore the significance of other well-worn phrases, such as "with Rosemary, as from a wedding" and "as from hunting." These and many others like them were, he contends, clear signals, immediately intelligible to actors and spectators alike, often serving as a kind of theatrical shorthand to portray actions that had just taken place off stage, and thus to widen the scope of the play in which they occurred.

Dessen is emphatically of the opinion that the plays which have survived from Elizabethan times are "theatrical scripts not literary texts." This view of them is shared by Random Cloud—a pseudonym that sounds right though it looks wrong, and neatly reveals through its transparent obfuscation. His "The Psychopathology of Everyday Art" has a target in sight—the modern editor of Shakespeare—but he approaches that target by a seemingly devious route. His point of departure is a close examination of George Bernard Shaw's use of variant speech prefixes in his *Press Cuttings*, *Pygmalion*, and, most strikingly, *Saint Joan*. Acutely bringing out the significance of these variations and the intimate connection between them and Shaw's whole method of composition, Cloud then proceeds to apply the same kind of biblioanalysis to Shakespeare's *Richard II*, as it appears in the First Quarto of 1597, where variant speech prefixes are common; in the New Penguin edition, where speech prefixes have been regularized; and in John Barton's promptbook for his production of the play in 1973, where variant speech prefixes are back again in a text that is "confused and incomplete and inconsistent in the ways a promptbook is not in theory supposed to be." There is certainly food for editorial thought here; but the challenge to editors would be much stronger than it is if Cloud had not ignored a crucial consideration: Shaw was his own publisher, and a demon proof-reader; whereas Shakespeare either did not read the proofs of such of his plays as were published in his lifetime, or was an execrably bad proof-reader.

The soliloquy, so common in Elizabethan plays, can set its own problems for editors and producers, since there is nothing in the early texts to show whether it is to be spoken directly to the audience or as though no audience were present. In some cases, such as Richard's opening speech in *Richard III* at one end of the scale, and Macbeth's "If it were done when 'tis done" at the other, there is no room for doubt; but between these two extremes there is a patch of grey, which attracts Herbert Weil's attention in his "'I Know You All': Possible

Assaults upon and Invitations to the Audience by Shakespeare's Characters." When Prince Hal makes his much debated speech at the end of I. ii of *1 Henry IV*, he has, Weil points out, spoken to two people only, Falstaff and Poins; and they, large though Falstaff is, seem insufficient to qualify as "all." It therefore follows, Weil goes on to argue, that the speech should be delivered not merely *to* but also *at* the spectators in the theatre. Drawing a nice parallel between this soliloquy and Cressida's speech at the end of I. ii of *Troilus and Cressida*, Weil suggests that in both cases the audience is being asked to think about the implications of what they are hearing, and are thus being drawn into the play, as it were. His most convincing example of this process is, however, Benedick's justification of his *volte-face* in II. iii of *Much Ado About Nothing*, which Donald Sinden in 1976 played just as he thinks it should be played.

The problem of how to secure participation from the audience was, perhaps, the most difficult that confronted the English actors who began to take plays to the countries of Northern Europe in the last two decades of the sixteenth century, for at that time their performances were given in English. Nevertheless, according to Fynes Moryson, recalling what he saw in Frankfort in 1592, the players managed to make themselves understood by "their gesture and Action." Jerzy Limon follows the fortunes of these men in his "English Players 'Beyond the Seas': Staging Problems." Round about 1600, he tells us, the travelling companies abandoned English and began to use German. At much the same time, they started to attach themselves to various courts. But while they became more secure as a result, they still relied heavily on music and dance, especially, one assumes, when they made their way to Limon's native Poland, taking with them not only their wives but also their theatre; for, he believes, a theatre built in Gdansk about 1610 was actually modelled on the Fortune.

When the people of Gdansk erected this building they were, quite unknowingly, anticipating a development which would not take place elsewhere until the nineteenth century, and which still continues today, as Jill Levenson shows in her "The Recovery of the Elizabethan Stage," an admirably lucid and concise survey of the fortunes of the Elizabethan stage after the closing of the theatres in 1642. For over a hundred years the subject was completely neglected, except in so far as the players of Shakespeare's day could be handily treated as whipping boys, and made responsible for the many "errors" in the plays. The first sign of a change in attitude is to be found in Dr. Johnson's notes to his edition, where there is a recognition that the plays were written for a particular kind of theatre. This trend was carried much further by Malone; but it was in Germany that Tieck sought to create something like an Elizabethan stage, and thus initiated a movement which was to lead to the experiments of William Poel, the building of the Festival Theatre at Stratford, Ontario, and, finally, the projects now under way for the building of replicas of the Globe in Detroit, Victoria, B.C., and on the Bankside in London. In its end the conference had returned to its beginning—playing places.

G. R. Hibbard
Department of English
University of Waterloo

"Inns, Inn-Yards, and Other Playing Places"

D. F. ROWAN

Something over fifty years ago W. J. Lawrence, in the Preface to *Pre-Restoration Stage Studies*, invited his audience "to climb certain craggy peaks of knowledge, all of which are trackless and most of them untrodden." With characteristic authority Lawrence went on to promise "the bringing to light of some [new] treasure-trove".[1] My topic is "Inns, Inn-Yards, and Other Playing Places," and I regret that I cannot repeat Lawrence's promise, or claim to guide you over trackless and untrodden terrain. Nevertheless, I do believe that it will be useful at this time to survey the paths and positions taken by past and present scholars in their attempt to place the inn and the inn-yard in the matrix of the Elizabethan theatre.

The baseline for such a survey is established by Edmund Malone when he writes in 1821:

> Many of our ancient dramatick pieces . . . were performed in the yards of carrier's inns, in which, in the beginning of Queen Elizabeth's reign, the comedians, who then first united themselves in companies, erected an occasional stage. The form of these temporary playhouses seems to be preserved in our modern theatre. The galleries, in both, are ranged over each other on three sides of the building. The small rooms under the lowest of these galleries answer to our present boxes; and it is observable that these, even in theatres which were built in a subsequent period expressly for dramatick exhibitions, still retained their old name, and are frequently called *rooms*, by our ancient writers. The yard bears a sufficient resemblance to the pit, as at present in use. We may suppose the stage to have been raised in this area, on the fourth side, with its back to the gateway of the inn, at

---

1. 1927; rpt. New York, 1967, p. [vii].

which the money for admission was taken. Thus, in fine weather, a play-house not incommodious might have been formed.[2]

In a footnote to these remarks Malone cites "the continuator of Stowe's Chronicle," who of the seventeen playhouses erected between the years 1570 and 1630 "reckons five *innes* or common *osteries* turned into playhouses." He notes as well the passing reference of 1664 in Richard Flecknoe's *Short Discourse of the English Stage*. The actors ". . . set up Theatres, first in the City, (as in the Inn-yards of the Cross-Keyes, and Bull in Grace and Bishops-Gate Street at this day is to be seen). . . ."[3]

Malone's statement hardened into dogma as the century advanced and the orthodox position was restated by T. Fairman Ordish in 1894. Writing of the travelling companies of professional players he notes that:

> The company usually waited on the mayor with their license, and after giving him a specimen of their quality, they gave a public performance in the guildhall, after which they were rewarded from the corporation treasury. These performances were often followed by performances given in the inns or inn-yards, when the players' reward was the largess of the guests and visitors.[4]

Whether the incipient heresy resting in the phrase "given in the inns or inn-yards" was deliberate or unintentional I cannot say, but Ordish goes on in the expected vein when he shifts from the provinces to London and writes:

> The inns in and about London became visited in this way very frequently; and it may be said that in the history of the London stage the immediate predecessor of the playhouse was the inn-yard. The resemblance of the ancient inn-yards to the interior of theatres . . . has been frequently pointed out.[5]

Notwithstanding this seemingly solid commitment to the inn-yard, Ordish had earlier glanced at the ancient amphitheatres in which religious plays were acted and had connected them with the bull and bear rings of the Bankside.

> Therefore, looking at the amphitheatres on the Surrey side of London, in accordance with the terms of our thesis, we may conclude that we have here

2. *The Plays and Poems of William Shakespeare*, "An Historical Account of the English Stage" (1821; rpt. New York, 1966), III, 71-72.
3. Cited from E.K. Chambers, *The Elizabethan Stage* (Oxford, 1923), IV, 369.
4. *Early London Theatres* (1894; rpt. London, 1971), p. 27.
5. Ibid., pp. 27-28.

a visible evidence of tradition which may have affected both the form in which plays were presented in London before the building of playhouses, and also the form of the playhouses themselves.[6]

E. K. Chambers in *The Mediaeval Stage* of 1903 neither cites Ordish nor comments on the amphitheatres; in fact he is squarely in the path of the true believers when he writes of the players that:

> In the towns they would give their first performance before the municipality in the guild-hall and take a reward. Then they would find a profitable pitch in the courtyard of some old-fashioned inn, with its convenient range of outside galleries.[7]

This comment on the inn-yard is only a passing reference in a general discussion of the players of interludes and we shall see that when Chambers comes to deal directly with the subject of the inn-yards, his position has been substantially modified.

In 1912 W. J. Lawrence, the self-proclaimed champion of the inn-yard, enters the lists by laying claim to "the mild honours of a pioneer" and stating that his collection of papers (*The Elizabethan Playhouse and Other Studies*) embodies "full details of the evolution of the English theatre in its primary and secondary stages, or, in other words, from its inception in the inn-yards until the close of the seventeenth century."[8] I might just note that it is easy at this date to patronize the flamboyant Lawrence who seems to have dreamed of taking all knowledge as his province, and who never hesitated to proclaim his findings as the gospel truth. Such scholars are vulnerable and it is easy to point to their errors, but one must remember as well the many points on which future scholarship has proved them correct. One should remember, for example, that it was Lawrence, not Joseph Quincy Adams, who first identified in 1913 the plans of the Cockpit-in-Court discovered and published by Hamilton Bell. Some years ago I noted this fact, as well as a bound collection of some ten articles and off-prints gathered together by Lawrence and bearing his autograph and the date, 1920.[9] One of the interesting features of this collection is the extensive marginalia in Lawrence's hand. The articles are asterisked and underlined and question-marked in pen and pencil. Sometimes a long comment fills the bottom of the page; sometimes a simple "no" or "wrong" is boldly written. T. S. Graves's well-known

6. Ibid., pp. 14-15.
7. Oxford, II, 189-90.
8. 1912; rpt. New York, 1963, p. viii.
9. "The Cockpit-in-Court," *The Elizabethan Theatre* [I], ed. David Galloway (Toronto, 1969), p. 94.

article, "The Act Time in Elizabethan Theatres," is particularly
scored with question marks and antagonistic comments, but I have
since been gratified to note that the upshot of all the "academic
graffiti" was a most generous review of Graves's study. More amusing
still—and perhaps most revealing of the probing and questioning
nature of Lawrence's mind—is the fact that the margins of his own
article, "The Elizabethan Stage Throne" are filled with the same
exclamations and question marks. Lawrence had evidently changed
his mind on a number of points since publication. Having paid what I
intend to be an honest tribute to the pioneering work of a scholar-
adventurer, I feel I can now return to a candid review of Lawrence's
position on the inn-yard.

In commenting on the circumstances which led to the building of
the Theatre in 1576 he writes:

> No evidence exists to show that up to the period when James Burbage solved
> a difficult problem by building the Theatre under protection of a royal
> patent, either players or playgoers were otherwise than content with the
> primitive histrionic conditions obtaining in the several inn-yards. For years
> it had been customary to give performances twice or three times a week on
> removable stages . . . in the yards of well-known hostells like the Cross Keys
> in Grace-church Street, the Bull in Bishopgate Street, and the Bell Savage on
> Ludgate Hill.[10]

Following Ordish, Lawrence writes that the players

> were forced to evolve a suitable playhouse out of their varied experiences
> both in public and in private, in town and country. For the reason that the
> old bull- and bear-baiting amphitheatres on the Bankside potently indicated
> how the greatest number of spectators could be accommodated in the least
> possible space, the Theatre was built, like them, of wood and circular or
> octagonal in shape.[11]

Noting the fact that both the Theatre and the Curtain were what
Glynne Wickham was to characterize as "multi-purpose arenas,"
Lawrence notes that the baiting of bulls and bears demands a clear
arena: "hence probably the main reason why the inn-yard principle of
the removable stage was adopted. . . ."[12]

To reinforce his belief in the primacy of the inn-yard in the genesis
of the playhouse he cites the fact that the space occupied by the

10. "The Elizabethan Playhouse," *The Elizabethan Playhouse and Other Studies*, (1912;
rpt. New York, 1963), p.p. 1-2.
12. Ibid., p. 4.

groundlings continued to be known as "the yard," a designation inherited from the past.

For a stage Lawrence posits "a simple rush-strewn platform, jutting out prominently into the yard," and then comes to a "point of departure" between the physical conditions of the inn-yard stage and the stage of the first public theatres.

> The paramount need of a readily accessible dressing room . . . led at once to the creation of the "tiring-house." . . . To some extent the aspect of the tiring-house recalled the background of the older stages in the inn-yards, but it would appear that at least one important hint had been taken from the screen of the banquetting halls in palaces, universities and inns of court, halls in which the players had occasionally given performances. From this source came the principle of the two frontal doors, forming the normal (but not complete) method of entrance and exit.[13]

The "abnormal" method of entrance and exit is through the "inner stage." Interestingly enough Lawrence makes no attempt to suggest an origin for this inner stage. He does, however, note its dramatic awkwardness and writes that "its employment was, to some extent, restricted by the remoteness and obscurity of its position, an inconvenience which almost invariably demanded the bringing in of lights at the commencement of all inner scenes."[14]

For our purposes the remainder of Lawrence's article is unimportant. He writes of the upper stage, the heavens, and even the three-tiered galleries, without a nod toward the inn-yard with its own galleries and upper areas. The "two narrow doors" of the Globe, however, are explained as "due to the continuance of the inn-yard and the bear-baiting system of preliminary payment at the door with subsequent 'gathering' inside."[15] The article ends with a discussion of the Blackfriars, and the use of music and lights in the private theatres.

It is at least a possibility that Lawrence's private but marked hostility to the academic judgments of T. S. Graves may arise from the fact that Graves in his 1913 dissertation, *The Court and the London Theatres during the Reign of Elizabeth*, argued for the rejection of the inn-yard as the progenitor of the public playhouse. Graves doubts that the actors would have preferred to act in the inn-yards "rather than in the great halls"[16] and consequently seeks to minimize the structural

13. Ibid., pp. 5-6.
14. Ibid., pp. 6-7.
15. Ibid., p. 10.
16. Menasha, Wis., 1913, p. 35.

influence of inn-yards on the theatres. Curiously enough Glynne Wickham seems to take no note of Graves's work when he in his turn comes to argue for the hall of an inn, rather than the yard, as the normal playing place.

E. K. Chambers similarly gives short shrift to Graves when he takes up directly the question of the relationship of the inn-yard to the theatres in *The Elizabethan Stage*, published in 1923. Graves is dismissed to a footnote in which Chambers writes of his "great hall" theory: "I do not think that he makes much of a case. Had the inns, indeed, 'great halls' at all?"[17]

Before examining Chambers' position in some detail I might just note in passing that Joseph Quincy Adams in *Shakespearean Playhouses* places himself squarely among the orthodox when he opens his book with this general statement:

> Before the building of regular playhouses the itinerant troupes of actors were accustomed . . . to give their performances in any place that chance provided, such as open street-squares, barns, townhalls, moot-courts, schoolhouses, churches and — most frequently of all, perhaps — the yards of inns. These yards, especially those of carriers' inns, were admirably suited to dramatic representations, consisting as they did of a large open court surrounded by two or more galleries.[18]

In the twenty years between *The Mediaeval Stage* and *The Elizabethan Stage* it is not surprising that a scholar of Chambers' calibre should have modified his position on the inn-yard. In the bibliographical note preceding the chapter on "The Public Theatres" both Ordish and Adams are cited, but, as noted above, Graves is not mentioned. Chambers opens his study proper thus:

> When the first Elizabethan theatres were built in 1576, it was the hall on the one hand, and the ring on the other, which determined the general structure of the two types of auditorium that came simultaneously into being.[19]

In a footnote he nods to Ordish but denies the direct influence of medieval entertainments: "a ring is so obviously the form in which the maximum number of spectators can see an object of interest, that too much stress must not be laid upon it as an evidence of folk 'tradition.'" It is important to note the explicit distinction introduced by Chambers between the public "public theatres" and the public "private theatres." (With an eye to the future I might say that it is to

17. *The Elizabethan Stage*, II, 527.
18. 1917; rpt. Gloucester, Mass., 1960, p. 1.
19. *The Elizabethan Stage*, II, 355.

this quoted passage that Glynne Wickham will take the strongest exception.) Having set forth this distinction, Chambers continues rather illogically to minimize its importance.

The distinction between "private" and "public" is an unessential one, depending probably upon some difference in the methods of paying for admission necessitated by the regulations of the City or the Privy Council. The performances in all the houses were public in the ordinary sense.[20]

In the same paragraph he goes on to add: "There was, however, another important factor, besides the baiting ring, which greatly affected the structure of the open-air theatre. This was the inn-yard." After commenting on and citing a number of instances where London halls were used by the players he moves on to write:

But an even more convenient hospitality was afforded by the great court-yards of the City inns, where there was sack and bottle-ale to hand, and, as the Puritans averred, chambers ready for deeds of darkness to be done, when the play was over. In these yards, approached by archways under the inn buildings from one or more streets, and surrounded by galleries with external staircases giving access to the upper floors, an audience could quickly gather, behold at their ease, and escape payment with difficulty. The actors could be accommodated with a tiring-room on the ground floor, and perform as on a natural stage between the pillars supporting the galleries. [I find this a curious turn of phrase, suggesting as it does something of an "inner stage."] An upper gallery could be used to vary the scene. The first performances in London inns upon record were at the Saracen's Head, Islington, and the Boar's Head, Aldgate, both in 1557. By the beginning of Elizabeth's reign the use of them was normal.[21]

Chambers goes on to cite in passing a number of city regulations and Privy Council orders which unmistakably refer to the acting of plays at the "greate innes." He does not comment on the possibility that these performances may have been in the inns themselves rather than in the yards. In his detailed discussion of five London houses—the Red Lion, the Bull, the Bell, the Bell Savage, and the Cross Keys—he cites the evidence for permanent modifications and alterations such as the "skaffoldes . . . mad at the house called the Red Lyon" but does not deal directly with a question, later to be raised by Wickham. That is whether these modified inns, or indeed any of the inns, continued to function as inns *per se* when plays came to be acted regularly in their yards. On balance it is clear that Chambers believed that the experi-

20. Ibid., 550.
21. Loc. cit.

ence of many years of playing in inn-yards exerted a powerful influence on the players when they came to erect their permanent playing places beyond the reach of the London authorities.

Clear as Chambers' commitment to the inn-yard appears to us, it was not enough for Lawrence when he returned to the question in two essays given pride of place in his *Pre-Restoration Stage Studies* of 1927. Citing Harley Granville Barker's review of chapters 20 and 21 of *The Elizabethan Stage* in which Granville Barker writes "that the distinguished stage historian makes a false start in underestimating the influence on the trend of acting and play writing . . . exercised by the early inn-yard playing places." Lawrence comments that "he might well have added on theatrical architecture and playhouse economy."[22] The purpose of Lawrence's paper is "to fortify Mr. Granville Barker's position, to clarify the befogged atmosphere, and uproot a baneful fallacy." The "baneful fallacy" is that of "the removable stage and the improvised auditorium." He notes that new evidence has forced him to the "public recantation of opinions long held and put years ago into cold print." In his earlier essay of 1912 Lawrence had accepted the necessity of a removable stage. He traces the growth of this fallacy from Malone who had supposed that the removable stage would have been built with its back to the gateway of the inn, at which the admission was taken. Lawrence finds this supposition attractive because "with the stage so positioned, the gateway, if bisected by a curtain or screen, could have been made to serve the double purpose of a rear stage and a dressing-room or property store," but he recognizes that in such a location, blocking the gateway of the inn, the stage must be removable. The problem is solved for Lawrence by the evidence of the New Inn in Gloucester which has two entrances to the yard.

> The grave inconvenience of having to keep putting the stage into position and removing it could have been obviated by building it in front of and into the back gateway, thus leaving the front entrance free at all times for the use of either carriers or playgoers.[23]

Citing, among other evidence, the "skaffolds" at the Red Bull, Lawrence goes on to add permanent seating as a complement to the permanent stage; a conclusion which no one who has followed the work of Herbert Berry on the Boar's Head in Whitechapel can deny. The conversion of the London inns to public theatres is not at

---

22. "The Inn-Yard Playing Places: Their Uprise and Characteristics," p. [3].
23. Ibid., p. 11.

question; at question is the continued use of these hostels by the carriers after conversion. Lawrence believes this to be so, and accepts the restriction of playing days.

What we particularly require to bear in mind is that the chief and larger of the London inns were carriers' inns, and that it was in their yards, because of their better accommodation that the players acted. But a serious drawback was allied with their choice. It restricted their days of playing. . . . This limitation of the playing days to a maximum of three per week was due to the fact that the players shared the use of the inn-yard with the carriers.[24]

The arguments of the first part of his paper are summed up, and Lawrence writes:

. . . at once you place the inn-yard playing places directly in the main line of architectural evolution. It would be idle to look further afield for the chief source of inspiration on which the builders of the first outlying theatres drew . . . Graves [has] gone sadly out of [his] way to deduce the primitive theatre auditorium from special court contrivances of a much earlier period and a purely temporary order.[25]

Lawrence moves on to the final section of his essay by writing:

No doubt the circular or polygonal shape of the regular theatres, when it came, was derived from the bull and bear-baiting circuses. . . . But everything else in the early theatres was the result of inn-yard experience: even the place where the groundlings stood was still styled the yard.[26]

His discussion of the inn-yard gathering system and its development in the public playhouses is well argued, but it is overshadowed by Lawrence's preoccupation with the fact that there was reported to be an outdoor staircase from the yard to the gallery nearby the gate in which he had placed his permanent stage at the New Inn. He moves from this particular instance to a general statement that "there are some grounds for thinking that this visible staircase afforded a model for a possible characteristic of the regular theatre stages whose existence is not commonly suspected."[27] The final pages of the paper are devoted to attempting to prove the existence of this "visible stage" from a complex of carefully selected stage directions and dramatic situations. He does not succeed, and this portion of Lawrence's paper warrants the neglect it has generated.

24. Ibid., pp. 5-6.
25. Ibid., p. 14.
26. Ibid., p. 15.
27. Ibid., p. 16.

Were it not for my desire to achieve relative completeness in this survey I should pass by Lawrence's second paper in silence. Dr. Leone Star in private correspondence has dealt with it with admirable dispatch: "This must take the prize for being the most erroneous and illogical article ever written on any aspect of the Elizabethan Theatre." There is not much more that one can say about "The Inn-Yard Play." In it Lawrence argues for a special kind of play which was written for performance in the inn-yards. While such plays share the dramatic tone of public theatre plays they may be distinguished from them in two ways:

> I think that when one comes across a sixteenth-century play whose title-page fails to convey by what company it was acted or where, one has reasonable grounds for believing that it was an inn-yard play.

Secondly:

> When we come across a late sixteenth- or very early seventeenth-century play which makes no mention of doors, indicating other modes of entrance or none at all, we are entitled to assume that we have discovered an inn-yard play.[28]

The use of negative evidence clearly has its dangers, and on that negative note I must leave W. J. Lawrence.

It would be mere fancy to suggest that the nearly forty-year silence which followed was due to Lawrence's paper. Nonetheless, it was not until 1963 that Glynne Wickham reopened the matter in Part I of Volume II of *Early English Stages*. Wickham's discursive style resists easy summation but his final position is perhaps fairly set forth toward the end of a long chapter on "Playhouses."

> This lengthy recital of the surviving evidence relating to inns has been necessary to establish two facts which I believe to be cardinal to any understanding of the Elizabethan stage. The first is that we have no justification for assuming from records which associate Inns with stage-plays and actors, that performances automatically took place in the yard or even out of doors. The second, its sequel, is that when trying to dovetail our interpretations of De Witt's drawing of the Swan to fit such knowledge as we can glean from surviving buildings of the period which are visually familiar to us, we are under no obligation—indeed, we have no right—to correlate that drawing with Tudor inn-yards to the exclusion of all other possibilities. . . . I do not wish to deny inn-yards their due as occasional places of performance, nor "other places" in and about the taverns and eating houses: but I do wish to

---

28. "The Inn-Yard Play," pp. 31, 33.

direct the reader's attention to the overwhelming predominance of indoor performances in churches, chapels, private rooms and a variety of halls, as attested in the surviving provincial records, over open-air performances, and to the equally impressive evidence from London to the same effect. In only seven of some thirty references associating plays and actors with inns is the yard mentioned at all: and of these one is of doubtful veracity while all the others speak of the yard as one of several possible sites including the interior of the "house" or "mansion."[29]

It should be remembered that Wickham's skepticism about inn-yard performances is only part of his much larger thesis more fully set forth in Part II of Volume II published nine years later in 1972. Central to his thesis is his insistence that the frame, stage, and tiring-house must be viewed as separate entities. Accepting this he writes:

> If James Burbage and John Brayne, with much larger financial resources chose to model their "frame" at the Theater on those of the gamehouses on Bankside . . . in order to accommodate a larger public and to swell their box-office receipts, this did not preclude their setting down within it a stage and tiring-house of the sort familiar to them in the Halls of the Earl of Leicester or of the Queen.[30]

Baldly stated, Wickham argues that conditions at court were the dominant and controlling factor in the development of the permanent, professional playhouses of the late seventeenth century. He speculates:

> Could it therefore be that the method of providing playhouses at Court standardized by the Office of Works during the sixteenth century suggested to London's theatrical impresarios and financiers the simplest means of providing the same facilities in a public environment? . . . Certainly such an assumption serves to remove most of the difficulties that stem from attempts to derive Elizabethan and Jacobean playhouse design from rings, rounds, innyards and other possible public prototypes, all of which relegate the Court to the limbo of afterthoughts. If, however, it is once granted that the prototype was the frame, stage and tiring-house implicit in the words "making ready," which occur repeatedly in the Works Accounts whether applied to the Great Chamber, Hall or the Banquet House, it is easy to see that little could be simpler than to copy that example in terms of a wide variety of public places already devoted to recreational activities.[31]

29. London, 1963, II, Pt. I, 196.
30. London, 1972, II, Pt. II, 160.
31. Ibid., 159-60.

With this major thesis I do not propose to meddle. It is clear that Wickham's skepticism about inn-yard playing is only a minor section of his much broader argument. If the possibility of influences stemming from inn-yards can be discounted, then a large obstacle to the acceptance of his general thesis has been removed. However, my brief today *is* concerned only with this minor element of Wickham's argument; but a minor element which poses a still-to-be-resolved major question of Elizabethan theatre scholarship and to that issue I must return.

In Part I Wickham had written:

> There is . . . a strong presumptive case for thinking that performances in provincial inns were rare, and that in those instances where performances can be proved to have been given in inns, they were presented indoors rather than out.[32]

Wickham advances three reasons for this conclusion. One is that the yard is virtually the only place in the inn that cannot be closed to traffic without paralysing all its services. Second is the fact that when the leading companies of James I's reign raised the capital to acquire permanent winter quarters, they found them in large halls, centrally situated and fully protected from the weather. He does not believe that this action marked a sudden innovation but rather a continuance of a normal practice.

> The third reason is that all the companies, Elizabethan and Jacobean, were obliged under the terms of their licences when touring the provinces to give at least one performance before the Mayor of every town visited in the Common Hall of that town: and the presumption must be that rather than strike the stage and equipment which they had set up there to go through the whole dreary process of setting up again at other places in the town they gave the other performances permitted by the Mayor in the same hall.[33]

I propose to return to these general arguments at the end of this paper; for now I will leave Wickham with one final summation and one final quotation. As part of his general argument against the use of inn-yards he notes that he has found only nine references in the two-hundred-year period from 1485 to 1685 in which either plays or players are specifically linked with the yard of an inn. Six of these are contained in a group of injunctions restraining plays which supply us with nothing more definite than a series of variants upon the phrase "dwellynge houses, yardes, or other places." One is simply the notice

---

32. Wickham, II, Pt. I, 189.
33. Loc. cit.

of the arrival of a group of players at an inn in Stourbridge in 1610; it does not tell us where the players played. Finally there is the already quoted post-Restoration testimony of Richard Flecknoe about two inns in London. I must grant Wickham the fact that the cited references are few and the wording vague in the majority of cases. In that light I allow him the final word:

> I have myself, however, become increasingly sceptical about the evidence, *contemporary with the plays and performances*, on which Chambers and other inn-yard style reconstructors of the playhouses saw fit to set performances at inns so firmly in the yard.[34]

Before leaving this question of the evidence I venture to call to your attention a paper presented at this conference in 1977. The paper is entitled "Records of Early English Drama in the Provinces and what they may tell us about the Elizabethan Theatre," and in it David Galloway brings to our attention the important evidence associated with the "affray in Norwich." Professor Galloway is, as always, witty and succinct and I cannot do better than quote him verbatim. He begins by citing Wickham:

> Where the provincial records are concerned the only notice to have come to light so far which links players even indirectly with the yard of an inn is an item from Stourbridge in Worcestershire dated 1610 which states that "plaiers with . . . their cartes and waggons" were then "at theire said Inne" [The Crown]. This certainly does not establish a performance as having been presented in the yard: only that the Innkeeper's guests have parked their waggons at the inn—possibly in the yard.

From the Norwich records, however, I can double the evidence, because there is clear-cut proof that the Queen's Men performed in the yard of the Red Lion Inn in St. Stephens on June 15, 1583. Chambers mentions the performance but does not note that it took place in the yard, possibly because he did not read the entire document and took his information from Halliwell-Phillipps who, in 1864, printed it in a limited edition of twenty-five copies, fifteen of which he destroyed. With that secretive jealousy so characteristic of many nineteenth century scholars, he did not give the source of his information, and I am grateful to Herbert Berry for finding it for me in the Public Record Office.

It was at this performance in the yard of the Red Lion that a famous "affray" took place—an affray which began when "one wynsdon

---

would have intred in at the gate but wold not haue payed vntyl he had been within. . . ." As a result, one of the actors, Bentley, "he wich played the duke came of the Stage and wyth his hiltes of his Sworde he Strooke wynsdon vpon the heade . . ." The upshot was that Bentley, followed by two other actors of the company, Singer and the famous Richard Tarleton, and with the aid of Henry Brown, "Sir william pastons seruant," pursued Wynsdon through the streets. Halliwell-Phillipps does not appear to have read the document very carefully, and neither do a number of scholars who follow him. He says, for example, that "the intruder," Wynsdon, was killed, when it was clearly not Wynsdon, but Wynsdon's servant, George. Chambers says that it was George who tried to gain entry to the play, when it was clearly not George but Wynsdon. Muriel Bradbrook says that the story of the "affray" "never seems to have reached London," although the Latin preamble to the document states that the depositions were sent to the Queen's Court at Westminster. (I suppose that there is a technical point as to whether or not we can call Westminster London.)

The "Affray at Norwich" is a fascinating document which, later, I hope to make the subject of a more detailed study. The evidence of thirteen witnesses, taken before the Mayor and Justices, agrees in essentials but varies in many particulars. Indeed, a latter-day Browning might consider it worthwhile to base on it a new *The Ring and the Book*. It is from one of these witnesses, "william kylbye of Pockthorpe worstedweuer,"' that we learn that the play was in the yeard: "this examynate sayeth that on satturnday last in the after noone he was at a play in the yard at the red lyon in St Sephans and hee dyd see three of the players rvnne of the Staige with there Swordes in there handes. . . ."[35]

Once declared, dogma has a powerful momentum of its own and Wickham's heresy appears to have had little impact on the "establishment" of theatre historians. Three major studies published, or reissued with new material, since 1968 present the orthodox position. C. Walter Hodges in *The Globe Restored*, revised and reissued in that year, cites *Early English Stages* in a Select Bibliography, and is cautious about the ultimate influence of the inn-yard on the permanent theatres:

---

35. *The Elizabethan Theatre VII*, ed. George Hibbard (Port Credit, Ont., 1980), pp. 97-98.

Certainly it was common at one time for plays to be performed in inn-yards, but more than this we do not know, and we are not justified in assuming that the inn-yard gave any other feature to the theatres than the convenience of the use of galleries; a feature which could in any case have been seen already in use at the bull- and bear-baiting arenas on Bankside.[36]

Nevertheless the first of a series of "Reconstruction Sketches" in Appendix A illustrates a booth stage set up against the wall of an inn which looks suspiciously like the New Inn in Gloucester; at any rate it presents Lawrence's famous (or infamous) staircase close to, but not contiguous with, the temporary stage.

Richard Leacroft in his finely illustrated architectural history, *The Development of the English Playhouse*, published in 1973, is generous in his recognition of Wickham's work and takes a position which makes the best of both worlds. Speaking of the travelling players he writes:

> These companies performed . . . in such halls and spaces as were available, which would have included the manor hall, the guild hall, and the large hall contained in many inns. In summertime they could also have made use of the inn yard or any other convenient enclosed space where it would have been possible to control the entry of an audience. . . .[37]

Richard Southern in his study of the staging of the Interludes, *The Staging of Plays before Shakespeare*, also published in 1973, presents an argument which is directly contrary to Wickham's central thesis. Discussing court staging in the sixteenth century he writes:

> When in the latter part of the period the information begins to include references to plays as well, it is almost certainly to a specialized form of play-presentation only, which was devised for command performance under the instruction of the Master of the Revels. But this specialized form may obviously not have the slightest reference to the way in which the same plays were presented on normal occasions outside the court.[38]

In the section on "Presentation in Civic Halls etc. 1538 onwards" Southern presents a vivid account of staging in a town hall based on the Chamberlain's Accounts in Norwich in 1541-42.

> Itm payd for sedge to strow the Halle ther when the prynces players playd an interlude ther, iid[;] dryncke for the players—iid[;] to ii laborers that fetchyd barrells and tymber and made a scaffold then—iid. . . .vi.d[39]

36. London, 1968, p. 27.
37. London, 1973, p. 25.
38. London, 1973, pp. 146-47.
39. Ibid., p. 333.

The discussion ends thus:

> It is also certain that at least as early as about 1540 there did exist in neigh-bouring countries a particular form of stage for the presentation of open-air plays at markets and fairs.[40]

Southern regrets that we have no certain evidence of the use of the "booth stage" in England but considers such a stage as "feasible" and uses it to illustrate a "public outdoor performance in an inn-yard"— once again the yard of the ubiquitous New Inn at Gloucester. He comments on the position of the stage:

> The position of the stage has been chosen at the middle of one of the "sides" of the yard leaving the "ends" free for access; in the end farthest from the spectator is seen the carriage-way from the street by which vehicles arrived at the inn-yard. Though some specialists [W. J. Lawrence] have suggested that the stage would be set up at that end instead of along one of the sides, I have ventured to put my stage as shown. The argument for the alternative of a stage at the end seems to be based on the opinion that the carriage-way opening might have been employed by the players as a sort of off-stage area from which to make their entrances. But it seems to me that the idea is rather based on the supposition, formerly unduly held, that a largish recess at the back, called the "inner stage," was a regular feature of the Elizabethan public-playhouse, and that this must therefore have had some similar predecessor when plays were performed in inn-yards.

Southern rejects "the inner stage" and closes:

> If I am right in this, then I think the carriage-way to the inn-yard would have been left free for spectators' access; and the stage would therefore be set up at the side of the yard and not at the end.[41]

Lawrence's staircase is not in evidence.

If my search of the standard bibliographies has been thorough, only a single scholar in the last decade has been concerned with the inn-yard and inn-yard theatres. O. J. Brownstein published two trenchant studies in 1971, and delivered a third at the 1975 meeting of the Shakespeare Association of America in Los Angeles (to the best of my knowledge it has not been published).

The first of the published papers, "The Saracen's Head, Islington: A Pre-Elizabethan Inn Playhouse" opens with a lively summation:

> Shifts in the tides of fashion in historical research have left the study of the inn-playhouses a back-water; except where earlier charted—often in-

40. Ibid., p. 345.
41. Ibid., p. 346, and Plate 4, after p. 264.

accurately—the interior of this region is characterized by darkness, mythology and ignorance. An important discovery by C. J. Sisson in the mid 1930's of the Boar's Head documents has gone virtually unnoticed [a neglect which has since been remedied by the work of Herbert Berry], besides which there has been very little additional information to that summarized by E. K. Chambers a half century ago. The subject may, indeed, be as unimportant as it has been treated, but this premature conclusion is drawn from current bias and flies in the face of contemporary testimony. On few historical subjects can there have been so much energy expended on speculation and so little on research.[42]

Brownstein sets to work with a will on the reference in Foxe's *Monuments* to John Rough, a Scot, who fled England at the beginning of Mary's reign but returned on 10 November 1557 and attached himself as minister to a secret group of religious dissenters. On 12 December 1557 he "was apprehended by the Vice-Chamberlain of the Queen's house, at the Saracen's Head in Islington, where the congregation had then purposed to assemble themselves to their godly and accustomable exercises of prayer, and hearing the word of God: which pretence, for the safeguard of all the rest, they yet at their examinations covered and excused by hearing of a play, that was then appointed to be at that place." Through his examination of this and related documents Brownstein demonstrates that two spaces—one for the prayer meeting and one for the play—were simultaneously required:

> It seems most likely, then, that two rooms—one quite large—or a yard and a room, or two yards were needed; indeed the larger inns of the period had three or four connecting yards.[43]

He closes his examination of the evidence by concluding that as early as 1557 plays at the Saracen's Head were a regular occurrence. "One must wonder how many [other] inns were showing plays regularly at that time, how regularly, and whether all of them were in the suburbs."[44]

In his second paper of 1971, "A Record of London Inn-Playhouses from c. 1565-1590," Brownstein extracts some most interesting information from *The Register of the Masters of Defense*. These dated accounts of the places used by fencers for their "prizes" provide the

---

42. *Theatre Notebook*, XXV, no. 2 (1970-71), 68.
43. Ibid., 70.
44. Ibid., 72.

earliest documentary evidence for the existence of the Theatre and the Curtain, and the playhouses in the Bell Savage and Bull Inns.

> Until now, without reference to the earliest entries in the Register, the first theatrical notice of the Bell Savage is in a work published in 1575, while another published in 1578 refers to plays at the Bull. . . . These notices show that playhouses were operating in the precincts of the Bell Savage Inn by the mid 1560's and at the Bull Inn by the early 1570's.[45]

Brownstein also finds in the records that

> following 1583 the prizes at the inn-playhouses were played . . . exclusively in cold months. . . . This seems clearly to mark the beginning of the well known seasonal migration from the city inn-playhouses to the suburban theatres.[46]

Most interestingly, to Brownstein "the evidence suggests that the seasonal migration was related to plague restrictions and precautions and not to the weather as such or to relative comfort."[47]

He notes as well in these records and elsewhere the absence of any contemporary reference to fencing at the Cross Keys or the Bell, two inn playhouses which for at least twenty years were rivals of the Bull and Bell Savage.

> Neither the Cross Keys nor the Bell Inn appears to have had the extensive system of yards and connecting passages that existed at the Bull and Bell Savage (each of which had at least four court and stable yards according to the earliest surveys).[48]

Brownstein closes this excellent paper by observing that "If by *playhouse* is meant especially constructed facilities for players and spectators, then it is quite obvious that the Bell Savage Inn contained the first public playhouse in London. . . ."[49]

In the third and unpublished paper of 1975, "The Bell Savage and the Innyard Playhouse Theories," scholars who persist in speculating rather than making use of the hard evidence already at hand are soundly rated. Both Wickham and Lawrence are firmly taken to task for basing their speculations and conclusions on the unique special inn which provides the expected single yard with two entrances surrounded by galleries—I refer, of course, to the New Inn in Gloucester. By bonding himself to a single galleried yard Lawrence is forced to

45. *Shakespeare Quarterly*, XXII (1971), 19-20.
46. Ibid., 21.
47. Ibid., 21-22.
48. Ibid., 23.
49. Ibid., 24.

postulate an "alternation" theory whereby the carriers use the inn on one day and the players on the next. Similarly, Wickham is forced to conclude that plays were either mounted in rooms in the inn, or in the inn-yard only after the inn has ceased to function as an inn.

Through a close study of the existing documentation Brownstein demonstrates to his satisfaction (and to mine) that performances took place in one of the yards of the Bell Savage, and that a special grandstand was built to accommodate the audience. He closes by stating that "there is neither logic nor evidence to keep us in the conceptual *cul de sac* of the New Inn court yard surrounded by integral galleries."

As I told you at the beginning of my paper I could promise you no treasure troves of knowledge, but I hope that our tour through the evidence of inns and inn-yards has not been without value. I agree with Wickham when he argues that travelling players in the provinces would prefer to continue playing in the town hall or guildhall, or wherever they presented the customary Mayor's play; but this would not always be possible, and I am confident that the thorough search of the provincial records being mounted by REED will turn up more records of performances in the inn-yards.

I am not as convinced as Wickham that the players were so firmly wedded to indoor playing places that they always preferred a room in the inn over the yard. If this were so why did they not build an enclosed playhouse when they moved to the suburbs? And why did they move from the great room in the inn to the inn-yard when they came to make permanent additions or modifications to the existing facilities? I know that the answer will be that economic pressures or reasons forced them to play in the place where the greatest number of paying spectators could be accommodated, and not in the place which they preferred, but I am not totally convinced that this was so.

I am most interested in Brownstein's thesis that the annual migration of the players to the suburbs and back was the result of plague restrictions and not for reasons of comfort. If this be so, a strong argument, with an appeal to spoiled twentieth-century scholars concerned with their comfort, for warm winter quarters inside the inns is rendered at least questionnable.

Brownstein's demonstration that many of the carrier inns of London had several yards makes Lawrence's "alternation" theory and Wickham's flight to the "great hall" unnecessary. Even in a single courtyard I believe that the players and the carriers could share the space. We tend to underestimate the flexibility and speed with which the players could mount their play, and I am struck by a passage in Fynes Moryson's *Itinerary* of 1617:

Likewise carriers let horses from city to city, with caution that the passenger must lodge in their inn, that they may look to the feeding of their horses, and so they will for some five or six days' journey let him a horse, and find the horse meat themselves for some twenty shillings. Lastly these carriers have long covered waggons, in which they carry passengers from city to city: but this kind of journeying is so tedious, *by reason they must take waggons very early, and come very late to their inns,* as none but women and people of inferior condition, . . . or strangers use to travel in this sort. (My italics)[50]

There is a lot of daylight between dawn and dusk and I am sure the players made good use of it. As always Shakespeare comes to mind and I think of II. ii. of *I Henry IV:*

Enter a Carrier with a lantern in his hand.

1 Carrier   Heigh-ho! an it be not four by the day, I'll be hanged. Charles' wain is over the new chimney, and yet our horse not packed. . .

2 Carrier   I have a gammon of bacon and two razes of ginger, to be delivered as far as Charing Cross. . . .

Gadshill asks what time they will get to London.

2 Carrier   Time enough to go to bed with a candle, I warrant thee.

As the wagons trundled toward London, I believe that the players mounted their play in the yard (or one of the yards) of the destined London inn, and were long gone when the carriers arrived.

50. Cited from John Dover Wilson, *Life in Shakespeare's England* (1911); rpt. Harmondsworth, Midd., 1949), pp. 110-11.

The King's Men on Stage: Actors and Their Parts, 1611-32

T. J. KING

This paper reviews the available evidence about the steps taken when actors prepared plays for performance in the time of Shakespeare. My purpose is to gain a clearer picture than we now have about the way parts were assigned to actors in Shakespeare's company, the King's Men. On this subject, some highly conjectural theories are advanced by T.W. Baldwin. From cast lists in plays by authors other than Shakespeare—most notably the lists of actors first printed in the Beaumont and Fletcher Folio of 1679—Baldwin attempts to define the personal characteristics of each actor and then to establish a "line of parts" that actor played throughout his career. Baldwin then projects this line backwards in time, and he attempts to identify the actor who first played each major role in Shakespeare's plays. According to Baldwin, when Shakespeare wrote his plays, "The play was regularly fitted to the company, not the company to the play. . . . These men did not act; they were themselves."[1] There is no direct evidence that Shakespeare wrote his plays to suit the characteristics of individual actors, but the author undoubtedly knew he could rely on the services of an extremely skilful and versatile acting company. The present paper demonstrates the versatility of the King's Men in ten of the plays they acted between 1611 and 1632.

Elizabethan acting companies took five important steps when they prepared a play for performance:

    1: the actors or their agent made partial payments to the author as

---

1. T.W. Baldwin, *The Organization and Personnel of the Shakespearean Company* (Princeton, 1927), pp. 197, 184.

he was writing the play, often with collaborators. The actors or their agent paid the author in full when he delivered "fair copy" of the "book-of-the-play."

2: the playhouse scribe copied the actors' parts from the book.

3: the book-keeper, who also served as prompter, conducted rehearsals from the book. My study examines three playhouse manuscripts that are prepared for performance by the book-keeper of the King's Men and censored by the Master of the Revels.

4: the book-keeper prepared a plot or outline of the play listing the characters who appear in each scene and identifying the actor who plays each part. This supplement to the book-of-the-play was posted in the tiring-house to remind the actors of the sequence of their entrances and to remind the stage-keepers of the required properties and effects. Four plots from Elizabethan plays are well enough preserved to provide evidence about the part or parts assigned to each actor.

5: before a play was first performed—or an old play revived—the actors sent the book to the Master of the Revels, who for a fee read the play and deleted those passages he considered objectionable. He usually affixed his licence and signature immediately after the last lines of the text and returned the book to the players.

In this review of playhouse procedures, I cite several documents from acting companies other than Shakespeare's, most notably the Lord Admiral's Men and Lady Elizabeth's Men. Nevertheless, these companies probably followed playhouse procedures similar to those followed by Shakespeare's company because Elizabethan actors frequently moved from one company to another just as companies moved from one playhouse to another.

The records of Philip Henslowe, the financial manager and money-lender to several Elizabethan acting companies, provide valuable evidence about the way these actors obtained new plays. In the usual procedure, one or more of the actors asked Henslowe to advance "earnest money" to an author or authors who had proposed an outline of a play.

The authors received further instalments as they wrote the play; when and if the play was finished, Henslowe paid the authors in full. When the play was performed, the actors repaid Henslowe from playhouse receipts. These procedures are explicitly described in articles of agreement drawn up between Nathan Field, the leading actor of Lady Elizabeth's Men about 1613, as one party, and, as the other, Philip Henslowe and Jacob Meade. The articles state that for three years Henslowe and Meade will "fynde and provide a sufficient howse or howses for the saide Company to play in" and will "lay out . . . somes of monny . . . for the furnishing of the said Company with playinge apparrell towarde the setting out of newe playes . . . and lay out . . . somes of monny . . . to be paide for any play which they shall buy or condition or agree for [provided that] the saide Company shall truly repay the saide Philipp and Jacob."[2]

Ben Jonson was the most important author for whose work Henslowe lent money to actors. For example, on 3 December 1597 Henslowe notes: "Lent vnto Bengemen Johnsone vpon a Bocke wch he was to writte for vs before crysmas next after the date herof wch he showed the plotte vnto the company I saye lente in Redy money vnto hime the some of xx s."[3] No further payments are recorded to Jonson in 1597, however, so he probably did not complete the play before Christmas as he had agreed. In the following year, Jonson took on collaborators, perhaps for the same play, and on 18 August 1598 Henslowe "lent vnto the company . . . to bye a Boocke called hoote anger sone cowld of mr porter mr cheattell and bengemen Johnson in full payment the some of vi li."[4]

Before the acting company made final payment, however, they expected to receive "fair copy," that is, a text free from the tangles and confusions usually associated with "foul papers." On 17 April 1613, Henslowe agrees to pay Robert Daborne twenty pounds for a tragedy, *Machiavel and the Devil*. In the next few weeks, Henslowe makes partial payments to Daborne as he sends the players sheets "fayr written." On 25 June, Daborne writes, "I have took extra-ordynary payns with the end and altered one other scean in the third act which they now have in parts."[5] Here the playhouse scribe apparently began to prepare the actors' parts even before the author had finished writing the play.

The only Elizabethan actor's part that survives is the one used by Edward Alleyn when he played the title role in Robert Greene's *Orlando Furioso*, probably with Lord Strange's Men at the Rose playhouse on 21 February 1592. Although the part is mutilated and defective in many places, it preserves about 530 lines of cues and speeches for Orlando written on strips of paper six inches wide and varying from ten to sixteen inches in length. When Alleyn used this part, the strips were pasted together to form a long roll. These strips

2. *Henslowe Papers*, ed. W.W. Greg (London, 1907), pp. 23-24.
3. *Henslowe's Diary*, eds. R.A. Foakes and R.T. Rickert (Cambridge, 1961), p. 73.
4. *Diary*, p. 96.
5. *Papers*, pp. 67-73.

have now been separated and bound as leaves in a volume preserved among Alleyn's papers at Dulwich College. Most of the part is in a secretary hand, probably that of the playhouse scribe. He was apparently unable to read all of the text from which he copied the part, and he leaves blank spaces into which the actor can insert the appropriate words at rehearsal. For example, toward the bottom of strip 8 the scribe leaves a space into which Alleyn inserts an entire line of iambic pentameter: "Inconstant, base, injurious and untrue."

The cues for Orlando usually consist of two or three words to the right of a line drawn across the strip. For example, on strip 5 the words "on his neck" are the cue for Orlando to "Enter with a man's leg" and to say:

> Villayns provide me straight a lions skyne
> for I thou seest, I am mighty Hercules
> See whers my massy club upon my neck
> I must to hell to fight with Cerberus.[6]

Elizabethan actors played in repertory, and in the years covered by this study Shakespeare's company introduced an average of five new plays a year.[7] This would require that the actors be in rehearsal much of the time. Usually the company rehearsed a new play in the morning and gave a public performance of another play in the afternoon. This procedure is implied in the only extant actor's contract from this period, an agreement dated 17 April 1614 between Robert Dawes, the actor, and Henslowe and Meade, managers of Lady Elizabeth's Men. The contract is to run for three years "at the rate of one whole Share according to the custome of players." Dawes agrees to "duly attend all suche rehearsall which shall the night before the rehearsall be given publickly out," and he agrees to be "ready apparrelled and to begyn the play at the hower of three of the clock in the afternoone."[8]

At rehearsals, a very important member of the company was the book-keeper. John Higgens, *Nomenclator* (1585), defines "book-keeper" as "he that telleth the players their part when they are out and have forgotten, the prompter or bookeholder."[9] Thus in Elizabethan usage the terms "book-keeper," "book-holder," and "prompter" are

---

6. As cited by W.W. Greg, *Dramatic Documents from the Elizabethan Playhouses*, 2 vols. (Oxford, 1931), II n.pag. Vol.I contains commentary, vol.II reproductions and transcripts.
7. In the years 1611-32, the King's Men probably first performed at least a hundred new plays. See Alfred Harbage, *Annals of English Drama 975-1700*, rev. S. Schoenbaum (Philadelphia, 1964).
8. *Papers*, p. 124.
9. As cited by E.K. Chambers, *William Shakespeare: A Study of Facts and Problems* (Oxford, 1930), I, 106, n. 4.

virtually synonymous. Hereafter, I refer to this person as the book-keeper. Three manuscript prompt books from the repertory of the King's Men are included here as evidence about actors in principal parts. In each of these manuscripts, the book-keeper notes changes in the text, adds the names of some, but not all, of the actors, and adds cues for some, but not all, of the required properties and effects.

It should be emphasized that these seventeenth-century manu-scripts differ from the prompt books prepared for present-day theatrical productions. A modern prompt book provides the com-plete text and stage directions for a given play, along with detailed information about the cues for lights, sounds, and scene changes, but the Elizabethan book-keeper did not enter all of this information in his prompt book. Instead, he prepared a plot or scene-by-scene outline that was hung in the tiring-house as a reminder for actors and stage-keepers. Thus when at rehearsals the book-keeper jotted in the book some actors' names and some of the properties and effects needed, he was probably making notes that he later transferred to the plot. At performances, the book-keeper followed the book to prompt the actors, but he also consulted the plot, which identified the actors and the parts they played at each performance.

When an Elizabethan acting company revived a play, the cast probably differed from the cast for the first performance. This would make it necessary for the book-keeper to draw up a plot and to record there the names of the actors for the revival. The separate functions of the book and the plot are indicated in *The Spanish Tragedy* (1592) at the play-within-the play:

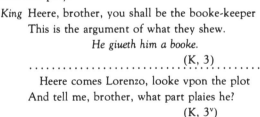

> *King* Heere, brother, you shall be the booke-keeper
> This is the argument of what they shew.
>> *He giueth him a booke.*
>>> (K, 3)
> . . . .
> Heere comes Lorenzo, looke vpon the plot
> And tell me, brother, what part plaies he?
>> (K, 3ᵛ)

The earliest extant manuscript prompt book from the repertory of the King's Men is the anonymous *The Second Maiden's Tragedy* (British Library MS. Lansdowne 807, ff. 29-56), probably by Thomas Middleton. The title is derived from the licence affixed to the last leaf and signed by the Master of the Revels, Sir George Buc: "This second Maydens tragedy (for it hath no name inscribed) may wth the reformations bee acted publikely 31 octobr. 1611. G. Buc."[10]

10. As cited by Anne Lancashire, ed. *The Second Maiden's Tragedy*, (Manchester, 1978) p. 5.

The book-keeper adds to the text the names of two actors, Robert Gough and Richard Robinson. Gough plays Memphonius, a noble at the court of the Tyrant; an eleven-line speech for Memphonius is added by the playhouse scribe, probably at rehearsal. In the left margin of the new speech, the book-keeper adds *Enter Mr. Gough*, probably as a reminder that this new entrance should be added to the plot and that these new lines should be added to this actor's part. Richard Robinson, a boy, plays the Lady who kills herself rather than yield to the lustful Tyrant. When the hero, Govianus, visits the tomb of the Lady, her Spirit appears to him. In the left margin, the book-keeper notes *Enter Lady Richard Robinson*, probably as a reminder that Robinson plays both the Lady and her Spirit and that this information should be added to the plot.

The manuscript prompt book of the anonymous *Sir John van Olden Barnavelt* (British Library, MS. Add. 18653), probably by Fletcher and Massinger, is a dramatization of contemporary Dutch history that deals with the unsuccessful attempt of Barnavelt to assert the sovreignty of the provincial estates against the claims of Maurice, Prince of Orange. Barnavelt was executed on 13 May 1619, and the play was probably written shortly afterward. The text is heavily censored by Sir George Buc, who adds a note of reprimand. As it now stands, this text does not include a revels licence, but Howard-Hill notes: "The evidence of damage which brought about loss of part of the manuscript at the end leaves the question of the license open."[11] The play was acted in August 1619, presumably at the second Globe playhouse.

Most of the text is in the hand of Ralph Crane, scrivener for the King's Men, and an unidentified book-keeper adds the names or initials of seven men and three boys to indicate the parts these actors play. Apparently these roles were assigned at rehearsal when the company was testing the possibilities for doubling. The identified parts in *Barnavelt* are assigned in such a way that each actor who doubles has sufficient time off-stage to allow for each change of costume. For example, the book-keeper identifies Richard Robinson as the Dutch Captain of the Guard in five scenes; then Robinson is off-stage for a full scene before he enters as Boisise, a French Ambassador. After his exit as Boisise, Robinson is off-stage for a full scene before he enters again as the Captain. The same plan for changes of costume is followed when John Rice plays the Captain of English mercenaries in six scenes, then doubles as an important Servant, and

---

11. *Sir John van Olden Barnavelt*, ed. T.H. Howard-Hill (Malone Society Reprints, 1979), p. iv.

later returns as the Captain. The book-keeper identifies five other men who play eight small parts and three boys who probably play two parts each.

The manuscript prompt book of *Believe as You List* (British Library MS. Egerton 1994) is a careful fair copy in the autograph of Philip Massinger.[12] This text is apparently a revision or an earlier draft for which the Master of the Revels, Sir Henry Herbert, refused a licence. Sir Henry notes in his office-book for 11 January 1630/1:

> I did refuse to allow of a play of Massinger's because itt did contain dangerous matter, as the deposing of Sebastian king of Portugal, by Phillip [the Second of Spain] . . . I had my fee notwithstandinge, which belongs to me for reading itt over, and ought to be brought always with the booke.[13]

In order to make the play acceptable to Sir Henry, Massinger revised the text, and for the story of Sebastian, deposed by Spain, Massinger substituted the story of Antiochus, a Syrian king deposed by Rome in 192 B.C. The revised play apparently met with Sir Henry's approval, and he adds his licence at the end of the text: "This play, called Believe as you list, may be acted this 6 of May 1631. Henry Herbert."

The book-keeper for *Believe as You List* is Edward Knight, who in preparing the play for performance cancels or writes over many of Massinger's stage directions. On the last leaf, Knight adds a property list that identifies indirectly six of the actors in principal parts. For example, the property list indicates "Act 3: 2 letters for Mr. Lowin." In the text at the start of Act III, Knight adds "wth 2 letters" to the stage direction for the entrance of Flaminius, the second largest part, probably played by Lowin. The property list also identifies indirectly the parts played by five other men: Taylor as Antiochus, Benfield as Marcellus, Robinson as Lentulus, Pollard as Berecinthius, and Swanston as Chrysalus. If the play were to be revived with a different cast, a new property list would be drawn up to include the names of these new actors, but it would not be necessary to change the prompt book.

In IV. i, Knight adds a warning for stage-keepers to be ready for an important entrance by Taylor: *Gascoine & Hubert below: ready to open the Trap doore for Mr. Taylor.* About fifty lines later, Knight adds

---

12. *Believe as You List*, ed. Charles J. Sisson (Malone Society Reprints, 1927), p. xii. Another manuscript prompt book from the repertory of the King's Men, *The Honest Man's Fortune* (Victoria and Albert Museum, MS.Dyce 9)—probably written by Nathan Field in 1613 with help from Massinger and Fletcher—is not included in this study because the text does not identify actors in principal parts.
13. *The Dramatic Records of Sir Henry Herbert, Master of the Revels, 1623-73*, ed. Joseph Quincy Adams (New Haven, 1917), p. 19.

another warning: *Antiochus ready under the stage*. In IV. ii, Antiochus speaks from *below* before he emerges from his dungeon. Knight identifies William Penn as Second Merchant, who appears in I. ii, II. ii, III. ii, and III. iii. Penn is then off-stage for IV. i before he doubles as the Jailer in IV. ii. Penn is then off-stage for IV. iii and IV. iv before he enters again as Second Merchant in V. i and V. ii. Knight also identifies John Honeyman as First Merchant.

Knight adds names or initials to identify seven men in minor parts, but there are inconsistencies and contradictions in role assignments. For example, the very small part of Demetrius, who speaks a total of six lines, is assigned to three different actors: Richard Baxter in three scenes, Rowland Dowle in two scenes, and William Patrick in one scene. Although it was common practice for actors to double in two or more parts, it is highly unlikely that the company would hire three actors to play the same small part at any one performance. A probable explanation for these apparent inconsistencies is that Knight made these notes at rehearsals when the company was trying out various hired men in various roles and testing the possibilities for doubling. When the casting of these minor parts was finally decided, the names of the actors and the parts they played were presumably entered in the plot; then the inconsistent notes that Knight had entered in the prompt book could be ignored.

As noted, four Elizabethan playhouse plots,—that is, scene-by-scene outlines that identify actors and the parts they play—are well enough preserved to provide important evidence about the casting requirements for acting companies in the time of Shakespeare. One plot is for a play acted by Lord Strange's Men about 1590; three plots are for plays acted by the Lord Admiral's Men between 1597 and 1602.

The platt of The secound parte of the Seven Deadlie Sinns (Dulwich College MS. XIX), preserved with the papers of Edward Alleyn at Dulwich College, is apparently derived from a version of Richard Tarlton's late morality play, *The Seven Deadly Sins*, possibly acted at Court by the Queen's Men in 1585. Tarlton died in 1588, and the play came into the repertory of Lord Strange's Men, who probably prepared this plot for performance at the Curtain about 1590.[14]

The plott of ffrederick and Basilea (British Library MS. Add. 10449, fol. 2) was probably prepared for the first performance of this anonymous play by the Lord Admiral's Men at the Rose on 3 June 1597.[15]

14. Greg, I, 105-18.
15. Ibid., 123-26.

The Plott of the Battell of Alcazar (British Library MS. Add. 10449, fol. 3) is the only Elizabethan play for which a complete printed text and a plot have been preserved. It was probably written by George Peele about 1589, and Henslowe's *Diary* shows that between 20 February 1591/2 and 20 January 1592/3 an amalgamation of Lord Strange's Men and the Lord Admiral's Men acted this play twelve times with the variant title *Muly Mollocco*. The anonymous title-page of the 1594 quarto states that the play was acted by the Lord Admiral's Men. The plot, probably prepared for a revival at the Rose sometime between 1 December 1598 and 1 March 1598/9, is mutilated; parts of it are lost, and it corresponds with only the first four acts of the quarto. The fifth act of the plot probably continued on its now lost back sheet.[16]

The plott of The First parte of Tamar Cam is lost, but a transcript by Steevens was printed by Isaac Reed in the 1803 Variorum Shakespeare. The first part of the play was apparently written before 28 April 1592, when Henslowe's *Diary* records that "the second pte of tamber came" was acted by the Lord Admiral's Men, then playing at the Rose. On 6 May 1596, Henslowe lists "tambercame" (probably the first part) as "ne," i.e., newly licensed for revival by the Lord Admiral's Men. Seven more performances of "tambercame" and "1 pte of tambercame" are recorded in 1596. The actors named in the plot were with the Lord Admiral's Men at the Fortune in 1602.[17]

Each plot is divided into scenes by rules drawn across its columns, but scenes are not numbered. Each scene begins with "Enter" followed by the names of one or more characters. The actor playing each role is usually identified at his first entrance in that role but not necessarily at subsequent entrances in that role. If after a scene begins one or more characters join others already on stage, this entrance is usually indicated by the words "to them," "to him," or "to her." In BA and TC, the directions *exit* and *exeunt* are included at the end of most scenes, but these closing directions are omitted from *7DS* and *F&B*.

As Table 1 indicates, the casting requirements for the four play-house plots are consistent with the requirements for ten King's Men

---

16. Ibid., 144-50.
17. Ibid., 160-65. Three other plots from Elizabethan playhouses survive, but none provides adequate evidence for the purpose of this study. *2 Fortune's Tennis* (1597-98) and *Troilus and Cressida* (1599) survive only in fragments, and neither text identifies actors in parts (Greg, I, 130-38). *The Dead Man's Fortune* (1590) lists "Burbage" as an actor, but the part he plays is uncertain. The only other actors listed are "Darlowe," "Robert lee," and "b samme," who play minor parts. A tire-man plays an attendant (Ibid., 94-101).

Table 1

	Principal				Minor				Totals	
	Men	Parts	Boys	Parts	Men	Parts	Boys	Parts	Actors	Parts
7DS	8	12	4	7	7	32	2	3	21 (plus 7 Vices and Mercury)	54
F&B	10	12	4	4	2	10	–	–	16 (plus Gatherers and Attendants)	26
BA	10	15	3	5	7	21	6	7	26	48
TC	8	15	2	2	8	51	2	5	20 (plus 6 men and 3 boys in final procession only)	73
SMT	8	8	4	5	7	13	–	–	19	26
DM	9	16	3	3	7	20	3	4	22	43
Barn.	10	16	5	9	10	37	–	–	25	62
DF	6	6	3	3	10	18	–	–	19	27
RA	9	11	5	5	8	24	–	–	22	40
Picture	8	8	4	4	6	20	3	3	21	35
SC	9	9	3	3	10	17	3	4	25	33
Swisser	9	9	3	3	6	15	1	2	19	29
BAYL	10	16	3	3	9	24	3	5	25	48
WGC	9	9	3	3	3	7	8	14	23	33

plays that identify actors in principal parts. In addition to the three manuscript prompt books already discussed, Table 1 lists the seven texts described below—two manuscripts and five printed plays from the repertory of the King's Men.

The Duchess of Malfi by John Webster was probably first performed in the season of 1613-14, and the title-page of the 1623 quarto states that the play was "*Presented privately at the Black-Friers; and publiquely at at the Globe, By the* Kings Majesties Servants." Two distinct casts are listed, one from before the death of Ostler on 16 December 1614, the other from after the death of Burbage on 13 March 1619 but before that of Tooley in June 1623.[18] Three of the actors in the earlier list, Burbage, Condell and Ostler are replaced in their respective roles by Taylor, Robinson and Benfield.

The Deserving Favorite is by Lodowick Carlell, a gentleman at the Court of Charles I; Bentley suggests the play may have been written as early as 1622.[19] The title-page of the 1629 quarto states that it was "lately Acted, first before the Kings Majestie, and since publikely at the *Blackfriers* by his Majesties Servants."

The Roman Actor by Philip Massinger was licensed for the King's Men by the Master of the Revels on 11 October 1626, and the title-page of the 1629 quarto states that the play "hath divers times beene, with good allowance Acted, at the private Play-house in the *Black-Friers*, by the Kings Majesties Servants."[20]

The Picture by Massinger was licensed for the King's Men by the Master of the Revels on 8 June 1629, and the title-page of the 1630 quarto states that the play "was often presented with good allowance, at the *Globe* and *Blacke-Friers* Playhouses by the Kings Majesties servants."[21]

The Soddered Citizen, by John Clavell, a gentleman highwayman, survives in a privately owned manuscript in which several hands have made cuts and emendations. G.E. Bentley describes the play as "a poor thing confused and contradictory that must have caused the company some embarrassment."[22] There is no record of a Revels licence, nor is this text censored, and it is possible that the company began rehearsals but then abandoned the project. The plot concerns

18. E.K. Chambers, *The Elizabethan Stage* (Oxford, 1923), III, 510-11.
19. Gerald Eades Bentley, *The Jacobean and Caroline Stage* (Oxford, 1956), III, 115-17.
20. Bentley, IV, 815-17.
21. Ibid., 808-10.
22. Ibid., III, 162-65. Also see the edition by J. H. P. Pafford (Malone Society Reprints, 1935).

the way in which an unscrupulous citizen, Undermyne, is mended or soldered by Dr. Makewell.

The Swisser (British MS. Add. 36759) is a careful calligraphic copy in the autograph of Arthur Wilson. The title-page states: "Acted at Blackfriars, 1631."[23]

The Wild Goose Chase by John Fletcher was acted at court in the Christmas season of 1621, and it was probably written earlier that year. It was revived in 1632 and first printed in 1652. The title-page states that "it hath been Acted with singular Applause at the *Black-Friers*." The cast list is probably from the revival of 1632.

Table 1 summarizes the casting requirements for men and boys in four playhouse plots and in ten King's Men plays that identify actors in principal parts. The distinction between principal parts and minor parts follows an Elizabethan theatrical convention observed by Ben Jonson, who in his *Works* (1616) lists William Shakespeare as one of ten "principal comedians" who acted *Every Man in His Humour* in 1598 and as one of eight "principal tragedians" who acted *Sejanus* in 1603.[25] The men who play principal parts are usually, but not always, sharers—that is, joint owners of the company who share the profits. The boys who play principal female roles are sometimes, but not always, apprentices to the leading actors of the company.

From six to ten men act all the principal male roles in each play, and from two to five boys act all the principal female roles. The men and boys in the larger principal parts do not double, but in lesser principal parts some actors play as many as three parts. Boys in female roles do not double in adult male roles, but in *BA* Dick Jubie, who plays Abdula Rais, a woman, doubles as a youth, Christophoro de Tavera, who speaks only one line and is described in the 1594 quarto as the "bedfellow" of Sebastian.[26] When an actor doubles in principal parts, he is usually off-stage for at least one full scene for each change of costume.

Most of the King's Men plays considered here do not identify actors in minor parts—those usually described by function rather than by name—but the playhouse plots identify almost all of the actors in minor parts. This evidence makes it possible to estimate the number of actors in minor parts for King's Men plays, and these estimates are included in Table 1. The plots require from two to ten men in

23. Bentley, V, 1273-74.
24. Ibid., III, 425-30.
25. Chambers, *Stage*, III, 359, 367.
26. George Peele, *The Battell of Alcazar* (London, 1594), C4.

minor parts, and the number of boys in minor parts varies from none to eight. Most of the actors in minor parts double, on the average, in four parts per play, and for about one-half the costume changes actors are off-stage for a full scene for each change. Some quick changes are required, but only rarely does an actor play more than one part in any given scene.

The playhouse plots usually specify that such minor parts as Attendants, Nobles, Soldiers and Guards are three in number. For example, in the fourth and fifth unnumbered scenes in 7DS, three soldiers enter with Ferrex and three soldiers enter with Porrex. In F&B, an unspecified number of Gatherers—men who collect money at the door or in the galleries—play Guards, Confederates and Soldiers. Also in this play, an unspecified number of Attendants—probably backstage helpers such as tire-men and stage-keepers—play Lords. TC identifies six men and three boys who wear exotic costumes in the final procession only. In 7DS, seven Vices and Mercury are played by eight unidentified supernumeraries.

Table 2 summarizes the evidence about casting for ten King's Men plays that identify actors in principal parts. In the left column are the names of nineteen actors, twelve of whom—Burbage, Taylor, Lowin, Ostler, Benfield, Condell, Robinson, Underwood, Rice, Tooley, Shank, and Gough—are among the twenty-six men named in the Shakespeare First Folio under the heading "Principall actors in all these plays."[27] The number after each part indicates its relative size. For example, on the top line Richard Burbage is listed as Ferdinand, the second-largest part in The Duchess of Malfi when it was acted in the season of 1613-14. Joseph Taylor is listed as Ferdinand in the cast list from the period 1619-23.

The casting for these ten plays clearly indicates the versatility of Shakespeare's company. First, we should note that boy actors play female roles and that when these same boys become young men they act adult male roles. For example, in 1611 Richard Robinson plays the Lady who kills herself rather than yield to the lustful Tyrant in The Second Maiden's Tragedy. About eight years later, Robinson plays the evil Cardinal who murders his mistress, Julia, by having her kiss a poisoned Bible in The Duchess of Malfi. John Rice was an apprentice to John Heminges in 1607;[28] about six years later, Rice plays the Marquis of Pescara, described as "as noble old fellow" in The Duchess

27. William Shakespeare, The First Folio: The Norton Facsimile, prepared by Charleton Hinman (New York, 1968), p. 17.
28. Chambers, Stage, II, 336.

Table 2: King's Men Identified in Principal Parts, 1611–1632

	2nd Maiden's Tragedy 1611	Duchess of Malfi 1613–14	Barnavelt 1619	Duchess of Malfi 1619–23	Roman Actor 1626
R. Burbage*	—	Ferdinand 2	—	—	—
J. Taylor*	—	—	—	Ferdinand 2	Paris 2
J. Lowin*	—	Bosola 1	—	Bosola 1	Caesar 1
W. Ostler*	—	Antonio 3	—	—	—
R. Benfield*	—	—	—	Antonio 3	Rusticus 7
H. Condell*	—	Cardinal 4	Captain 8	—	—
R. Robinson*	Lady x	—	Ambassador	Cardinal 4	Aesopus 9
J. Underwood*	—	Delio 5 Madman	—	Delio 5 Madman	—
J. Rice*	—	Pescara 6y Madman	Captain 4 Servant	Pescara 6 Madman	—
N. Tooley*	—	Malateste 8 Forobosco Madman	—	Malateste 8 Forobosco Madman	—
R. Pallant, Jr.	—	Cariola x	—	Doctor y Officer v	—
J. Shank*	Memphonius 8	—	—	—	—
R. Gough*	—	Silvio 7y Madman	—	—	—
T. Pollard	—	Duchess x	Holderus y Servant	Silvio 7y Madman	Stephanos 6
R. Sharpe	—	—	—	Duchess x	Lamia
E. Swanston	—	—	—	—	Parthenius 3
A. Smith	—	—	—	—	Aretinus 4
W. Penn	—	—	—	—	Philargus 8
J. Honyman	—	—	—	—	Domitilla x 1st Tribune 5y
C. Greville	—	—	—	—	Latinus

	Deserving Favourite 1629	The Picture 1629	Soddered Citizen 1630	The Swisser 1631	Believe as You List 1631	The Wild Goose Chase rev. 1632
R. Burbage*	—	—	—	—	—	—
J. Taylor*	Duke 2	Mathias 1	—	Arioldus 1	Antiochus 1	Mirabell 1
J. Lowin*	Jacomo 4	Eubulus 2	Undermyne 1	Andrucho 3	Flaminius 2	Belleur 2
W. Ostler*	—	—	—	—	—	—
R. Benfield*	King 3	Ladislaus 6	Makewell 5	Antharis 5	Marcellus 4	De Gard 4
H. Condell*	—	—	—	—	—	—
R. Robinson*	Orsinio 5	—	—	—	Lentulus 6	Le Castre 6
J. Underwood*	—	—	—	—	—	—
J. Rice*	—	—	—	—	—	—
N. Tooley*	—	—	—	—	—	—
R. Pallant, Jr.	—	—	—	—	—	—
J Shank*	—	Hilario 5	Hodge 8	—	—	Servant 8
R. Gough	—	—	—	—	—	—
T. Pollard	—	Ubaldo 3	Brainsick 2	Timentes 6	Berecinthius 3	Pinac 3
R. Sharpe	Lysander 1	Ferdinand 8	Wittworth 3	King 2	—	—
E. Swanston	Utrante 6	Ricardo 4	—	Alcidonus 4	Chrysalus 5	Lugier 5
A. Smith	Gerard 7	—	Clutch 7	Asprandus 7	2nd Merch. 8 Jailer	—
W. Penn	—	Baptista 7	—	Clephis 8	—	Nantolet 7
J. Honyman	Clarinda x	Sophia x	Sly 6y	Iseas 9y	1st Merch. 7y 3rd Merch. 9y	Yng. Factor 9y
C. Greville	—	—	Mountayne 4y	—	—	—

* = Shakespeare First Folio List of Principal Actors. Figure after a part denotes its relative size. x = boy. y = hired man.

35

of Malfi. In the earlier cast of this play, Robert Pallant, Jr. plays Cariola, a young woman; in the later cast, he doubles in the minor roles of a Doctor and an Officer.

Richard Sharpe, who plays the Duchess of Malfi, probably became a sharer in the King's Men in 1624.[29] Thereafter, he plays adult male roles: Lysander, a young lover; Parthenius, a young man; Ferdinand, a general; Wittworth, a young Lord; and the King of the Lombards. John Honeyman was baptized in 1613,[30] and at nine he plays Clarinda; at thirteen, Domitilla; at sixteen, Sophia. At seventeen he plays the adult male role of Sly, a tricky servant; at eighteen, the First Merchant; at nineteen, the Young Factor.

Actors also show their versatility when they double, often in markedly different roles. In *The Duchess of Malfi*, John Underwood plays Delio, the good friend and confidant of Antonio, the steward secretly married to the Duchess; Underwood doubles as one of the eight madmen who torment the sleep of the Duchess when they "sing and daunce, And act their gambols to the full o'th'moone" (I 3). Nicholas Tooley plays three roles; the cowardly Count Malateste; Forobosco, a comic servant; and another of the madmen.

When a character assumes a disguise, he is, in effect, playing another role-within-the-play. The audience is usually made aware of this double identity, but most of the other characters do not penetrate this disguise until late in the play. For example, in *The Swisser* John Lowin plays Andrucho, who is really the banished Count Aribert in disguise. An actor can readily assume a disguise by putting on a false beard, but in this play John Lowin wears *two* beards. One is his real beard that he wears as Aribert; the second beard he wears for his disguise as Andrucho. Late in the play he reveals his true identity to Arioldus and confides to him: "I have reduced my beard to the old shape." But Arioldus warns him: "keepe this falce one on: The King is coming" (f. 58). Finally, when Andrucho *discovers* to reveal his true identity and his real beard, he also reveals that the captive maiden, Eurinia, is really his daughter Eugenia, the long-lost love of the King. Characters assume disguises in three other of these plays. Robinson appears as a Hermit who reveals himself to be Count Orsinio; Anthony Smith plays Clutch, who assumes the disguise of Querpo, a "decayed gentleman;" Swanston plays Lugier, a "Tutor to the Ladies" who assumes the disguise of an Italian Merchant.

In *The Picture*, Hilario, a jester played by John Shank, attempts to

29. Bentley, II, 570.
30. Ibid., 476.

cheer his melancholy mistress, Sophia, and "put her out of her dumps with laughter." Hilario enters "with a long white hayre and beard, in an anticke armour "(D, 3ᵛ). After reciting a few lines of doggerel, Hilario forgets his part; he says "I am out." He tries to recover, but Sophia, still very melancholy, banishes him from her household. Her maid, Corsica, scorns Hilario's poor performance and says:

> You have made
> A fine peece of work on't: how do you like the quality?
> You had a foolish itch to be an actor,
> and may strowle where you please.
>
> (D4ᵛ)

In each of the plays considered here, each of the leading actors usually plays only one major role, but over the years each of the leading actors plays a wide variety of parts. As noted, Richard Burbage was the first actor to play Duke Ferdinand, the evil twin brother of the Duchess of Malfi. In Act V the Duke becomes ill with "a very pestilent disease ... they call Licanthropia." A doctor describes the symptoms:

> In those that are possess'd with't there ore-flowes
> Such mellencholy humour, they imagine
> Themselves to be transformed into Woolves
> Steale forth to Church-yards in the dead of night
> And dig dead bodies up ...   (L2)

The mad scene of the Duke is a *tour de force* for an actor, and undoubtedly Burbage was a howling success. Joseph Taylor also plays Duke Ferdinand and Paris, the Roman actor; the Duke who wins Clarinda; Mathias, a faithful husband; Arioldus, a gentlemen who leaves retirement to become a successful general; Antiochus, the deposed and aging King of Syria who has wandered in exile for twenty-two years; and Mirabell, a young Benedick who finally succumbs to love and marriage.

John Lowin was apparently skilful as villains and tyrants, but he also plays sympathetic roles. He plays Bosola, the villain who spies on the Duchess of Malfi and who supervises her execution; Caesar Domitian is a tyrant, and Jacomo is a villain, but Eubulus is an old windbag courtier reminiscent of Polonius. Undermyne is an unscrupulous citizen, but, as noted, Andrucho is the sympathetic Count Aribert in disguise; Flaminius is a tyrannical Roman consul who persecutes Antiochus, but Belleur is the companion of Mirabell and the bashful lover of Rosalura.

There should be no need to multiply examples. Evidence shows that each of the other actors on this list plays a wide variety of parts. The most important consideration in casting a given part was not the type of role to be acted but the *size* of that part. It should come as no surprise that the leading actors of the company almost invariably play the largest parts, a practice that continues in the theater of our own day.

Perhaps the most instructive play for the purpose of this paper is *The Roman Actor*, in which the players perform three distinctly different plays-within-the-play. With the first play, Paris attempts to help a young man, Parthenius, who has a miserly father, Philargus. Paris suggests that a possible remedy for the father's obsession with money would be to have him watch a play showing a character with the same obsession. In describing this process, Paris paraphrases Hamlet's lines about "guilty creatures sitting at a play" who "have proclaimed their malefactions" (II.ii, 617, 620). Paris says:

> I once observ'd
> in a Tragedie of ours, in which a murther
> Was acted to the life, a guiltie hearer
> Forc'd by the terror of a wounded concience,
> To make discoverie of that which torture
> Could not wring from him. Nor can it appeare
> Like an impossibilitie, but that
> Your Father looking on a covetous man
> Presented on the Stage as in a mirror
> May see his owne deformity, and loathe it.   (D2)

The young man agrees. He pays Paris a fee for a performance of the first play-within-the-play, *The Cure of Avarice*; he says that he will ask Caesar to command his miserly father to observe the play. In this, Paris plays the Doctor of Physic who attempts to cure the miser-within-the-play, but Philargus, the miserly father who observes the play, is not reformed.

However, Caesar's wife, the Empress Domitia, in watching the play becomes infatuated with Paris. After the actors leave, she says to Caesar:

> The Fellow
> That play'd the Doctor did it well by *Venus*:
> He had a tunable tongue and neate delivery
> And yet in my opinion he would performe
> A lovers part much better. Prethee *Caesar*
> For I grow wearie let us see tomorrow
> *Iphis* and *Anaxerete*.   (E3)

Caesar agrees, and the next day Paris acts in this second play-within-the-play. When Paris, as Iphis, is spurned by the hard-hearted Anaxarete, he threatens to hang himself. But the Empress Domitia becomes so emotionally involved that she stops the performance. Before she leaves the scene, however, she says "Come to me, Paris, Tomorrow for your reward" (G2)

When they meet, Domitia says that she loves Paris and that he is worthy of her love because he must *be* like the noble characters he plays:

> Thou whom oft I have seene
> To personate a Gentleman, noble, wise,
> Faithfull, and gainsome, and what vertues else
> The Poet pleases to adorne you with
> Thou must be reallie in some degree
> The thing thou dost present. Nay doe not tremble,
> We seriouslie beleeve it, and presume
> Our *Paris* is the volume in which all
> Those excellent gifts the Stage hath seene him grac'd with
> Are curiouslie bound up.   (H2)

But here the Empress labours under the same misapprehension about actors and their parts that appears to have misled T.W. Baldwin when he asserts: "These men did not act; they were themselves." Paris, in his reply to the Empress, describes one of the qualities essential to the art of acting:

> The argument
> Is the same, great *Augusta*, that I acting
> A foole, a coward, a traytor or cold cinique
> Or any other weake and vitious person
> Of force, I must be such. O gracious Madam,
> How glorious soever, or deform'd,
> I doe appeare in the Sceane, my part being ended,
> And all my borrowed ornaments put off,
> I am no more, nor lesse, then what I was
> Before I enter'd.   (H2)

As the scene continues, Domitia attempts to seduce Paris—her stage direction reads: *Courting Paris wantonly*—but Caesar, who has been secretly observing them from above, intervenes. At first, Caesar seems to be merciful to Domitia and Paris, and he asks Paris if the actors can perform a play called *The False Servant*. Caesar describes the argument: a great lord, who suspects his wife of infidelity, pretends to go on a journey but returns home to surprise his wife attempt-

ing to seduce a servant. Paris remembers the play and says that the
actors are ready to perform it. In this, the third play-within-the-
play, Paris is to act the Servant, and Aesopus is to play the Lord. But
before the actors can begin, Caesar insists that he himself play the
Lord:

> We can perform it better.
> Off with my Robe and wreath. Since *Nero* scorn'd not
> the publike *Theater*, we in private may
> Disport ourselves. This cloake and hat, without
> Wearing a beard or other propertie,
> Will fit the person.   (H4^v—I).

But one of the actors asks Caesar to use a property sword instead of
his real one:

> Sir a foyle
> The point and edge rebutted when you act
> To doe the murder. If you please use this
> And lay aside your owne sword.   (I)

But Caesar insists on keeping his own sword, and, apparently playing
the part of the irate Lord, Caesar stabs Paris to death. *The Roman
Actor* requires the work of several extremely versatile performers,
and this play alone should serve to dispel Baldwin's erroneous notions
about actors and their parts.

In closing, I cite an observation about the versatility of Shakespearean actors by William Hazlitt, who writes in *The Examiner* of
5 January 1817:

> Players ... are the only honest hypocrites. Their life is a voluntary
> dream; a studied madness. The height of their ambition is to be *beside
> themselves*. Today-kings, to-morrow beggars, it is only when they are them-
> selves that they are nothing. Made up of mimic, laughter and tears, passing
> from the extremes of joy or woe at the prompter's call, they wear the livery
> of other men's fortunes; their very thoughts are not their own. They are,
> as it were, train-bearers in the pageant of life, and hold a glass up to
> humanity, frailer than itself. We see ourselves at second-hand in them;
> they show us all that we are, all that we wish to be, and all that we dread to
> be.[31]

Hazlitt's comments are appropriate for the great actors of his own day
as well as for the actors of Shakespeare's company, the King's Men.

---

31. William Hazlitt, *Selected Essays*, ed. George Sampson (Cambridge, 1917), p. 72.

The Staging of Shirley's
The Lady of Pleasure

RONALD HUEBERT

The first performance of *The Lady of Pleasure* took place in late October or early November, 1635. The play was licensed for performance on 15 October,[1] and by 5 or 6 November it had attracted sufficient notice to deserve mention in John Greene's diary. Referring to the party of guests which gathered to celebrate his sister's wedding, Greene wrote as follows: "wee were at a play, some at cockpit, some at blackfriers. The play at cockpit was Lady of pleasure, at blackfriers the conspiracy."[2] A month later, on 8 December, Sir Humphrey Mildmay recorded in his account book the expenditure of 1 shilling for admission to the play, and in his diary he added the following description: "dined w[i]th Rob[ert] Dowgill wente to the La[dy] of pleasure & sawe that rare playe came home late Supped."[3]

Very little can be inferred with confidence from these laconic observations by members of Shirley's audience. Indeed, Greene may not have been a member of this audience at all, if he was among those wedding celebrants who chose to see *The Conspiracy* at Blackfriars rather than Shirley's play at the Cockpit. Still, Greene's notation confirms one fact and one assumption: it agrees with the title page of the quarto (1637) and with the Lord Chamberlain's list (10 August 1639)[4] in assigning *The Lady of Pleasure* to the Cockpit in Drury Lane, otherwise known as the Phoenix theatre; and it supports the view of

---

1. "*The Lady of Pleasure*, by James Shirley, licensed" (*The Dramatic Records of Sir Henry Herbert*, ed. Joseph Quincy Adams [New Haven, 1917], p. 37).
2. See Gerald Eades Bentley, *The Jacobean and Caroline Stage* (Oxford, 1941-68), V, 1125.
3. Bentley, II, 677. Whenever I quote from old-spelling texts or manuscripts, usage of *i/j*, *u/v*, and long *s* is silently modernized.
4. Bentley, I, 330-31.

some theatre historians that by 1635 the Cockpit and Blackfriars were theatrical institutions of virtually equal prestige.[5]

Mildmay's jottings, however cryptic, will reward more detailed inspection. First, the shilling which Mildmay spent on 8 December 1635 appears to have been the normal minimum price of admission for a cavalier gentleman. I doubt that Sir Humphrey would have been satisfied to pay the absolute minimum of sixpence, if by such thrift he were to risk the social opprobrium which Shirley attaches to unsophisticated spectators in the Prologue to *The Example* (1637):

> Nay, hee that in the Parish never was
> Thought fit to bee o'th jury, has a place
> Here, on the Bench for six pence, and dares sit
> And boast himself commissioner of wit. (sig. *2)

Indeed, in his recorded decade of playgoing, Mildmay never paid less than a shilling for a performance at a professional theatre.[6] He often paid exactly a shilling, as he did when he saw "a pretty & Merry Co[m]edy att the Cocke" (6 June 1633), or when he visited Blackfriars to see *The Wits* on one occasion (22 January 1633/4), *The Elder Brother* on another (25 April 1635). Frequently Mildmay paid more than a shilling: "a Newe play Called the spartan Lady" (1 May 1634) cost him a shilling and threepence, a "base play att the Cocke pitt" (20 March 1633/4) cost him one and six, and an unnamed play at the Globe (18 July 1633) one shilling ten. When he was "with company" Mildmay's expenditures reflected his hospitality, ranging from about three shillings up to eleven. On these occasions, no doubt, Mildmay wanted to be thought well of, to be "held the witty man, / [Who] censures finely, rules the Box, and strikes / With his court nod consent to what he likes."[7]

When he paid his shilling to see *The Lady of Pleasure*, then, Mildmay was doing what was typical and unpretentious for a person of his social class and theatrical tastes.[8] And, in attending the theatre between his

5. See William B. Markward, "A Study of the Phoenix Theatre in Drury Lane, 1617-1638" (Dissertation, University of Birmingham, 1953), p. 166; Bentley, I, 224-26: T. J. King, "Staging of Plays at the Phoenix in Drury Lane, 1617-42," *Theatre Notebook*, 19 (1964-65), 146; and Andrew Gurr, *The Shakespearean Stage, 1574-1642* (Cambridge, 1970), p. 43.

6. See the records printed in Bentley, II, 674-80. Two expenditures of sixpence each do not qualify as exceptions: the first pertains to a masque performed at Whitehall (18 February 1633/4), the second "To a Playe of Warre" (16 November 1643) which took place after the closing of the theatres. Neither of these events is necessarily comparable to attendance at a professional theatre.

7. Prologue to *The Example*, sig. *2. It is disconcerting to find that, in the metaphor of the gallant who "censures finely" from his position "on the Bench" as if he were "commissioner of wit," Shirley is heavily indebted to Jonson; see the Induction to

midday meal (when he "dined") and his evening meal (when he "Supped"), Mildmay was engaging in perfectly normal behaviour both for himself and countless others. When he described *The Lady of Pleasure* as "that rare playe," however, Mildmay was breaking with his personal habits: though in the space of a decade he recorded sixty-one theatrical excursions, he seldom confided his judgment to the diary. On three occasions he expressed distaste for a play, and on three occasions he recorded approbation. In the eyes of its first critic, *The Lady of Pleasure* appears to have been an outstanding theatrical achievement.

The external stimulus provided by the assignment of editing *The Lady of Pleasure* is largely to blame for my interest in Mildmay's opinions, and indeed for my central concern in the pages which follow: namely, to recover some rough impression of the nature and quality of Sir Humphrey Mildmay's experience on the afternoon of 8 December 1635. Without being able to see what he saw or hear what he heard, it becomes necessary to rely on such historical evidence as may have a bearing on three principal subjects: the design of the playhouse which Mildmay visited, the talents of the theatrical company engaged in the performance, and the staging requirements of the play being performed. These, for purposes of clarity, will be the stages of my argument; in those few instances where I violate my own division, I ask for indulgence by appealing to the more exacting

Bartholomew Fair, ed. E. A. Horsman, The Revels Plays (London, 1960), 11. 98-107: "It is also agreed, that every man here exercise his own judgement, and not censure by contagion, or upon trust, from another's voice, or face, that sits by him, be he never so first in the commission of wit: . . . and not to be brought about by any that sits on the bench with him, though they indict and arraign plays daily." Both passages, of course, are describing conventional behaviour which could have been as easily observed at the Hope in 1614 as at the Cockpit some twenty years later.

8. That a shilling should be treated as a normal charge for admission can be confirmed by citing the dedicatory verse (by W. B.) to *The Bondman* in *The Plays and Poems of Philip Massinger*, ed. Philip Edwards and Colin Gibson (Oxford, 1976), I, 314:

> And (Reader) if you have disburs'd a shilling,
> To see this worthy STORY, and are willing
> To have a large encrease; (if rul'd by me)
> You may a MARCHANT, and a POET be.
> 'Tis granted for your twelve-pence you did sit,
> And *See*, and *Heare*, and *Understand* not yet.
> The AUTHOR (in a Christian pitty) takes
> Care of your good, and Prints it for your sakes.
> That such as will but venter Six-pence more,
> May *Know*, what they but *Saw*, and *Heard* before.

This play was licensed for performance at the Cockpit on 3 December 1623, and was printed in the following year. The bookseller must have been grateful to W. B. for pointing out that the cost of a printed quarto was only half of the normal admission charge at the theatre.

demands of an untidy and intractable world of external fact.

The playhouse in which *The Lady of Pleasure* was first performed came into being when Christopher Beeston, a prominent member of Queen Anne's company at the Red Bull, planned and sponsored the construction of the Cockpit in Drury Lane in 1616 and 1617. On 9 August 1616 he leased for thirty-one years

> All that edifices or building called the Cockpittes and the Cockhouses and the shedds thereunto adjoining . . . Togeather alsoe with one tenement or house and a little Garden therunto belonging next adjoyning to the said Cockpittes . . . and one part or parcell of ground behinde the said Cockpittes.[9]

Within seven months the buildings had been renovated and the new playhouse was in operation. But not for long. On Shrove Tuesday, 4 March 1616/17, an unusually vigorous apprentice riot interrupted Beeston's enterprise; one part of the mob,

> making for Drury Lane, where lately a newe playhouse is erected, . . . besett the house round, broke in, wounded divers of the players, broke open their trunkes, & what apparell, bookes, or other things they found, they burnt & cutt in peeces; & not content herewith, gott on the top of the house, & untiled it, & had not the Justices of the Peace & Sherife levied an aide, & hindred their purpose, they would have laid that house likewise even with the grownd.[10]

Undaunted by this disastrous beginning, Beeston set about having the damage repaired, and within three months (by 3 June 1617) the playhouse was ready to open again.[11] Perhaps the alternate name for the theatre, the Phoenix, was Beeston's attempt to make good publicity out of the near destruction and quick revival of his edifice. In any case, the public continued to prefer the traditional name, the Cockpit, as the remarks of Sir Humphrey Mildmay (already quoted) indicate. On this question of usage, I will follow Sir Humphrey's taste, so that "the Cockpit" (unqualified) may be understood as referring to Beeston's theatre, and should not be confused with the Cockpit-in-Court, of which more later.

No direct documentary evidence about the design of the Cockpit has been discovered. The earliest verbal description occurs in James Wright's *Historia Histrionica* (1699), cast in the form of a dialogue between Truman, an "Honest Old Cavalier" who remembers a great

---

9. Bentley, VI, 48.
10. The account is contained in a letter by Edward Sherburne (8 March 1616/17), and is printed in Bentley, VI, 54.
11. Ibid., 56.

deal about the good old days before the closing of the theatres, and Lovewit, a persistent interrogator who today might be either the host of a talk-show on daytime TV or a Professor of Oral History. "What kind of Playhouses had they before the Wars?" asks the genial interviewer. Truman replies:

> The *Black-friers*, *Cockpit*, and *Salisbury-court*, were called Private Houses, and were very small to what we see now. The *Cockpit* was standing since the Restauration, and *Rhode's* Company Acted there for some time.

"I have seen that," Lovewit interposes, and the old gentleman continues:

> Then you have seen the other two, in effect; for they were all three Built almost exactly alike, for Form and Bigness. Here they had Pits for the Gentry, and Acted by Candle-light. The *Globe*, *Fortune* and *Bull*, were large Houses, and lay partly open to the Weather, and there they alwaies Acted by Daylight.[12]

Since a great many of Truman's assertions have been confirmed by modern scholarship, we ought to treat his claim about the resemblance between the Cockpit and the other "Private Houses" with some respect. If it is true that the "Bigness" of the Cockpit was roughly the same as that of Blackfriars, then we might suppose it to have occupied a space 46 feet by 66 feet with a seating capacity not much in excess of 500 spectators.[13] If it is true that the "Form" of the Cockpit resembled that of the other two, then we can suppose it contained a platform stage somewhat smaller than that specified in the Fortune contract (43 feet by 27 feet 6 inches);[14] that the stage was

---

12. The relevant extracts are printed in Bentley, II, 694.
13. The dimensions are those given by Richard Hosley in his essay on "The Playhouses" in *The Revels History of Drama in English*, ed. Clifford Leech and T. W. Craik, III (London, 1975), 206. Irwin Smith estimates the capacity of Blackfriars at 516 In *Shakespeare's Blackfriars Playhouse* (New York, 1964), p. 297. The highest known receipt for a single Blackfriars performance is £19 15s (see Bentley, VI, 22). At the putative average price of a shilling per admission, this would mean 395 spectators. But of course, on the occasion in question, the house may not have been full or even very near to full. The estimate of 516 would seem to be a safe maximum, if there is any truth in Wright's claim that the Caroline private houses were "very small" compared to Restoration playhouses; Wren's Drury Lane reputedly held about 600 to 800 spectators, or so Richard Southern claims in *The Revels History of Drama in English*, ed. T. W. Craik, V (London, 1976), 110.
14. For a review of the evidence concerning stage sizes, see Leonie Star, "The Middle of the Yard, Part II: The Calculation of Stage Sizes for English Renaissance Playhouses," *Theatre Notebook*, 30 (1976), 65-69. Star estimates the dimensions of the Blackfriars stage as 30 feet in width by something less than 30 feet in depth; this compares favourably with Hosley's calculations of 29 feet by 18 feet 6 inches (*Revels History*, III, 210) and with William A. Armstrong's observations about the relative smallness of the stage at Blackfriars (*The Elizabethan Private Theatres: Facts and Problems* [London, 1958], p. 5).

flanked on either side by high-priced gentleman's boxes; that opposite the stage was a pit, furnished with benches "for the Gentry" instead of a yard for the groundlings in the outdoor manner; and that the pit was surrounded on three sides by a U-shaped configuration of galleries, in either two or three tiers.[15] Some of these inferences by analogy can be confirmed by indirect evidence drawn from plays performed at the Cockpit. In the Prologue to *The Example*, quoted above, Shirley refers to the man of wit who "rules the Box" from which he observes the play, and contrasts him with a less officious spectator who "has a place / Here, on the Bench." The Prologue continues, in a passage not yet quoted, with a reference to a stage-keeper who "beares / Three-footed stooles in stead of Juory chaires" (sig. *2). This allusion to the practice, peculiar to the private houses, of allowing some spectators to sit on the edges of the stage, is consistent with other available evidence, like the imaginary portrait by Hemminges and Condell of a gallant who "sit[s] on the Stage at *Black-Friers*, or the *Cock-pit*, to arraigne Playes dailie."[16]

To return briefly to Wright's claims about the private houses, I should point out that in two respects his remarks are quite uncontroversial: he asserts indirectly that the private houses were indoor theatres, and directly that the stages were lit by candles. There is no reason to doubt the truth of either of these claims, or their pertinence to the design of the Cockpit.

But there is one highly controversial inference to be drawn from Wright, and I shall mention it without presuming to solve the problem it creates. If the Cockpit was anything like Blackfriars or Salisbury Court in "Form," then it should be visualized as a rectangular structure. No matter how diligently the Burbages renovated the Upper Frater of the Blackfriars monastery, the result must have been a rectangular auditorium. And since the builders of Salisbury Court began with a barn on a plot of ground measuring 42 feet by 140 feet, it is difficult to imagine them achieving anything but a rectangular playhouse.[17] Yet it has been a favourite belief among students of the Cockpit that they are dealing with a round or octagonal structure.[18]

15. This is not the place to demonstrate that these features were common to both of the other private houses mentioned by Wright, but a good case could be made by comparing Hosley's carefully documented reconstruction of Blackfriars (*Revels History*, III, 205-17) with the evidence assembled by Bentley (VI, 86-115) pertaining to the Salisbury Court theatre.
16. From the address "To the Great Variety of Readers" prefixed to *Mr William Shakespeares Comedies, Histories, & Tragedies* (London, 1623), sig. A3.
17. See Bentley, VI, 88-92.
18. See Markward, pp. 182-83, 363-64; and Bentley, VI, 50.

This belief is based on three separate kinds of evidence: first, the conventionally circular or polygonal shape of buildings used for cockfighting in the seventeenth century, and hence the plausible assumption that the cockpit leased by Beeston was also "round";[19] secondly, the hazardous assumption that Inigo Jones's drawing of the octagonal interior he designed for the Cockpit-in-Court bears a rough resemblance to the design of Beeston's Cockpit; and thirdly, the hasty supposition that references to "this sphere of love" in Cockpit plays can be understood as describing the shape of the galleries.[20] The second and third lines of argument are, without documentary support, little more than fanciful guesswork. The first hypothesis, based on what is known about the design of cockhouses, does bear on a crucial question: namely, what was Beeston up to when, in 1616 and 1617, he converted a plain ordinary cockpit into *the* Cockpit in Drury Lane?

In order to arrive at a possible answer to this question, I will begin by taking a brief detour along a road already travelled by members of this conference under the guidance of D.F. Rowan in 1969. I am referring, of course, to Rowan's discovery of the Jones /Webb theatre drawings (7B and 7C in the collection at Worcester College, Oxford) which, in one of the few ironies of theatre scholarship, can no longer be described as neglected.[21] After a thorough review of the evidence connected with the drawings themselves and some speculations about their significance, Rowan concludes that "there can be no doubt that they represent a real or proposed private 'professional' theatre."[22] This conclusion, though temperate enough to invite eager assent, is also decisive enough to affect in significant ways our interpretations of staging practices in the private houses. But this is a question to which I shall later return.

At present my concern is the ground-plan in the Jones/Webb project. This drawing shows a semicircular shape (housing the pit and galleries) combined with a square shape (housing the stage, boxes, and tiring-house). John Orrell has argued, on what is admittedly "circumstantial evidence," that this ground plan and the drawings which

19. For a review of the evidence, see John Orrell, "Inigo Jones at the Cockpit," *Shakespeare Survey* 30 (1977), 163-65.
20. See the Prologue to *The Coronation* in *The Dramatic Works and Poems of James Shirley*, ed. William Gifford and Alexander Dyce (London, 1833), III, 459.
21. See "A Neglected Jones/Webb Theatre Project, Part II: A Theatrical Missing Link," *The Elizabethan Theatre* II (1969), pp. 60-73. See also "A Neglected Jones/ Webb Theatre Project: Barber-Surgeons Hall Writ Large," *New Theatre Magazine*, 9 (168-9), 6-15, and an abridgement of the same article in *Shakespeare Survey* 23 (1970), 125-29.
22. "Missing Link," pp. 72-73.

accompany it are in fact the designs for the Cockpit in Drury Lane.[23] If Orrell is right, then we have encountered a highly unusual compromise between the rectangle and the circle. The ground plan is in one sense a rectangle, with two of its corners rounded: enough of a rectangle, that is, to allow James Wright to compare its "Form" without qualification to Blackfriars and Salisbury Court. But the ground plan includes a semicircle as well: enough of a circle, that is, to betray the cockhouse origins of the edifice and to allow its galleries to be referred to as a "sphere." Still, to make the association between the Jones/Webb drawings and the Cockpit, though highly enticing, remains a temptation rather than a virtue, at least until there are further documentary witnesses.

Sir Humphrey Mildmay has paid his shilling and been seated, at last, probably on one of the fairly desirable benches in the pit or the first gallery (not on the stage, nor in a private box, nor in an upper gallery seat, I would suppose), and as he looks around him, he sees the interior of either a rectangular playhouse, or a circular playhouse, or a combination of both. More important, as he looks toward the stage, what does Sir Humphrey see? He sees a platform, a façade with doors, hangings, and an above; but these are features which I will discuss in connection with the staging requirements of *The Lady of Pleasure*. As soon as the play begins, he sees costumed actors; upon them will depend the success or failure of the performance, and it is to the players themselves that I should now like to turn.

Of the actors in Queen Henrietta Maria's company in 1635, at least twelve can be securely identified. Collectively, they possess all of the talents one would expect of a first-class company put together by a shrewd theatrical entrepreneur. The members include the sedate if ageing leading man, the fresh-faced adolescent already admired for his female roles, the former adolescent now being groomed for romantic leads, the veteran comedian who has never been averse to earning a laugh by exploiting his unusually skinny physique, and a sprinkling of character actors who habitually expend their energies on assorted merchants, dukes, old men, and servants. In short, Queen Henrietta's men were a repertory company in the best sense of the term: their well-balanced and amply diversified abilities must have been perfectly suited to a play like *The Lady of Pleasure*, which requires stylish collaboration among the actors who play the sixteen speaking roles, and which distributes responsibility rather evenly among the players who take the eight principal parts.

23. "Inigo Jones at the Cockpit," pp. 157-68.

If the company had a star actor, it would be Richard Perkins (c. 1585-1650). I qualify his status in this way because, among the virtues attributed to Perkins by his contemporaries is the one which star performers shun: professional modesty. Perkins played Barabas in the Cockpit revival of Marlowe's *The Jew of Malta* (1633); in the Prologue which Heywood wrote for this occasion, Edward Alleyn is described as "peerless" in his creation of the original Jew for Lord Strange's men; Perkins is awarded the lesser laurel of "merit" which is said to be consistent with his own view of the matter: "nor is it his ambition / To exceed or equal [Alleyn], being of condition / More modest."[24] However surprising, Heywood's assertion should not be lightly dismissed, for his association with Perkins was of long standing, dating back more than thirty years to an earlier theatrical generation when Perkins, Heywood, and Christopher Beeston were all actors with the Earl of Worcester's men. The earliest known reference to Perkins' career, in Henslowe's *Diary*, is remarkable for its quaint anticipation of a professional friendship: "Lent unto Richard perkens the 4 of septemb[er] 1602 to bye thing[s] for thomas hewode playe . . . xvs."[25] Probably seventeen years of age, Perkins was obviously very much the apprentice in 1602. But a decade later he had acquired the skills to attract an unprecedented compliment from Webster. Now a member of Queen Anne's men at the Red Bull, Perkins had played in the first staging of *The White Devil*: a generally unsuccessful production, to judge by Webster's grumblings in the preliminary letter "To the Reader" of the published play. Whatever the causes of Webster's disappointment, the actors' performances were not among them, for he acknowledges their efforts in a note appended to the final scene, concluding his commendation as follows: "in particular I must remember the well approved industry of my friend Master Perkins, and confess the worth of his action did crown both the beginning and end."[26]

By 1635, at the age of fifty, Perkins was a veteran performer. His known roles, aside from Barabas, are Sir John Belfare in Shirley's *The Wedding* (c.1626), Captain Goodlack in the first part of Heywood's *The Fair Maid of the West* (c.1630), Fitzwater in Davenport's *King John*

---

24. *The Complete Plays of Christopher Marlowe*, ed. Irving Ribner (New York, 1963), p. 178.

25. *Henslowe's Diary*, ed. R. A. Foakes and R. T. Rickert (Cambridge, 1961), p. 213.

26. *The White Devil*, ed. John Russell Brown, The Revels Plays (London, 1960), p. 187. Brown infers that, only if Perkins were playing the part of Flamineo could he be described as crowning "both the beginning and end," since Bracciano dies long before the conclusion ("Introduction," p. xxiii).

and Matilda (c.1634), and Hanno in Nabbes' *Hannibal and Scipio* (1635). All of these parts he played for Queen Henrietta's men, whom he joined in about 1626 and with whom he remained until their dispersion in 1637.[27] In one of them he earned a tribute from Andrew Pennycuicke, a man who claimed to be a fellow actor and whose edition of *King John and Matilda* (1655) informs us that the part of Fitzwater was played by "M[aster] Perkins, Whose action gave Grace to the Play."[28]

Of these roles, the one which most clearly concerned Shirley is that of Sir John Belfare in *The Wedding*. Here Perkins played the part of a dignified father, a man who behaves with surprising restraint in his dealings with his marriageable daughter, but who is nevertheless prepared to defend her honour with firmness and vigour. When Belfare makes comfortable allusions to his advancing age, or when he refers to his "gray hairs" (III. ii),[29] Shirley seems to be indulging in his habit of writing with even the personal appearance of a particular actor in mind. This impression can be confirmed by observing the attitude of candid confidence and whimsical frankness on the cavalier-style face in the only known portrait of Perkins (Dulwich College, no. 423).

When Shirley wrote *The Lady of Pleasure* he must have visualized Perkins in one of the principal roles. I believe Sir Thomas Bornwell to have been the only genuinely suitable part. His is the only "straight" role which could be effectively played by an actor of fifty. As the exceptionally tolerant husband of Aretina, Bornwell combines authority, good humour, and restraint in a manner quite reminiscent of Sir John Belfare in *The Wedding*. Since modesty, industry, and grace were characteristics apparently within Perkins' command, he would have been eminently qualified (both by experience and by nature) to take on Bornwell's part. It should not be surprising to find such easy compatibility between the player and his role in a company where, as in this case, the working relationship between star actor and leading dramatist extended over approximately nine years.

The outstanding comic among Queen Henrietta's men was William Robbins, evidently a professional thin man, who appears to have been generously assisted by William Sherlock, a professional fat man. In the *Historia Histrionica*, Wright names "*Robins* a Comedian" among "those of principal Note at the *Cockpit*."[30] Shirley seems to have

---

27. See Bentley, II, 526-28.
28. See Bentley, II, 528.
29. Shirley, *Works*, I, 415.
30. Bentley, II, 693.

placed considerable confidence in his talents, for in *The Wedding* it is Robbins in the role of "Rawbone, *a thin citizen*" who remains on stage at the close to speak the Epilogue and ask for the spectators' applause. Physically emaciated and morally avaricious, Rawbone repeatedly draws attention to these comic faults, as do other characters, who refer to him as "a piece of folly! / A thing made up of parchment," or little more than "an anatomy" (I. iii).[31] Robbins' other known roles include "Carazie, *an Eunuch*" in *The Renegado*[32] and Antonio, the title role, in *The Changeling*.[33] William Sherlock appears in *The Wedding* as "Lodam, *a fat gentleman*" with a penchant for obvious lines, like "I have no stomach to your acquaintance" (II. iii) or "love is worse than a Lent to me, and fasting is a thing my flesh abhors" (III. ii).[34] His other roles include "Mr Ruffman, *a swaggering Gentleman*" in the first part of *The Fair Maid of the West*.[35]

This pair must have played two of the three principal comic roles in *The Lady of Pleasure*: Sir William Sentlove, Master Haircut, and Sir John Littleworth. Just which was which is a matter of speculation, but I am tempted—on grounds of girth—to cast Sherlock as Littleworth. In Act V, after an offstage dunking in the Thames, Littleworth enters "*wet*" (V. ii. 57.1) and complains that his "belly" has disgorged "a tun of water, beside wine" (V. ii. 61, 64).[36] Sir William Sentlove, the trickster and ringleader among the comedians, might well have been Robbins' role.

John Sumner, a regular though not a leading member of the company, would have been the obvious choice for the part of Alexander Kickshaw. He seems to have played roles demanding sexual charisma, like that of Marwood in *The Wedding* or Mustapha in *The Renegado*. In *The Wedding*, Beauford's jealousy is confirmed by his assessment of Marwood's masculinity: "He has a handsome presence and discourse, / Two subtle charms to tempt a woman's frailty" (II. ii).[37] These qualities are exactly what Kickshaw needs, if Aretina's behaviour in *The Lady of Pleasure* is to be credible.

Among the adolescent actors of the company, Ezekiel Fenn is the most likely candidate for one of the female leads. He played the

---

31. Shirley, *Works*, I, 366, 372, 375.
32. Massinger, *Plays*, II, 12.
33. Bentley, II, 401, 548.
34. Shirley, *Works*, I, 366, 393, 409.
35. Bentley, II, 572-73.
36. Citations from *The Lady of Pleasure* refer to my own edition, in preparation for The Revels Plays.
37. Shirley, *Works*, I, 385.

pathos-laden parts of Sophonisba in *Hannibal and Scipio* (1635) and Winifride in a revival of *The Witch of Edmonton* (c. 1635). Since both of these demanding roles were probably acted in the same season as *The Lady of Pleasure*, we can assume that Fenn was at the height of his powers as a "woman actor" when Shirley's play was staged. At fifteen he was already experienced, and his voice must have broken late, for he played his first "mans part" four years later—an event celebrated by Glapthorne in the 1639 edition of his *Poems*.[38] Fenn would have played either Celestina or Aretina, but in the absence of other evidence, it is impossible to be more specific.

The speculative casting I have so far engaged in still leaves plenty of room for such journeymen actors as William Allen, Robert Axen, George Stutville, and Anthony Turner. There is also room for Michael Bowyer, who frequently played male romantic leads, but may have left the company before *The Lady of Pleasure* opened.[39] And there is additional room on both sides of the sexual divide for Theophilus Bird, Hugh Clark, and John Page, all of whom played women's parts, but all of whom may have been too old for anyone but Madam Decoy by 1635, when they were gradually taking on more and more responsibility as adult male actors. Michael Mohun, a boy actor already well known by 1637, may have joined the company in time to play one of the female leads.[40] But at this point speculation becomes rainbow-chasing. It is time to abjure the rough magic of conjecture to return to Sir Humphrey Mildmay as he watches a scene develop on the reliably substantial pageant of the Cockpit stage.

In order to place the actors into their customary environment, I wish to rely in part on four familiar specimens of visual evidence: the elevation showing the stage in the series of Jones/Webb drawings already discussed, the frontispiece for *The Wits* (1662), and the two vignettes from the title pages of *Roxana* (1632) and *Messalina* (1640).[41] It is possible that none of these visual specimens represents the stage of the Cockpit in 1635, but let us assume that even indirect visual evidence can assist us where it corroborates or illuminates the evidence drawn from the stage directions of Cockpit plays.

My interpretation of the verbal evidence in particular is heavily indebted to William B. Markward's unpublished thesis, "A Study of the Phoenix Theatre in Druary Lane, 1617-1638" (University of

---

38. Bentley, II, 433-4.
39. See Bentley, II, 386-7.
40. Bentley, II, 511-12.
41. The last three illustrations are often reprinted, most conveniently in *The Riverside Shakespeare*, ed. G. Blakemore Evans et al. (Boston, 1974), pls. 8 and 10 following p. 494.

Birmingham, 1953); to William A. Armstrong's published lecture, *The Elizabethan Private Theatres: Facts and Problems* (1958); to an article by T. J. King, "Staging of Plays at the Phoenix in Drury Lane, 1617-42" (*Theatre Notebook*, 19 [1964-65], 146-66); and to the compendious resources contained in the seven volumes of Gerald Eades Bentley's *The Jacobean and Caroline Stage.* The scholars just named would, in varying degrees, be at odds about how the available evidence should be treated. Markward's thesis, for example, is based on all of the conceivably relevant information: on the texts of plays written specifically for the Cockpit, those revived at the Cockpit, and on those possibly staged at the Cockpit though not published until the interregnum. I shall call this procedure a *promiscuous* treatment of the evidence. King's inquiry is based on a selection: that is, on plays incontrovertibly written for and staged at the Cockpit, whose texts or manuscript copies bear marks of association with performance in the theatre. By calling this a *chaste* interpretation of the evidence, I am admitting something about my own predilections. But I should add that, in the following attempt to visualize *The Lady of Pleasure* in performance, I have been guided not only by the scholar's obligation to test his evidence, but also by the editor's responsibility to make sense of a scene even where final proof is wanting.

The process of reconstructing the action and spectacle devised by Shirley for the Cockpit stage can safely begin with a platform, thrust forward from the tiring-house wall, and surrounded on three sides by spectators. The façade of the wall in all four of the visual specimens mentioned above is divided into two levels: a level contiguous with the stage and an above. The design of the above varies significantly from drawing to drawing, but on the evidence of the Cockpit plays we can infer that it was often used as an observation post from which one or more actors could look down on and comment upon the action on the platform below.[42] Three of the visual specimens show hangings covering all or part of the lower façade, and the presence of these is nowhere better confirmed than in Celestina's instructions to her Steward in *The Lady of Pleasure:*

> Cel. . . . What hangings have we here?
>
> Stew. They are arras, madam.
>
> Cel.   Impudence, I know't.
>
> I will have fresher and more rich, not wrought
> With faces that may scandalise a Christian,
> With Jewish stories stuffed with corn and camels;
>   . . . I say I will have other,

42. See King, pp. 159-60.

> Good master steward, of a finer loom.
> Some milk and silver, if your worship please
> To let me be at so much cost. (I. ii. 11-22)

In addition, though of the drawings only the Jones/Webb project provides for them, the tiring-house façade required doors for entrances and exits. If Jones and Webb were designing the Cockpit, they certainly wanted three doors: two of normal size at either edge of the façade, and a larger arched doorway at upstage centre. Three doors are stipulated by Markward, who promiscuously exploits the possibly contaminated evidence offered by Nabbes' *Covent Garden* and Heywood's *The English Traveller*.[43] King's chaste analysis of the thirty pure Cockpit plays yields only two necessary doors. This debate could be prolonged by citation of and interpretation of stage directions. I propose to suspend it, for the present limited purposes, by leaving the left-hand and right-hand doors exactly where they are, and by drawing the hangings from either side of the stage façade neatly together until they meet, thus enclosing the arched aperture at upstage centre. Now, at least, we have accommodated the stage direction from *The English Traveller* (1633): "*Enter at one doore an* Usurer and his Man, *at the other*, Old Lionell *with his servant: In the midst* Reginald."[44] The compromise I propose has the advantage of giving Heywood credit for knowing the difference between a door and an aperture which is not a door. And an entrance "*In the midst*" can be visualized as nothing more serious than what is going on between the two panels of hangings in the frontispiece to *The Wits*.

The features of the Cockpit stage thus visualized are perfectly adequate for most scenes in *The Lady of Pleasure*. They are adequate even when stage directions are fairly elaborate, as in the opening of the third act: "*Enter* Lord *unready*; HAIRCUT *preparing his periwig, table, and looking-glass*" (III i. 0.1-2). I am fully aware that *unready* is an adjective meaning "not completely dressed" and that the stage direction requires the actor to finish his adornment onstage. But, since this nobleman has been given no proper name, I refer to him throughout by the nickname "Lord Unready" in order to avoid verbal confusion with any other personages, terrestrial or celestial.

Before the scene in question opens, in the musical interval between Acts II and III, anonymous hirelings have, I presume, placed the specified table and the unspecified but necessary stool or chair into a

---

43. Markward, pp. 329-32.
44. Sig. F1ᵛ.

reasonably prominent downstage position. The looking-glass may also have been placed in position on the table, perhaps by Master Haircut, who could enter during the final minute of the interval to ensure that all is well for the beginning of Act III. While the last bars of music are being played, Lord Unready enters by one of the two doors, crosses to the table, and sits. He adjusts the mirror to allow himself to watch Haircut arranging the wig to best advantage and completing the application of his cosmetic powers. Conversation begins, only to be interrupted by the Secretary's arrival at the other stage door to announce the approach of Madam Decoy. She now enters and requests a private audience; to oblige her, Lord Unready asks the Secretary and Haircut to "Wait i'th' next chamber till I call" (III. i. 13), upon which they go out through the door from which Decoy has just entered.

The rest of the scene can be managed in precisely the same way, though embellished with many hand-held properties. The Secretary must produce, perhaps from a hiding-place in the table, a pen, an inkwell, and a sheet of paper. He must sit while writing the letter which Lord Unready dictates, and must produce sealing-wax, melting it no doubt by using the nearest convenient candle. After Sentlove and Kickshaw enter, Lord Unready must produce a miniature of his dead mistress (Bella Maria) from a pocket in his costume, and Kickshaw will study the image with affected nonchalance. At the end of the scene, the stage will be cleared, though presumably the table and chair will remain in place until the end of the act.

The scene which follows immediately (III. ii) takes place in the lodgings of Bornwell and Aretina in the Strand. No changes of scenery are required, but a special problem arises in relation to exits, entrances, and eavesdropping. Near the beginning of the scene, Aretina extracts promises from Littleworth and Kickshaw to the effect that they will use their combined wits to humiliate Celestina, the Bornwells' guest. But, Aretina specifies, "Begin not, till I whisper you" (III. ii. 85). Now Bornwell, Celestina, Mariana, and Isabella enter, and a highly social conversation (much of it in French) ensues. Aretina's Steward and her nephew Frederick join the party, and after further badinage, a stage direction reads: "*Ex[eunt] all but* CEL[ESTINA], ALEX[ANDER], *and* LITTLE[WORTH]" (III. ii. 201.1). At this point Aretina says, "Now, gentlemen" (201); that is, she gives the promised cue to Kickshaw and Littleworth. The two gentlemen subject Celestina to verbal abuse which continues without a halt even after the stage direction, "*Enter* BORNWELL" (III. ii. 224.1). Bornwell's two brief lines—"How's this?" (224) and "A conspiracy!" (268)—have no effect whatever on some fifty lines of dialogue during which the flyting continues. At last he addresses Celestina as "Brave soul!" and vilifies her abusers as a "brace of horse-leeches" (283-84). Encouraged by Bornwell, Celestina takes the initiative, gains verbal revenge for some thirty lines, and then asks Bornwell: "How shall I / Acquit your lady's silence?" (321-22). After a brief exchange of graceful exit lines between Bornwell and Celestina, Aretina unexpectedly asks, "Is she gone?" (326).

Here there is confusion in plenty. How is it that Bornwell's presence fails to intrude on the action for fifty lines? Why does Celestina remark on Aretina's silence, if indeed she has been offstage for more than a hundred lines? Even more oddly, how can an absent Aretina suddenly resume her place in the dialogue without the stage direction, "*Enter* ARETINA"?

I believe the answers to these questions lie in the use of the above, even though there is no authority for such a notion in the quarto. We can be sure, from its specified function in eleven bona fide Cockpit plays, that the theatre had an above; and we can infer that communication between the platform and the above was remarkably rapid and easy. In the final act of Davenport's *A New Trick to Cheat the Devil* (1639), Master Changeable, after announcing that the Devil will soon appear, says to his Wife: "will you ascend and guide my Lord to a / Convenient place, where you may view this object?" The stage direction which follows is uncompromising: "*They ascend.*"[45] Eight lines of dialogue cover the ascent, after which the Wife and three other characters "*Enter above.*" At the climax of this scene the Wife offers to leap down to the platform below, but is warned that she may break her neck and advised that "The Stair-case will doe better."[46] This is presumably a permanent, backstage staircase which allowed the ascent to be made in the first place, and which allows the Wife to descend while twelve further lines of dialogue cover her actions.[47]

45. Sig. K1.
46. Sig. K2.
47. In the spoken version of this paper I argued largely on the basis of this scene that the Cockpit was equipped with a visible, onstage staircase, but I am no longer convinced that this was the case. Cf. Markward, who believes that the "rapid entrances" in *The English Traveller*, *A Tale of a Tub*, and *Claricilla* "seem to hint that there may have been an inner stairway leading from lower to upper stage situated very near one of the side doors" (p. 408). There is no reason to doubt that Queen Henrietta's men could have produced a staircase for any production that required one. The Lord Admiral's men, in an inventory of properties held on 10 March 1598/9, are said to have owned a "payer of stayers for Fayeton" (*Henslowe's Diary*, p. 319). But the logical step from a possibly to a necessarily visible staircase is a dangerous one, as I now realize, thanks to the convivial warnings issued by members of the Waterloo conference.

Once the above is allowed its normal function as an observation post, the apparently confusing action in *The Lady of Pleasure*, III. ii, falls readily into place. Aretina, after giving her instructions to Littleworth and Kickshaw, goes out with the general "Ex[eunt]" (III. ii. 201.1), leaving only Celestina and her two assailants on the platform. By a backstage route, Aretina ascends and reappears silently at the observation point, above. "*Enter* BORNWELL" (III. ii. 224.1) means that he appears on the platform, taking a position reasonably distant from the characters involved in the game of insults. From this position, his two brief lines (224, 268) can be spoken as asides without interrupting the scene. But when Bornwell cries out "Brave soul!" (283) he attracts the attention of the other characters on the platform. While Celestina completes her verbal revenge, Bornwell approaches her in order to be quite near her when she inquires, "How shall I / Acquit your lady's silence?" (321-22). The reference, of course, is to the silent but visible Aretina at the observation point above. Now Aretina retreats and, retracing her backstage route, descends to the platform level. She enters just as Bornwell and Celestina go out, and hence addresses Littleworth and Kickshaw with the most natural question: "Is she gone?" (326).

In the two scenes which I have chosen to discuss, indeed in *The Lady of Pleasure* as a whole, the broad outlines of Shirley's theatre craft are remarkably clear. He allows actions of major significance to be played out on the platform, where the actors' voices and gestures will be most effective. He frequently calls for properties, but most of these are small hand-held articles which not only contribute to the action but also reveal the social circumstances or personal inclinations of his characters. Numerous asides, many of them not clearly marked in the quarto, and frequent references to goings-on in this or that chamber just offstage are among the techniques Shirley uses to build the conspiratorial atmosphere which characterizes the world of the play.

In selecting two scenes for analysis, I have necessarily slighted others, among them the crucial actions of Act IV, in which Kickshaw is led in "*blind[fold]ed*" (IV. i. 0.2), bribed by Madam Decoy, and bedded by Aretina. When Decoy presses her offer, showing Kickshaw "a prospect / Of the next chamber" and asking him to "observe / That bed" (IV. i. 84-90), I believe that the action has moved to upstage centre, where Decoy is enticing her confused client to enter Aretina's bedroom by going out through the gap between the hangings. If this is the case, then it is another instance of Shirley's shrewdness: if this unusual exit ("*in the midst*") is used at all, it is fitting that it should be used here, and used only once.

To follow Madam Decoy a single step further would be an error of crude self-indulgence. I shall resist, and I shall conclude by gathering a few indications of the quality of Shirley's theatrical style in *The Lady of Pleasure*. Something of Shirley's taste in this matter may be inferred from his address to the reader prefixed to *The Grateful Servant*. In response to adverse criticism from Blackfriars partisans, Shirley takes a stand which he hopes will "do the comedians justice, amongst whom, some are held comparable with the best that are, and have been in the world, and the most of them deserving a name in the file of those that are eminent for graceful and unaffected action."[48]

Just what actions will qualify as free of affectation is always open to question, especially in the theatre; but in this context it is fair to assume that, in the relatively small, indoor, artificially lighted Cockpit playhouse, an actor like Richard Perkins, whose background included the Hope and the Red Bull, would reduce the volume of his voice and the scale of his gestures in accordance with the modesty of his nature and the dimensions of his new environment. In doing so, Perkins would have increased his attractiveness in the eyes of a playwright who designed each scene with a special alertness to social nuance. An acknowledged runner-up in his re-creation of Marlowe's towering passions, Perkins may well have been "comparable with the best that are" when the script required ingenious adjustments of mood within an intricately balanced network of social relationships.

"Graceful . . . action," in Shirley's terms, was undoubtedly very considerable praise. A playwright who repeatedly places his characters into dance-like formations, and who thinks of a Lord as unready until he is armed with his periwig, is admitting a taste for elegance. And actors who deal in mirrors and miniatures rather than tankards and targets will need to be graceful in both bearing and speech. As the leading playwright of Queen Henrietta's men in 1635, Shirley knew the resources of his theatre, the talents of his actors, and the tastes of his audience. In response to these external influences, he created the "graceful and unaffected action" of *The Lady of Pleasure*: "that rare playe" by which he earned, in its first production, the admiration of

48. *Works*, II, 5.

Sir Humphrey Mildmay, and for which he is awarded, even today, "a name in the file of those that are eminent" for impeccably crafted comedy of social artifice.

"The Getting up of the Spectacle": The Role of the Visual on the Elizabethan Stage, 1576-1600

BARBARA A. MOWAT

Even though Aristotle assures us that the spectacle, "the stage appearance of the actors," is the sixth and least important part of drama, having "least to do with the art of poetry" and being more the province of the costumier than the dramatist,[1] we know that Elizabethan drama is often as dependent on spectacle, on what the viewer sees, as on what the words say. Thanks to the work of the scholars who have been exploring the role of the visual on the Elizabethan stage, we now generally accept the fact that spectacle was very often the province of the playwright, who gave attention to costumes, props, and gestures, and made them an integral part of the play.[2] Yet Aristotle's comment raises an interesting question that, so far as I know, has thus far been investigated only in an ad hoc fashion:

---

1. I am here using the Bywater translation of *Poetics*. Aristotle's denigration of Spectacle is found in chapter 6 of *Poetics*. Interestingly, at other points in *Poetics*, (e.g., in chapters 15 and 17), Aristotle makes it clear that the dramatist of necessity must visualize the characters and the action as if he were present at the actual event. Gerald Else, in his *Aristotle's Poetics: The Argument*, suggests that the solution to this dilemma lies in the fact that Aristotle knew that the dramatist must visualize the important physical characteristics of his characters (i.e., Shakespeare must "see" Othello as a black man and Lear as a kingly old man), but that the costuming, the "look" of the character is the concern not of the dramatist but of the costumer (Cambridge, Mass., 1957), pp. 232-35, 274-79, 486-89.
2. See, e.g., Alan S. Downer, "The Life of Our Design: The Function of Imagery in the Poetic Drama," *The Hudson Review*, II, 2 (1949), 242-63; Alan C. Dessen, *Elizabethan Drama and the Viewer's Eye* (Chapel Hill, 1977); Brownell Salomon, "Visual and Aural

namely, to what extent, and for what ends, did the Elizabethan dramatist incorporate the visual into his plays? How much, judging by the texts of the plays, did he depend upon specific visual effects for his play to make sense to the spectator? As he imagined and shaped the play, how much of his attention went to what Aristotle called "the getting up of the Spectacle"?

In these pages, I would like to make a start toward answering such questions by focusing on one aspect of the visual: namely, the costuming. This single aspect is an attractive one to investigate for a variety of reasons. First, as Hal H. Smith has argued persuasively, there is considerable evidence that not only large sums of money but also serious thought was given to the proper costuming of major dramatic figures, to emblematic figures, and to national "types."[3] This interest in stage apparel should not surprise us, given the fact that, in the Elizabethan period, clothing itself had such importance. The period is noted for the attention attached to sartorial display; foreign clothing was admired and imitated; clothing was used systematically to transmit messages about the wearer. Colour symbolism sent messages about his state of mind, just as particular fabrics and styles sent messages about his or her rank, occupation, and sex. Interestingly, these sartorial messages were not always truthful, as we learn from the sumptuary laws, proclaimed on ten separate occasions during Elizabeth's reign, designed to halt the wearing of apparel which sent false messages about one's rank in society.[4] In a social world so conscious of clothing, stage apparel could hardly be a matter of

Signs in the Performed English Renaissance Play," *Renaissance Drama* n.s. 5 (1972), 143-69; Dieter Mehl, "Visual and Rhetorical Imagery in Shakespeare's Plays," *Essays and Studies,* n.s. 25, ed. T. S. Dorsch (1972), 83-100; Inga-Stina Ewbank, "'More Pregnantly than Words': Some Uses and Limitations of Visual Symbolism," *Shakespeare Survey 24* (1971), 13-18; Jocelyn Powell, "Marlowe's Spectacle," *Tulane Drama Review* 8 (1964), 195-210; Barbara A. Mowat, "The Beckoning Ghost: Stage-Gesture in Shakespeare," *Renaissance Papers 1970* (1971), 41-54.

3. Smith's important essay appeared as "Some Principles of Elizabethan Stage Costume," in the *Journal of the Warburg and Courtauld Institutes* 25 (1962), 240-57.
4. For "the importance attached to sartorial display" and the fascination with foreign clothing, see, e.g., Cecile de Banke's discussion of Elizabethan clothing in her *Shakespearian Stage Production: Then and Now* (New York, 1953), pp. 141 ff. Miss de Banke discusses colour symbolism on pp. 151 and 157-61. See also M. Channing Linthicum, *Costume in the Drama of Shakespeare and His Contemporaries* (New York: 1963), and Don Cameron Allen, "Symbolic Colors in the Literature of the English Renaissance," *PQ,* XV (1936), 81-92. The sumptuary laws are discussed by Frances Elizabeth Baldwin, *Sumptuary Legislation and Personal Regulation in England* (Baltimore, 1926), and by Wilfred Hooper in "The Tudor Sumptuary Laws," *English Historical Review* XXV, (1915), 433-49. As B. L. Joseph notes in his *Shakespeare's Eden: The Commonwealth of England 1558-1629* (London, 1971), p. 90, "Elizabeth issued ten Proclamations insisting on the enforcement of the Sumptuary Act of 1533, chiefly to perpetuate

indifference to the audience, to the producer, nor, one would assume, to the playwright.

By the end of the sixteenth century, as we know, costume was used by dramatists so complexly that the critic of the visual can profitably devote a full-scale study to a single play or to a single important artifact within a play. I simply remind you of Alan Downer's study of Richard's crown and Macbeth's armour and robes, and of Alan Dessen's tracing of Hamlet's sword as it moves visually through Hamlet's drama.[5] Rather than beginning, then, with the richly complex clothing images of the turn of the century—Hamlet's inky cloak, for instance, or Rosalind's doublet and hose—I prefer to turn our attention first to earlier phases of sixteenth-century drama, when the dramatists' purposes were more single and their use of costume for meaning therefore more susceptible of elucidation.

When we look at plays of the earlier sixteenth century, we find that dramatists used costume for one of two distinct reasons: either to lead the minds of the audience *through* the fiction being enacted—the "game," as Glynne Wickham calls it[6]—and toward the "earnest" which lies behind or beyond it; or, conversely, to draw the audience more deeply into the "game" itself, into the dramatic illusion, into

social distinctions." H. E. Neale, too, in his *Elizabeth I and her Parliaments, 1559-1581* (London, 1953), p. 354, describes "a bill reforming excess in apparel" debated in the Parliament of 1576, as "a measure attuned to that age, which accepted as its philosophy that people should dress according to their station in society, and that the State should enforce this by penal legislation."

As noted by C. H. Williams, editor of *English Historical Documents, 1485-1558* (London, 1967), p. 249, "Early Tudor legislation provides a detailed survey of the ranks and order of society in the statutes passed for the regulation of dress." Williams prints "An Act against wearing of costly apparel. St. 1 Hen. VIII, c. 14, 1510 (Stat. Realm, III, 8)," "the first exemplar of Tudor sumptuary legislation and . . . the model for all later acts. It defines the degrees in great detail and was prohibitive rather than permissive" (pp. 249-52). Elizabeth's ten proclamations (the earliest dated October 1559, and the last dated July 1597) are collected in *A Booke containing all Such Proclamations as were published during the Raigne of the late Queen Elizabeth* (London, 1618).

Sumptuary legislation, which "reached its height in England" under the Tudors (Baldwin, p. 275), died under James, but as late as 1661 John Evelyn published a book, *Tyrannus or the Mode: in a Discourse of Sumptuary Lawes*, urging Charles to institute sumptuary legislation requiring persons to dress according to class and occupation (sig. B2^v, B4), with "all degrees of Men whatever [having] some Badge to distinguish them by."

The best single summary of what is actually known about Elizabethan stage costuming practices is to be found in Andrew Gurr's *The Shakespearean Stage 1574-1642*, 2nd ed. (Cambridge, 1980), esp. pp. 177-88. See also Stella Mary Newton, *Renaissance Theatre Costume and the Sense of the Historic Past* (London, 1975). I am grateful to T. J. King for the reference to Newton's work.

5. Downer, "The Life of Our Design"; Dessen, *Elizabethan Drama*, pp. 91-109.

6. *Early English Stages 1300 to 1660, Volume Three: Plays and their Makers to 1576*

imaginative engagement with the characters and the action. We can see this distinction at its simplest if we think, for example, of the way the scholar's gown is used as a costume in Redford's *Wyt and Science* and in Gascoigne's *Supposes*, the first a hybrid morality written in the 1530s or 1540s, the second an Italianate comedy first performed at Gray's Inn in 1566.[7]

The scholar's robe, off-stage, is itself a kind of costume, a symbolic garment worn by young men in pursuit of an academic degree. Redford, in *Wyt and Science*, takes the symbolism inherent in the robe and builds a moral lesson upon it. His hero, Wyt, dressed in his academic gown, represents the mind in proper pursuit of knowledge. When Wyt casts off the robe in order to dance with Honest Recreation, we are to understand this as self-betrayal. He soon falls asleep in the arms of Idleness and is there dressed in a Fool's robe. After he is beaten by Shame he repents, and Reason takes away the Fool's robe and gives him back his gown. At the play's happy ending, to celebrate his betrothal to Knowledge, he receives the "gowne of knoledge" (probably a master's gown, according to T. W. Craik).[8]

Redford, then, has his hero wear, discard, and resume again the scholar's robe as a didactic device. The audience is asked to translate the visual symbol into abstract terms, to become aware of the moral lesson being dramatized: namely, that when one's mind pursues pleasure instead of knowledge, one is in danger of sinking into idleness and sloth, in danger of becoming a fool. Redford gives his morality play the shape of comic romance, presenting the choice of the life of the mind as a wished-for betrothal, and showing the life of pleasure as a trap of sloth and folly. This moral lesson he drives home visually through the symbolism of the robes.

George Gascoigne's *Supposes* is designed to teach no moral lesson, as the author makes clear in the Prologue. Those who suppose that the play will deal with "sophistical handling of subtle suppositions" or will "decipher . . . quaint conceits" are supposing wrongly, he says, for "our Suppose is nothing else but a mistaking . . . of one thing for another."[9] In *Supposes* the hero Erastrato "cast[s] aside both long

(London, 1981), p. 67.

7. In my discussion of the hybrid moralities and the transitional romances, I am indebted especially to T. W. Craik's *The Tudor Interlude: Stage, Costume, and Acting* (Leicester: 1958) and to David M. Bevington's *From "Mankind" to Marlowe: Growth of Structure in the Popular Drama of Tudor England* (Cambridge, Mass., 1962).

8. *Tudor Interlude*, p. 86. Both Craik and Wickham give attention to the symbolic use of clothing in *Wyt and Science*.

9. I quote here from the text in *Elizabethan Plays*, ed. Arthur H. Nethercot (New York, 1971).

gown and books" when he falls in love with young Polynesta; in order to be near her, he "exchange[s] . . . name, habit, clothes, and credit with his servant" and gains service in the household of her father. There, Erastrato wins her love, and there he is cast into prison when the liaison is discovered. Only his own father's unexpected appearance saves his life and makes possible a return to his scholar's gown and to union with the heroine.

For the characters who inhabit the world of *Supposes*, the garb of scholar and of servant function much as they would do in the real world of the sixteenth century: Erastrato's servant-costume proclaims him to be a servant, suitable for employment, but criminally unsuitable to woo the master's daughter; at the same time, the scholar's gown worn by the servant enables him to win respect and to compete openly for the hand of Polynesta. For the audience, who know from the beginning that the clothes do not properly identify the hero's class and occupation, the interest lies in the discrepant awareness set up by the disguise. From our position of superior awareness, we watch the knots of misunderstanding tangle, we wait for the knife-stroke that will cut the knots, for the discovery that will save the young man from death and unite him with the heroine. At no point are we encouraged to meditate upon the meaning of academic gowns or servants' costumes, except insofar as the meaning they carry in the social world affects the fate and happiness of the hero.

The visual shape of *Supposes* is remarkably like that of *Wyt and Science*: in both plays, the hero puts off the scholar's robe and dallies with pleasure; he is dressed in garments that signify a fall in estate; he suffers humiliation and danger; he is saved and is returned to his original robes and to a marriage. But where the audience, in *Wyt and Science*, is forced to ask, "What does it mean?" the audience of *Supposes* is encouraged to ask, "What will happen next?"

Given the difference in dates between Redford's and Gascoigne's plays, one might assume that Gascoigne's represents a later stage in the use of visual effects, a chronological move toward representational, illusory drama such as that traced by O. B. Hardison in the development of the vernacular play from the ceremonial drama of the Mass.[10] Yet such seems not to be the case. Rather, the plays seem to reflect two different styles of drama, two different traditions of significant costuming—symbolic costuming and illusionary costuming—both of long standing and both quite alive in 1576. In that year,

10. *Christian Rite and Christian Drama in the Middle Ages* (Baltimore and London, 1967), esp. pp. 230-36.

the year in which permanent theatres first began to appear in London, both late moralities and transitional romances were being written, the first using symbolic costume to point elaborately to larger, detachable meanings outside the play, the second using illusionary costuming just as elaborately, but for disguise and plot complication. In Wapull's *The Tide Tarrieth No Man* and in Lupton's *All for Money*, costumes are emblematic, allegorical, symbolic; in the anonymous *Common Conditions* and *Clyomon and Clamides*, costumes belong to the world of illusion and carry much of the burden of character identification, plot complication, and suspense.[11] Again, a simple comparison makes the point. Consider the use of knightly armour, shield, and sword in *The Tide Tarrieth No Man* and in *Clyomon and Clamides*.

In Wapull's late morality (as in the earlier *Wyt and Science*), characters are dressed so as to represent abstractions: Greed is represented iconographically as a rich merchant, Pride as a courtier; Despair is dressed according to its nature in "some ougly shape." A character enters late in the play dressed in armour, carrying a shield and a sword; on the sword hangs a title-board which, on the side facing the audience, reads "pollicy"; on the shield, a title-board that reads "riches." The character's opening speech is a gloss on this puzzling costume:

> Christianity I doe represent,
> Muse not though the sword of pollicy I beare:
> Neyther marveile not what is mine intent,
> That this fayleable Shield of Riches I weare.

He goes on to tell the audience that, because "Greedy great will have it so," and because he cannot withstand their "cruel force," Christianity

---

11. The terms "late morality" and "transitional romance" are borrowed from David Bevington. George Wapull's *The Tide Tarrieth No Man*, published in 1576, is assigned in the Harbage/Schoenbaum *Annals of English Drama* to that year; Thomas Lupton's *All for Money*, published in 1578, is assigned in the *Annals* to 1577. *Common Conditions*, registered in 1576, seems to present an example of a play in which the playwright gave little thought to the visual, in that, even though disguise is the controlling dramatic device, the costumes are seldom described and only briefly mentioned. This play, though, is so problematical and is flawed in so many ways that one hesitates to speculate much upon it. See Tucker Brooke's edition of the play (New Haven, 1915), esp. pp. xii-xv, and Brooke's interesting note on p. 68. *Clyomon and Clamides*, assigned in the *Annals* to the year 1570 (with the limiting dates given as 1570-83?), seems, to David Bevington, "to have heralded the arrival of a permanent London stage," (p. 71); see also pp. 62, 103, and 196 for Bevington's dating of the play c. 1576. Betty J. Littleton, too, in her *Clyomon and Clamides: A Critical Edition* (The Hague and Paris; 1968), argues persuasively for a dating of 1576, claiming that "the anterior limit for the play's production may be set with some certainty at 1576, the year when James Burbage constructed The Theatre, or at the latest, at 1577, when the Curtain was constructed" (p. 32).

must "beare this deformed sword and shield." Observing this character and listening to his words, the audience perceives that the weapons of the true Christian, the "sword of God's word" and the "shield of faith" prescribed by St. Paul in the Letter to the Ephesians, have been turned into instruments of that very power—worldly success and riches—against which the Christian is supposed to arm himself. The play's most significant moment comes when, after Greediness has died and the Vice has been hanged, the title-boards are turned so that the audience can see that Christianity's sword is now labelled "the word of God" and his shield "Faythe." The figure of the armed knight, then, is in this play an elaborate double emblem, a commentary on Ephesians 6, on the true armour of Christianity.

Knightly garb in *Clyomon and Clamides* is also complex, but in quite a different way. The costume carries some symbolic overtones, but it functions primarily as a crucial element in the play's action. In the first scene, Juliana gives Sir Clamides a silver shield, saying to him: ". . . as thou seemest in thine attire, a Virgin Knight to be, Take thou this Sheeld, likewise of white. . . ."[12] She names him "The White Knight of the Silver Sheeld" and sends him off with instructions to bring back the head of the deadly flying serpent and thereby win her hand. Sir Clamides kills the serpent, but is charmed asleep by the cowardly Bryan sans Foy, who steals Clamides' armour, shield, and sword, along with the serpent's head. Bryan, as he sets out in the white armour to claim Juliana, admits that the clothes of "the noble Knight" belie his true nature:

> . . . though I do usurpe his name,
> His sheeld or ensigne here,
> Yet can I not usurpe his heart,
> Still Bryan's heart I beare (xxi, 1971 ff.)

But the usurped costume wins for Bryan the hand of Juliana, who turns on the true Clamides as a "dissembling wretch," a "counterfeit": "Where is my glittering sheeld?" she demands. After the false Clamides is challenged to a duel and his cowardly nature forces him to admit to being Bryan, Juliana accepts the true Clamides, who praises her for her constancy—constancy, one assumes, to the costume.

The golden armour and shield of Clyomon function in an analogous way in the second plot-line. They identify Clyomon as the Knight of the Golden Shield to the princess Neronis, who falls in love with him, is abducted by the Norway King, escapes disguised as a shepherd boy,

12. Littleton edition, i, 81 ff.

and then follows Clyomon in the disguise of a page. The most dramatic moment for the Golden Shield comes at the point where Clyomon leaves the shield to mark the grave of the Norway King, whom he has killed. Neronis finds this memorial, interprets it to mean that Clyomon is dead, and is saved from suicide only by Providence, who descends from the Heavens to suggest that she read the note on the shield which explains whose grave it marks.

For the characters within the world of *Clyomon and Clamides*, the armour and shield of the two knights function primarily to identify the wearer to other characters, sometimes correctly, sometimes disastrously incorrectly. For the audience, the two sets of armour are important parts of the web of signals that make up the play. The dramatist accepts the symbolic associations conventionally assigned to armour, shield, and sword, but rather than elaborating on those associations or using the armour to point to external meanings, he uses it to counterpoint visually the shifts in roles within the play, to show up the cowardliness of Bryan, to illustrate the fact that the world of appearances can be deceiving, and to create suspense and patterns of expectation by allowing the audience always to know the truth behind the disguise.

From any of the plays of circa 1576, it seems a long step to the drama of the 1580s and early 1590s. When we look at Lyly's *Gallathea*, for instance (dated c. 1585), we find that this play depends upon *both* of the costuming traditions, and uses both with a new subtlety. Cupid, for example, is dressed in proper symbolic style, but his wings and bow and his scar from Psyche's molten wax serve to make him seem alive and real as a dramatic, not an abstract, character; and the fact that he abandons this costume for female disguise so as to gain access to Diana's nymphs places him, for the bulk of the play, in the illusionary tradition. Note, though, that when he is returned to Venus, his treatment at the hands of the nymphs is portrayed in proper symbolic style: his wings, as Venus notes, have been singed. The disguise of the young heroines as pages, too, carries with it more substance than Neronis's disguise as a boy in *Clyomon and Clamides*. In the elaborate mythological complex of Lyly's play, maleness and femaleness are principles of godhood and of nature; attempts to hide one's sexual identity in a disguise and thereby escape one's fate are futile and an affront to the gods.

In *Gallathea*, then, the symbolic and the illusionary uses of costuming are beginning to blur. Most of the costuming is illusionary: that is, most of the characters dress as they do because their roles in the story demand it; disguises serve to complicate or further the plot. But along the way the clothes themselves take on meaning. The young heroines meditate at length on what masculine clothes *mean*; an elaborate connection develops between the supernatural nymph-virgins who serve Diana and the mortal virgin-maidens to be sacrificed to Neptune; finally, Neptune's attraction to Venus having led him to make peace with the female element in the universe, the maidens are released from the threat of virgin sacrifice and one of the girls is promised a miraculous transformation so that her male garb will reflect a newly-made male body, and the longed-for marriage can take place. The costuming, then, though first of all a part of a plot that appears to be non-didactic, yet takes on meanings that enlarge the play, so that the disguisings link interestingly and subtly to what Peter Saccio sees as the play's quasi-allegorical theme of the necessity of submitting our mortal wills to the gods.[13]

If we look at other plays from the 1580s and 1590s, we find examples comparable to what we see in *Gallathea:* that is, we see references to costuming in which the clear line between the symbolic and the illusionary tends to blur. More interesting, though, we find that in its many references to costume, *Gallathea* is, by 1585, rather rare. In most plays of the period, dramatists have come to depend upon a kind of stock costuming to which they seldom refer in the dialogue, but which they clearly envision as they shape the play.[14] If one examines a play like Lyly's *Midas,* for example, where dialogue references to costumes are almost non-existent, one sees that the dramatist assumes readily identifiable costumes as he plans the scenes, in that the audience can follow the plot only if the boy actors playing the King, the Princess, and the nobles are dressed according to their fictional stations, only if the sub-plot characters are recognizable on

13. *The Court Comedies of John Lyly: A Study in Allegorical Dramaturgy* (Princeton, 1969).
14. This discovery lends support to the argument put forth by E. A. J. Honigmann in "'Dramatis Personae' Lists and 'Othello,' " *The Stability of Shakespeare's Text* (London, 1965), pp. 44-46. Honigmann argues persuasively that "lists of characters" in the different plays must have existed in the theatres; he speculates that they would probably have been a part of the "author-plot" rather than of the "book of the play," the manuscript, or the prompt-book. In the one author-plot which has thus far been discovered, there is in fact just such a list, which gives not only the names of the characters, but also enough identifying characteristics (nationality, rank, sex, occupation) that the author could be assured of identifiable costuming. See Joseph Quincy Adams, "The Author-Plot of an Early Seventeenth Century Play," *The Library,* XXVI, (1945-46), 17-27. The list of characters can be found on p. 21 (p. 1 of the "plot"). The vexing, but fascinating, questions about "dramatis personae" lists as they appear (or, more often, fail to appear) in plays printed during the years between 1576-1600 is far too complicated to go into here.

sight as pages, barbers, waiting-maids, and shepherds, and only if the actors playing Bacchus, Apollo, and Pan carry identifying insignia. Yet, except for brief dialogue comments about Midas' ass's ears and Pan's flute, the play nowhere mentions the costumes. We see this same easy confidence at work as Marlowe shapes the *Jew of Malta*, where Jews, friars, nuns, bassoes, knights, slaves, Turks, Spaniards, carpenters, courtesans and gentlemen enter, interact, and exit, and where nothing but readily identifiable costumes would allow an audience to make the first sense of the action; yet the only references to costuming that we find in the play are Ithamore's line about Bellamira: "I know she is a courtesan by her attire," and Ithamore's reference to the Jew's "bottell nose" (a piece of symbolic costuming which, according to Craik, links Barabas to the Devil-figure in earlier English drama.[15])

As I noted above, however, one does find plays in this period in which the dramatist includes discussion and description of costumes. When, in *Friar Bacon and Friar Bungay*, for instance, Robert Greene has the Fair Maid of Fressingfield appear dressed as a nun, he includes extensive dialogue comment:

He has her father say to Lord Lacy:

> See where she stands clad in her nun's attire,
> Ready for to be shorn in Framlingham.
> She leaves the world because she left your love. (xiv, 49-51)

He has her say:

> Adieu to dainty robes! This base attire
> Better befits an humble mind to God
> Than all the show of rich abiliments. (xiv, 31-33)

And when the Fair Maid, offered the chance to choose "Either a solemn nunnery, or the court;/God or Lord Lacy. Which contents you best . . . ?" she announces her decision with the words "Off goes the habit of a maiden's heart . . . ; all the show of holy nuns, farewell" (xiv, 82 ff.).[16]

In a similar fashion, Marlowe in *Tamburlaine*, Part I, has Tamburlaine elaborately discuss his shepherd's robe; he has characters explain at length Tamburlaine's white, red, and black garments; and the several crowns in the play are repeatedly identified and commented upon (this in sharp contrast to *Tamburlaine*, Part II, which, like Part I,

---

15. *Tudor Interlude*, p. 51.
16. I quote here from the text in *Elizabethan Plays*.

depends for audience understanding on elaborate costuming for rank and nationality, but which contains not a single costume description or comment).

What we have in the "nun's apparel" scene in *Friar Bacon*, and throughout *Tamburlaine I*, are, I suggest, examples of one kind of situation in which dramatists of the period around 1590 did choose to specify and comment upon costumes: that is, these are examples of situations in which the dramatist wished to make clear the way, or ways, in which a particular garment, with its several possible associations, actually reflects the character wearing it. Margaret's putting on of nun's attire is a gesture signalling her giving up of sexual love; her taking off of the habit signals her acceptance of sexual love. To make sure that we follow this largely symbolic action, Greene elaborates on it through the dialogue. Throughout most of the play, where Margaret appears as the Keeper's daughter, Greene does not mention Margaret's clothing, nor does he, in the final scene, describe her wedding garment. For the play to make sense, these garments must indicate visually the discrepancy between her two social positions, but, unlike Dekker, who will focus attention on Grissell's gown throughout her play, Greene simply assumes that Margaret's dress speaks for itself—just as he assumes that the friars, kings, emperors, scholars, Germans, magicians, hostesses, and devils will be dressed in garb that will properly identify them to the audience. The nun's apparel is different. Margaret's wearing it could signal many things; it actually reflects her character in one particular way. Hence, Greene explains it.

The situation with Tamburlaine and the shepherd's robe is analogous, but much more interesting. Tamburlaine is dressed as a shepherd when he enters with the captive Zenocrate. She comments on his "mean" attire: he himself discusses the "weeds" which he will soon "disdain to wear." Again, as with Greene's description of Margaret's nun's attire, Marlowe's intention is to make clear the ways in which the garment reflects on the character. On the most immediate level, the robe indicates Tamburlaine's birth, the social level from which he came; Tamburlaine acknowledges this. On a second level, the shepherd's robe belies Tamburlaine's martial and noble nature; he acknowledges this as well, and takes off the robe to reveal his armour and curtle-axe, "adjuncts more beseeming Tamburlaine." On a third level, the shepherd's robe paradoxically links Tamburlaine to Jove. Throughout the play, Tamburlaine will take Jove's climb to supreme power as the model for his own aspiration: "What better precedent than mighty Jove?" Thus Tamburlaine finds it fitting that he appear briefly as a shepherd, since "Jove sometimes masked in a shepherd's weed."

When Tamburlaine removes his shepherd's robe to reveal the armour beneath—a device hardly inspired to sustain the illusion of reality—we seem very close to morality costuming. We seem even closer in those scenes where his emblematic white, red, and black costumes are described, and closer yet in, say, Kyd's *Spanish Tragedy*, where the ending of the play is prefigured by the entrance of Hymen dressed "in sable with a saffron robe." When dramatists of this period have characters discuss a costume in order to make its meaning clear, we seem in the presence of a late, sophisticated use of morality costuming. But not all instances of described costume from this period are in this tradition. In many cases, the dramatist comments on the costume not because he wants to make its symbolic meaning clear, but because, as in the earlier dramatic romances, it is functioning as a disguise, and its effectiveness for audience involvement is dependent on the audience's knowledge that the costume is hiding rather than revealing identity.

As in the romances, the dramatists' rule of thumb seemed to be that when a costume disguises the character, the costume is described and discussed. We think of Lord Lacy in *Friar Bacon and Friar Bungay*, disguised as a farmer "tired . . . in rags . . . to win fair Peggy's love" (vi, 116 ff.), of Lucentio dressed "in the habit of a mean man" to court Kate's sister Bianca. We think of Shakespeare's Julia, a latter-day Neronis, off to find her Proteus, dressed in the habits of a page. These and other disguises—so innocent when compared with those of such Jacobean disguisers as Face, Vindici, Volpone, and Aspatia—are described, thought about, sometimes moralized upon. As with the disguises in *Gallathea*, some may easily fall over into the category of the moralized costume: one thinks of the scene in *Friar Bacon*, where Rafe, Henry's fool, appears disguised as the Prince of Wales at the very time that the Prince is most playing the fool in his attempt to win Margaret. But, in general, clothing for disguise in the plays of the late 1580s and early 1590s carries on the tradition of *Clyomon and Clamides* or *Supposes*, the illusionary tradition of costuming used to pull the reader into the play through discrepant awareness and suspense.

I would suggest, then, that by the mid-1590s, three costuming traditions co-existed on the London stage. Two of these involve dialogue comment. First, when a dramatist wished to introduce an abstract figure into a play, or to signal the larger significance of a piece of clothing, or to make clear the specific way in which a costume was appropriate for the character wearing it, then he used explanatory dialogue comments reminiscent of the morality tradition. Envy with her arms covered in blood, Richard addressing his crown, Mucedorus dressing as a hermit because such a garment "befits his state of mind" —these are all examples of morality costuming as it was used in the 1590s. Second, when a dramatist used costume for disguise, he included dialogue comment reminiscent of earlier plays in the illusionary tradition. We think, for example, of Musco, in the 1598 version of *Every Man in His Humour*, going through a series of trans-formations, each time discussing the disguise with the audience before proceeding to use it to gull another unwary victim. Rarely, by the way, does either the morality or the illusionary costume tradition appear in its pure state in plays of the 1590s: Mucedorus's emblematic hermit's robe serves the purpose of a disguise while, say, Portia's disguise as a lawyer can be said to carry symbolic meanings, as she becomes, in effect, a young Daniel, as if the robes allow her to express a part of her personality that would not so readily appear in the normal garments of the mistress of Belmont.

These two traditions, used when clothing was to take on an extra burden of meaning or to play a special role in the action, were super-imposed on the stable costuming pattern that made up the third, prevailing tradition—that is, the dramatist's casual dependence on what was clearly stock costuming to identify a character's rank, sex, age, and occupation. This tradition has roots in the early moralities: consider the costuming of Mankind in *The Castle of Perseverance*, where his costumes reflect throughout his age and his changing fortunes; it also has roots in the *commedia* tradition. But it is most closely rooted, one suspects, in a social world governed by the idea— indeed, the law—that certain clothes belong to certain ranks in the social hierarchy. Costuming at this level, even if undescribed in the dialogue, is meaningful—is part of the dramatist's conception of the play—in that the dramatist knew that he and his audience shared a world in which clothing almost always identified, or at least classified, the wearer. Thus, without description or elaboration, clothing *placed* the character, and he functioned both as himself and in his socially, professionally, or sexually defined role.[17]

Interestingly, the stock costuming of the 1590s, as far as I can tell from studying the texts and Henslowe's inventories, differs sig-

17. Alan Dessen has called my attention to yet another use of stock costuming which he is himself investigating—namely, the use of a character clothed in an identifiable way present on the stage to silently identify a *place*—as the garb of a tapster would signal to us "tavern."

nificantly from that of, say, the *commedia dell'arte*. Where the stock costuming and the masks of the *commedia* identify character type, the Elizabethan costume identifies social role. In London drama of the 1590s, as in the world which that drama mirrors, clothing sends messages not about how we can expect a character to behave, but rather about his status, his role in society. The way is open, then, for plays in which the character's actions and his growth can be placed within or against the costume he wears, for plays in which the character is tragically or comically at odds with the clothing, for plays in which the stage appearance of the actor is deliberately supported by, or deliberately at variance with, what the character says and does. The stage has been set, then, for Macbeth in his borrowed robes, for Coriolanus in the "napless vesture of humility," for the Duchess of Malfi's brother in his Cardinal's robes, though in the 1590s we are still some way from such potent visual images.

In the 1590s the plays often contain two or more of the three traditions, one overlapping the other. *The Taming of the Shrew*, an earlier play, uses all three. Against a background of stock costuming, Kate and Petruchio play out their story around symbolic costuming, while Bianca and her suitors (drawn from Gascoigne's *Supposes*) ring all the changes on romance disguise. *The Merchant of Venice* is more typical in its superposition of one tradition—the disguise—onto a general dependence on stock costuming for role identification. Here Christian and Jewish merchants, old and young men, masters and servants would be dressed appropriately to set up the oppositions visually. Shylock, who sees his Jewishness as the focus of the hatred against him, mentions his Jewish costume, his "gaberdine." Otherwise, discussion of costuming is saved for the random mocking comments about the clothing of Portia's suitors, and for the disguises: the page's costume for the embarrassed Jessica, and the lawyer's and clerk's robes used to transform Portia and Nerissa. In *Richard II*, Shakespeare sets intricate symbolic scenes focusing on the crown against a general background of stock costuming. And in a play like *Mucedorus*, we find a fascinating amalgam of the three traditions, beginning with Comedy and Envy in their iconographical clothing, and moving on to a romance in which most of the characters—kings, princesses, nobles, and wild men—are dressed for ready audience identification, but in which disguise also plays an elaborate, and moralized, role.[18]

---

18. Particularly nice is the *trompe l'oeil* effect achieved by the 1610 reviser of *Mucedorus*, when he has Prince Mucedorus choose as his first disguise a shepherd costume worn by his friend in a masque at court.

I noted earlier that the multiple functions of even one of the intriguing, richly complex costumes from the period around 1600 repay extensive study. I would now like to suggest that much of that complexity derives from the dramatist's superposition of the various traditions onto given garments. Consider, briefly, Hamlet's black cloak, a stock costume used to indicate a noble character in mourning (the Vice-Roy of Portugal wore such a garment, we recall, in *The Spanish Tragedy,* and claimed that Fate could take everything away from him except his cloak of sable). When Hamlet and others enter in I. ii, the cloak is not discussed or described; it silently sets Hamlet against the rest of the court in their wedding/coronation finery, and does so without verbal elaboration. At line 68, though, it becomes the focus of the struggle between Hamlet and his aunt/mother and uncle/father. They would have him "cast [his] nighted colour off," put away "those mourning duties" those signs of "unmanly grief." Their words show that they understand the symbolism of black clothing, its denotation of grief and melancholy, and that they assume that both the state of mind symbolized and its symbol can be cast aside at will. One is hard put to say whether they see the black garb as a kind of disguise—a costume deliberately assumed in order to hurt and defy them, something that Hamlet can easily "throw to earth"—or whether they see it as truly emblematic of a state of mind that they claim to see as peculiar, unbalanced, but one which, thrown aside, will free the mind to proceed healthily.

Hamlet's own discussion of his mourning garb is even more complex. He accepts the colour symbolism of blackness as a sign of grief, but seems to see it, as did others in Elizabethan England, as also a sign of constancy, of "a love which lives beyond death" of a love "constant in death," a sign of "firmness in intent."[19] Hamlet's interpretation of the meaning of the clothing, then, is quite different from that of Claudius and Gertrude: this is not a robe, or an emotional state, to be easily changed. Nevertheless, he himself describes his black garments as a kind of costume:

> 'Tis not alone my inky cloak . . .
> Nor customary suits of solemn black
>
> That can denote me truly. These indeed seem . . .
>
> But I have that within that passeth show—
> These but the trappings and the suits of woe.

19. See Don Cameron Allen, "Symbolic Colors," pp. 83-84.

We are here plunged into a world in which a stock costume simultaneously identifies the character—in this case identifies the son who is still in mourning—, expresses symbolically the emotions that he in fact feels, is equated by others with an attitude they want changed, and is acknowledged by the wearer to be a costume, mere "trappings." In such a dramatic world, only the foolish critic would try to separate the symbolic or emblematic from the characterizing, or even from disguise. The costume is all of these, though not as ambiguous and disturbing, perhaps, as Hamlet's antic garb, which again may or may not be a disguise, but which is certainly richly complex.

If we look back, now, at Aristotle's words: "the Spectacle (or stage-appearance of the actors) . . . though an attraction, is the least artistic of all the parts [of drama], and has least to do with the art of poetry. The . . . effect can be obtained without performance or actors; and besides, the getting up of the Spectacle is more a matter for the costumier than the poet"—we realize anew just how inadequate a description that is of English drama. If we return, with O. B. Hardison, to the very earliest beginnings in liturgical drama, we see that the visual—and especially the costuming—has been highly significant at every point. If we trace through English drama of the fifteenth and earlier sixteenth centuries with T. W. Craik and Glynne Wickham, we see again that what the viewer saw—especially in terms of significant costume changes—remained a central interest of the dramatist. And during the years following the building of permanent theatres in London, the visual aspect of the drama was, it seems, always a focus of the playwright's imagination.

Given the theatrical roots in liturgical and morality drama, given the influence of classical and Italian comedy, and given, especially, the fact that "the reign of Elizabeth marks an era of unprecedented activity in the history of restraints on apparel,"[20] we should not be surprised that playwrights depended on costuming to carry many dramaturgical burdens, nor that they used particular costumes to reflect in special and meaningful ways on the characters wearing them.

If we look at the use of costuming in the years between 1576 and 1600 from the perspective of such later plays as *Macbeth*, *Coriolanus*, *Volpone*, *The Revenger's Tragedy*, *The Alchemist*, or *The Tempest*, we see even *Hamlet* as being a mere precursor of what is to come. Significant costuming in Jacobean drama carries richer meanings, serves better to structure drama, combines more excitingly with poetic images, fills the stage with more flamboyant characters, opens our imaginations

20. Hooper, "Tudor Sumptuary Laws," p. 436.

further. But the ground for all of this was laid in those earlier years in which the separate traditions of significant costuming developed, came together, and overlapped, until a single costume and the words surrounding it could move audience imagination into and out of the play in a drama both illusionary and symbolic—a drama in which spectacle is very close to the poetic art, very much the province of the playwright.

Interpreting Stage Directions: Elizabethan Clues and Modern Detectives

ALAN C. DESSEN

Given the shortage of external evidence, any attempt to reconstruct the staging of plays in the age of Shakespeare must depend primarily upon the stage directions in the extant manuscripts, theatrical "plots," and printed texts. To work with these stage directions, however, is quickly to encounter frustration and confusion. Thus, many scenes in which meaning is closely linked to decisions about staging have no directions whatsoever (as in the nunnery scene in *Hamlet* where the reader today can never be certain when Hamlet becomes aware of the eavesdroppers if, indeed, he notices them at all). Moreover, the signals that *are* provided are often uninformative or confusing or inconsistent (as with the many situations where a character is given no exit but nonetheless is directed to re-enter: e.g., Osric at the close of *Hamlet*). Such murkiness is characteristic not only of printed texts (which may be one or more removes from the playhouse or may show the effects of compositorial error) but also of those texts and manuscripts that actually may have been used as the basis for performance. Thus, I find it chastening to remember that whoever annotated the manuscript of Heywood's *The Captives* for the theatre let stand the marginal stage direction for a murderous assault: "*Eather strykes him with a staffe or Casts a stone*" (MSR, ll. 2432-34).[1] At any per-

---

1. To reduce the number of notes (since so many stage directions and other snippets of evidence will be cited in this essay), references will be included in my text to Malone Society reprints (MSR), Tudor Facsimile Texts (TFT), Scolar Press facsimiles (Scolar), editions in the Revels Plays series (Revels), and editions in the Regents Renaissance Drama series (RRD). Similarly, for brief citations from seventeenth-century editions I cite only STC or Wing numbers.

formance the actor had to make a choice, but even with what appears to be the playhouse "book" in front of us we cannot be certain what that choice would have been.[2]

Even when we make allowances for missing and ambiguous stage directions, we are still left with some basic (and perhaps insurmountable) obstacles to interpretation. Quite simply, these signals, such as they are, are not directed at us. Thus, fifty years ago R. B. McKerrow noted shrewdly "that the original manuscript of a play would not have been written with any thought of the press. It was not intended for the study, or for the minute discussion of students three hundred years away in the future. It was not a literary document at all." Rather, for McKerrow, that original manuscript "was merely the substance, or rather the bare bones, of a performance on the stage, intended to be interpreted by actors skilled in their craft, who would have no difficulty in reading it as it was meant to be read."[3] Those manuscripts, then, were theatrical *scripts*, written to be performed by Elizabethan theatrical professionals, not literary *texts*, written to be read by modern critics. Furthermore, those scripts assumed a language shared by actor and spectator that went beyond the words alone to include stage conventions, emblematic properties, and an overall logic that today we may no longer recognize or appreciate.

To deal justly with the surviving stage directions is therefore to be conscious of the various pitfalls awaiting the modern detective working with these Elizabethan clues. Like McKerrow, I would assume that the original actors knew their craft well and, indeed, often did not need specific stage directions from the dramatist to tell them how to achieve particular effects. What may therefore seem murky to us now most likely made excellent sense then, with or

2. In his excellent discussion of this problem, W. W. Greg notes that playhouse manuscripts "all preserve stage-directions and other features of a literary type very imperfectly assimilated to the requirements or the point of view of stage representation," so that "even when they have been extensively worked over by a stage reviser the assimilation to a technically theatrical type and language has been but imperfectly effected" (*Dramatic Documents from the Elizabethan Playhouses*, 2 vols. [Oxford, 1931], I, 87). Citations from the theatrical "plots" are taken from volume two of this work. See also pp. 208-21 for discussion of stage directions (with specific mention of the "permissive" direction from *The Captives*). In his discussion of an otherwise unknown edition clearly used as a prompt copy, Charles Read Baskervill finds the carelessness in the entries "almost inconceivable," but is forced to conclude that "the apparent fact that the book was in use for many years and that a number of people contributed to the preparation of it suggests that a disregard for errors and inconsistencies in the text was not unusual." See "A Prompt Copy of *A Looking Glass for London and England*," *Modern Philology*, 30 (1932), 51.
3. "The Elizabethan Printer and Dramatic Manuscripts," *The Library*, 4th Series, 12 (1931), 266.

without specific signals from the playwright. However, without access to that language of the theatre shared then by dramatists, actors, and spectators, the scholar today can only work with whatever scraps of evidence have chanced to survive and then indulge in inference, hypothesis, and conjecture, all to recapture what would have been obvious to an untutored groundling at the Globe. And the only substantial basis for such conjectures and often labyrinthine reasoning lies in those unsatisfying, inconsistent, puzzling, and often tantalizing stage directions.

Unlike Agatha Christie, I can offer no ingenious solution to pluck out the heart of the mystery raised by these theatrical clues. However, I do wish to argue for the advantages to the modern detective of considering related stage directions as part of a larger group or genus. Other scholars have advocated such an approach, at least in general terms. Thus, in his paper for this conference in 1973, T. W. Craik concluded that the ideal interpreter of stage action "will read each play with every other Elizabethan play simultaneously in mind."[4] More recently, E. A. J. Honigmann has provided several examples of how editors can be misled when they look "too narrowly at a single play." Rather, as he observes, "we are only ready to interpret stage directions when we have identified them as members of a group."[5] Since philologians, linguists, and iconographers have demonstrated the advantages of such a comparative approach for the reconstruction of lost meanings, should not such a method also be appropriate for recovering the lost language of the theatre?

Needless to say, much then depends upon what constitutes such a group for the editor or stage historian. As a point of departure, consider the brief stage direction provided by Massinger in *A New Way to Pay Old Debts*: "Overreach *as from dinner*" (III. iii. 0.s.d.).[6] Subsequent dialogue establishes that Sir Giles has left the table in anger; thus Marral enters to say: "Sir the whole boord is troubled at your rising" (l.13). To the editor or critic viewing this scene in isolation, "as from dinner" may appear to be a "literary" stage

4. "The Reconstruction of Stage Action from Early Dramatic Texts," *The Elizabethan Theatre V*, ed G R. Hibbard (Toronto, 1975), p. 91.
5. "Re-Enter the Stage Direction: Shakespeare and Some Contemporaries," *Shakespeare Survey*, 29 (1976), 124. In this brief section, Honigmann deals with *stand forth*, *music still*, and *silence*; elsewhere in his essay he discusses misplaced stage directions, asides, "*all*" speeches, and what he calls "crypto-directions" (e.g., the use of "O!-O!").
6. Quotations from Massinger are taken from *The Plays and Poems*, ed. Philip Edwards and Colin Gibson, 5 vols. (Oxford, 1976). Besides *A New Way to Pay Old Debts*, this set of plays includes *The Unnatural Combat*, *The Emperor of the East*, *The Bondman*, *The Bashful Lover*, *The Great Duke of Florence*, *The Duke of Milan*, and *The Picture*.

direction geared to the reader of a text rather than to an actor or spectator and may conjure up no clear picture of stage action.

But Massinger's terse signal makes more sense when seen as part of a larger group or series in which other examples supply revealing details. For example: "*Enter* Tucca *brushing of the crumbes*" (*Satiromastix*, III. i. 98.s.d.);[7] enter "*Robin* hauing his napkin on his shoulder, as if hee were sodainly raised from dinner" (*The Downfall of Robert Earl of Huntingdon*, MSR. ll. 166-68); "*Enter Ayre, Hodge, Firke, Rafe, and other shoemakers, all with napkins on their shoulders*" (*The Shoemakers' Holiday*, V. iv. O.s.d.); "*Enter Master Frankeford, as it were brushing the Crummes from his clothes with a Napkin, as newly risen from supper*" (*A Woman Killed With Kindness*, II. 118);[8] enter Neatfoot "*with a napkin on his shoulder, and a trencher in his hand as from table*" (*The Roaring Girl*, I. i. O.s.d.); "*Enter hastely at seuerall doores: Duke of Lancaster. Duke of yorke, the Earles of Arondell and Surrye, with Napkins on ther arms & kniues in ther hands*" (*Woodstock*, MSR, ll. 1-3); "*Enter* Petruchio *and* Nibrassa *with napkins, as from supper*" (*Love's Sacrifice*, STC 11164, Hl[r]). In *The Wise Woman of Hogsdon*, figures not included in an off-stage meal are joined by a servant "*with a Trencher, with broken meate and a Napkin,*" who then re-enters moments later "*with a bowle of Beere and a Napkine*"; finally, "*enter* Chartly *with his Napkin as from Dinner*" (V, 335-36). This final "as from dinner" completes the circle started by Massinger's identical phrase, but not before a sense has emerged of a shared effect provided by different plays that span several decades. Such recurring details as real or imaginary crumbs, napkins, trenchers, and eating implements establish how an "as from dinner" effect can be signalled simply yet effectively for a spectator.

Similar "as from . . ." signals recur throughout the extant plays, both with and without suggestive details. Thus, figures are directed to enter: "*as newly come from play*" (*The Wise Woman of Hogsdon*,

---

7. Quotations from Dekker are drawn from *The Dramatic Works*, ed. Fredson Bowers, 4 vols. (Cambridge, 1953-61). Besides *Satiromastix*, this set of plays includes *The Shoemakers' Holiday*, *The Roaring Girl*, *Patient Grissill*, 1 *The Honest Whore*, *The Witch of Edmonton*, *Northward Ho*, *The Famous History of Sir Thomas Wyatt*, *Match Me in London*, *Westward Ho*, and *Lust's Dominion*.

8. With the exception of *The Captives*, quotations from Heywood are taken from *The Dramatic Works*, 6 vols. (London, 1874); references in my text are to volume and page numbers in this edition. In addition to *A Woman Killed With Kindness*, this set of plays includes *The Wise Woman of Hogsdon*, *The English Traveller*, *The Four Prentices of London*, *The Late Lancashire Witches*, *A Maidenhead Well Lost*, 1 and 2 *Edward IV*, *The Golden Age*, *The Silver Age*, *The Brazen Age*, 1 and 2 *The Iron Age*, 1 *The Fair Maid of the West*, *The Rape of Lucrece*, *Love's Mistress*, *The Royal King and the Loyal Subject*, and 2 *If You Know Not Me You Know Nobody*.

V, 279); "*as at Dice*" (*The Tragedy of Valentinian*, IV, 17);[9] "*in their shirts, as from Torments*" (*A Shoemaker, a Gentleman*, STC 21422, H3ʳ); "*as rob'd*" [i.e., robbed] (*Love's Pilgrimage*, VI, 262); "*as in the field*" [i.e., awaiting a duel] (*The Little French Lawyer*, III, 391); "*as it were in retire*" from a battle (*Coriolanus*, I. vi. 0.s.d.);[10] and "*as from Walking*" (*The English Traveller*, IV, 44). Some of the more vivid examples include: enter "*as being thrown off his horse, And falls*" (*The Yorkshire Tragedy*, MSR, l. 632); "*as out of a caues mouth*" (*Sophonisba*, STC 17488, E2ᵛ); "*as out of a Bush*" (*The Two Noble Kinsmen*, IX, 325); "all wett as newly shipwracke and escapt the ffury off the Seas" (*The Captives*, MSR, ll. 653-54); and "*as newly landed & halfe naked*" (*The Four Prentices of London*, II, 176). To my knowledge, no play provides "as from fishing," but Dekker does give us: "*Enter Ianicola with an Angling rod, Grissil with a reele*" (*Patient Grissill*, V. i. 56.s.d.), and Field provides: "*Enter Sir Abraham throwing down his Bowles*" (*A Woman is a Weathercock*, STC 10854, F3ʳ). Similarly, I know of no "as from battle" signal, but (in addition to the bloody sergeant in *Macbeth*) Marston provides a messenger from the front with "his sword drawne, his body wounded, his shield strucke full of darts" (*Sophonisba*, B2ʳ). Quite a few plays set up off-stage weddings and then direct figures to enter "*as from the Church*" (*A Woman is a Weathercock*, D3ᵛ) or "*as from Church over the Stage*" (*The Spanish Gipsy*, M 1986, H3ᵛ) or exeunt "*going to be Married*" (*The Scornful Lady*, I, 281), presumably setting up a wedding procession rather than the wedding itself. Other scripts, however, provide at least one revealing detail. Thus, at the outset of *The Woman's Prize*, a group enters "*with Rosemary, as from a wedding*" (VIII, 2); such rosemary then recurs in the stage directions or dialogue of quite a few plays (i.e., *Eastward Ho*, TFT, D2ʳ; *A Fair Quarrel*, RRD, V. i. 36.s.d., 40-42, 119, 123-24, 133-34; *The Pilgrim*, V, 229; *The Scornful Lady*, I, 235).

9. Unless otherwise noted, quotations from Beaumont and Fletcher are drawn from *The Works*, ed. Arnold Glover and A. R. Waller, 10 vols. (Cambridge, 1905-12); references in my text are to volume and page numbers in this edition. In addition to *Valentinian*, this set of plays includes *Love's Pilgrimage*, *The Little French Lawyer*, *The Two Noble Kinsmen*, *The Scornful Lady*, *The Woman's Prize*, *The Pilgrim*, *The Prophetess*, *The Queen of Corinth*, *The Nice Valor*, *The Honest Man's Fortune*, *The Lover's Progress*, *Thierry and Theodoret*, *The Coxcomb*, *Rule a Wife, Have a Wife*, *Cupid's Revenge*, *The Humourous Lieutenant*, *Wit Without Money*, *The Noble Gentleman*, *The Custom of the Country*, and *The Captain*.
10. Unless otherwise noted, quotations from Shakespeare are from *The Complete Pelican Shakespeare*, gen. ed. Alfred Harbage (Baltimore, 1969). Citations from the First Folio are from the Norton Facsimile, ed. Charlton Hinman (New York, 1968).

Perhaps the most interesting examples are found in the many plays that call for figures to enter "*as from hunting*" (*The Late Lancashire Witches*, IV, 171) or, more commonly, "*from hunting*" (e.g., *The Taming of the Shrew*, Induction, i.13.s.d.; *The Taming of a Shrew*, TFT, A2ʳ; *Titus Andronicus*, II. iv. 10.s.d.; *Demetrius and Enanthe*, MSR, l. 187). Even the theatrical "plot" of 2 *The Seven Deadly Sins* calls for Tereus to appear "*from Hunting with his Lords.*" To achieve this effect, the dramatists and actors relied heavily upon sound effects. Indeed, "*wind horns*" appears in so many plays it is pointless to list titles. Thus, in *A Maidenhead Well Lost*, "*Sound Hornes within*" is followed by the on-stage comment: "It seems the Duke is Hunting in the Forrest" (IV, 122). One sequence in *The Shoemakers' Holiday* provides: "*Hollowing within*"; "*A noise of hunters within*"; "*Hunting within*"; and "*Hornes sound within*" (II. i. 0.s.d., 9.s.d., II. ii. 0.s.d, 9.s.d.). In *A Trick to Catch the Old One*, Hoard associates a falconer and a huntsman with their characteristic sounds ("Sa ho, sa ho, sa ho" and "There, boy, there boye, there boye"—Scolar, F4ʳ). Or consider the stage picture evoked in *Summer's Last Will and Testament*: "*Enter Orion like a hunter, with a horne about his necke, all his men after the same sort hallowing and blowing their hornes*"; these figures then exeunt "*blowing their hornes, and hallowing, as they came in*" (STC 18376, D3ᵛ, E2ʳ).[11]

In addition to such sound effects, "from hunting" often was linked to costume. As just noted, Nashe's Orion was to enter "*like a hunter*"; similarly, in *The Insatiate Countess* Guiaca twice is directed to enter "*in his hunting weedes*" (STC 17476, Flʳ, F2ᵛ); elsewhere, figures enter "*all like Hunters*" (*Patient Grissill*, I. i. 0.s.d.) or "*like hunters*" (*The Shoemakers' Holiday*, II. i. 0.s.d.). Often these hunting weeds are linked specifically to the colour green. Thus, Henslowe's inventory includes green garments for Robin Hood and Marian;[12] then, in Munday's play, the two figures are to enter "all in greene" (*The Downfall of Robert Earl of Huntingdon*, MSR, l. 1260). In various Heywood plays, figures are directed to enter "*in greene*" (1 *Edward IV*, I, 40) or "*like a wood-man in greene*" (*The Silver Age*, III, 146) or "*with Iauelings, and in greene*" (*The Brazen Age*, III, 187), while a group in Peele's *Edward I* enter "*all clad in greene*" (MSR, l. 1368). At the same time, many plays specify no sounds or costumes or colours but rather establish a forest locale or the atmosphere of the hunt by

11. For other extensive sound effects associated with the hunt, see the opening of *Patient Grissill*, Act II of *The Brazen Age*, and Act I of *The Royal King and the Loyal Subject*.
12. See *Henslowe's Diary*, ed. R. A. Foakes and R. T. Rickert (Cambridge, 1961), p. 317, ll. 20-21.

calling for the presence of huntsmen or woodmen (e.g., *Philaster; Thierry and Theodoret; The Martyred Soldier; 3 Henry VI; James IV; Patient Grissill; A Maidenhead Well Lost*).

To spell out further "as from hunting," quite a few plays call for weapons or other portable properties: a falconer's lure (*Look About You*); crossbows (*3 Henry VI*); various combinations of bows, quivers, and javelins (*The Custom of the Country; 1 Edward IV; The Downfall of Robert Earl of Huntingdon; The Humourous Lieutenant; The Brazen Age; The Golden Age*). In *Woodstock*, the treacherous masquers enter *"like Dianas knights, led In by (4.) other knights: (In Greene) with hornes about ther necks & borespeares in ther hands"* (MSR, ll. 2119-20). In the quarto of *2 Henry VI*, where the royal party is to enter "as if they came from hawking," the queen appears "with her Hawke on her fist" (C1ᵛ). To climax a successful hunt, Munday brings on a stag's head (*The Death of Robert Earl of Huntingdon*); Heywood brings on Hercules *"with the Lyons head and skinne"* (*The Silver Age*, III, 131); and Fletcher brings on Diocles *"with a Boar"* (*The Prophetess*, V, 325). By far the most elaborate example is the hunt for the Caledonian boar in *The Brazen Age*. Heywood starts with Venus dressed *"like a Huntresse,"* horns sound off-stage as "the summons to the chace," a group of heroes *"with Iavelings, and in greene,"* and Atlanta *"with a Iauelin."* Then follow: *"Enter Adonis winding his horne . . . . a great winding of hornes, & shouts"*; cries of "charge, charge" and reports of wounds and pursuits; *"Hornes and shouts . . . Hornes. . . . After great shouts, enter Venus . . . A cry within."* After the dying Adonis is carried on and off and *"the fall of the Boare being winded,"* the successful hunters enter *"with the head of the Boare"* and *"with their iavellins bloudied"* (III, 184-94).

Although providing no startling new insights, this group of "as from ..." stage directions does bring into focus some distinctive features of Elizabethan staging. Readers familiar with these plays will have no difficulty compiling a list of banquets or weddings actually presented on stage, but, for various practical or aesthetic reasons, certain types of scenes (e.g., hunts, fires, shipwrecks, public executions) often were not displayed, either to increase the narrative flow or to sidestep significant problems. Remember, for the most part we are dealing with repertory companies presenting four to six plays per week on a bare platform stage using mostly portable properties and having no access to formal sets, variable lighting, or a fourth wall curtain. With or without the accompanying details, the "as from ..." stage direction represents an essential part of the strategy for using such a stage, a strategy that builds upon a few clear signals and the actor's skill to convey, deftly and economically, a recently completed or continuing action. What results is a theatrical shorthand for the spectator, an alternative to a full scene or more extensive narrative detail. To be sure, in a Shakespearean play such details often form part of a larger metaphoric or symbolic effect (so in *Titus Andronicus* the entrance of Marcus "*from hunting*" in II.iv clearly is linked to the maimed Lavinia and the Andronici as prey), but the general usage is more basic, even elementary—a way of telling a story on stage in an economical yet theatrically telling fashion. At its best, such a technique can create for the spectator a sense of a rich, busy, very "real" world just off-stage.[13]

Many modern readers, particularly actors and directors, will have no difficulty translating "as from dinner" or "as from hunting" into appropriate stage action, with or without support from other plays of the period. Indeed, a recent modern dress production of *Timon of Athens* (Oregon Shakespearean Festival, 1978) used costume and properties to display two of Timon's false friends entering "*as from tennis*" and "*as from swimming*." But some stage directions will call upon associations shared by actors and spectators then but less accessible, even lost today (an equivalent, in the popular theatre, to the emblems and icons in the learned tradition). Deciphering such visual signals today therefore requires both a good sense of theatre (again, a distinction between scripts and texts) and fluency in a language for the eye that may at times be as difficult to translate into a modern idiom as Caliban's *scamels*.

Consider, for example, the following series: "*Enter Ophelia distracted*" (*Hamlet*, Folio, l. 2766); "*Enter* Bellafronte *mad*" (1 *Honest Whore*, V. ii. 299.s.d.); "*Enter* Ann Ratcliff *mad*" (*The Witch of Edmonton*, IV. i. 172.s.d.); "*Enter* Merione (*as newly ravished*)" (*The Queen of Corinth*, VI, 17); "*Enter* ... Lauinia, *her handes cut off, and her tongue cut out, & rauisht*" (*Titus Andronicus*, Q-1, E2^r). This signal even turns up in one of the theatrical "plots": "*Enter* carynus madde to him prelyor madde" (*The Dead Man's Fortune*, IV. iii).

Granted, the scholar cannot assume the presence of any one signal or set of signals to denote madness or rape; rather, the responsibility for conveying such an effort must fall largely upon the actor. Nonetheless, a significant number of plays in the age of Shakespeare does provide one such signal, especially for the boy actor playing a female

13. For further discussion of similar techniques, see Alan C. Dessen, "Elizabethan Audiences and the Open Stage: Recovering Lost Conventions," *The Yearbook of English Studies*, 10 (1980), 1-20.

figure distraught with madness, shame, extreme grief, or the effects of recent violence. Most familiar are the various Shakespearean examples: "*Enter Cassandra with her haire about her eares*" (*Troilus and Cressida*, II. ii, Folio, ll. 1082-83); "*Enter the Queene with her haire about her ears*" (*Richard* III, II. ii, Folio, l. 1306); "*Enter Ofelia playing on a Lute, and her haire downe singing*" (*Hamlet*, Q1, G4ᵛ). In the manuscript of *Dick of Devonshire*, Eleonora, who has just been raped, enters "loose haired, & weeping" (MSR, ll. 687-89); in Massinger's *The Unnatural Combat*, after an off-stage rape, "*The* Souldiers *thrust forth* Theocrine, *her garments loose, her haire disheveld*" (V. ii. 185.s.d.); in *A Warning for Fair Women*, after the corruption of Anne Sanders has been acted out in dumb show, Chastity enters "with her haire disheueled" (TFT, E3ᵛ). Hair about the ears can indicate public shame (*2 Edward* IV, I, 165; *The Insatiate Countess*, STC 17476, H3ᵛ; *The Bloody Banquet*, TFT, G4ᵛ; *The Emperor of the East*, V. iii. 0.s.d.) or high passion (*Northward Ho*, V. i. 194.s.d.) or mourning (*Swetnam the Woman Hater*, TFT, G2ʳ) or, of course, madness ("*Enter* Cassandra *with her haire about her eares*"—1 *The Iron Age*, III, 269). A few examples of male figures with disordered hair can also be noted (e.g., Humber in *Locrine*, MSR, ll. 1573-75; Saturn in *The Golden Age*, III, 38), but most of the examples are female. One famous modern example can be found in Peter Brook's landmark 1955 production of *Titus Andronicus* in which Lavinia, as played by Vivian Leigh, *did* enter with her hair down in this manner; in contrast, in the 1977 production of *Richard* III at Stratford Festival Canada, Maggie Smith as a grief-stricken Queen Elizabeth did not change her hair for her entrance.

Such choices made in recent productions can be instructive, for what may seem an intrusive or impractical detail to the modern actress may, in contrast, have been easily accessible for the boy actor and visually meaningful for the Elizabethan spectator. Thus, unlike the actress today who must worry about her coiffure, the original boy actor need only have changed his wig to set up a strikingly different image that, in turn, could convey a severe change in the state of the character. Such an entrance can then be particularly effective if previously the viewer had seen the same figure impeccably attired. For example, early in 1 *The Honest Whore* Dekker provides Bellafront with an elaborate dressing scene in which, among other things, she "*curles her haire, cullers her lips*" (II. i. 12.s.d.). If then in Act V she does enter with her hair about her ears (the stage direction only specifies "*mad*"), this climactic visual configuration would be in striking contrast to our image of her throughout the play. In addition to aiding narrative economy, such an effect can also provide a clear visual display of the falling away from or the destruction of a previous image of order. One thinks as well of Hamlet's new antic costume in Act II as described by Ophelia ("his doublet all unbraced, / No hat upon his head, his stockings fouled, / Ungartered, and down-gyved to his ankle ... "—II. i. 78-80), or, similarly, from *The Nice Valor*: "*Enter the passionate Cosin, rudely, and carelesly apparrell'd, unbrac'd, and untruss'd*" (X, 170). For other clear violations of orderly patterns, remember too the interrupted dance at the end of Prospero's masque in Act IV of *The Tempest* or the opening stage direction of *The Malcontent* which calls for "*the vilest out of tune Musicke*" (Scolar, B1ʳ). Without undervaluing the importance of the actor's skill in playing madness or distress, the scholar can still recognize the metaphoric and symbolic potential in "loose" or "disheveled" hair, a potential that can extend beyond the psychological state of the individual character.

Nor can the metaphoric potential in visible stage details be limited to disordered hair and clothing. As a point of departure for a large group of stage directions, consider the following: "*Enter as it were in haste*" (*The Downfall of Robert Earl of Huntingdon*, MSR, l. 142); "*King in great hast*" (*The Life of Sir John Oldcastle*, TFT, F1ᵛ); "*enter a Messenger hastily*" (*Coriolanus*, I. i. 217.s.d.). Particularly with messengers and clowns, such haste can be conveyed through the speed of the entrance alone: "*enter a messenger runinge*" (*Edmund Ironsides*, MSR, ll. 735, 1332);˙ "*Enter Clem running*" or "*falling for haste*" (*1 The Fair Maid of the West*, II, 330, 315); "*enter Zanthia running*" (*The Bondman*, II. ii. 141.s.d.). The theatrical "plot" of *2 The Seven Deadly Sins* provides "*to them Lucius Running*" (l. 44) and "*to him will foole Runing*" (ll. 62-63). To convey a hasty arrival is well within the province of the actor (and can be a good source of comedy).

But a wealth of evidence is available to document a specific bit of theatrical shorthand to enhance this effect. For example, in *The Famous History of Sir Thomas Wyatt* Northumberland asks: "Sir Thomas booted and spur'd, / Whether away so fast?" (I. i. 21-22); in *The Life of Sir John Oldcastle* Scroop says of the hero: "here comes the man himselfe / Booted and spurrd, it seemes he hath beene riding" (TFT, E1ᵛ); in *The Widow's Tears* Tharsalio asks Lysander: "What, sir, unbooted? Have you been long arrived?" (Revels, V. iii. 87). Also cited regularly are other items of costume that serve the same function: "*Enter Longueville with a riding-rod*" (*The Honest Man's Fortune*, X, 255); "*Enter sir Petronell in Bootes with a ryding wan*" (*Eastward*

Ho, TFT, C2ʳ).[14] An appropriate signal was available for the ladies: *"Enter* Winnifride *in a riding-suit"* (*The Witch of Edmonton*, I. i. 155.s.d.); *"Enter* Jane *in haste, in her riding-cloak and saue-guard, with a pardon in her hand"* (*2 Edward* IV, I, 139).[15] But the recurring detail most often associated with haste or a journey recently completed or a journey about to be undertaken is the stage boot. Thus, when a group of figures arrive at an inn in *The Merry Devil of Edmonton*, the stage direction calls for *"the men booted, the gentlewomen in cloakes and safeguardes"* (TFT, B1ʳ); in *The Fair Maid of the Exchange*, a figure about to go on a journey is *"booted"* but his friend, who is not to depart, is not (MSR, ll. 1197-98). For one who reads widely in these plays, *enter booted* is a very familiar stage direction.[16]

Often dialogue spells out associations to be linked with boots and riding apparel. Thus, in *Friar Bacon and Friar Bungay* the gentlemen arrive *"booted and spurd"* (TFT, H3ʳ), with Lacy announcing: "we haue hied and posted all this night to Frisingfield" (H4ʳ). *Northward Ho*, with its many journeys and quick exits, has an unusually large number of stage directions that call for boots (see I. i. 0.s.d.; IV. i. 207.s.d.; IV. iii. 0.s.d.; V. i. 454.s.d.); at one point, Mayberry concludes: "Come, bootes boy, we must gallop all the way ..." (IV. i. 276-77). Such connotations are best developed in Act V of *2 Henry* IV. First, Justice Shallow urges Falstaff not to depart, with the injunction: "Come, come, come off with your boots" (V. i. 48). Falstaff's reaction to the news of Henry IV's death then includes "get on thy boots. We'll ride all night" and "boot, boot, Master Shallow. I know the young king is sick for me. Let us take any man's horses" (V. iii. 128, 131-32). While awaiting the coronation procession, Falstaff argues that his zeal, devotion, and "earnestness of affection" will be evident in his willingness "to ride day and night" and "not to have patience to shift me" but rather "to stand stained with travel, and sweating with desire to see him" (V. v. 13-27). The boots and travel-stained costume are thereby interpreted by the wearer as an index to his commitment—"as if there were nothing else to be done but to see him" (26-27).

14. For other wands and rods, see *Amends for Ladies*, STC 10852, G1ʳ; *Wit Without Money*, II, 170; *The History of King Leir*, MSR, ll. 398-99, 408-9.
15. See also *Perkin Warbeck*, Revels, V. i. 0.s.d.; *The Yorkshire Tragedy*, MSR, l. 296; *The Picture*, I. i. 0.s.d.; 1 *Edward* IV, I, 39; *The Witch*, MSR, ll. 909-10; *The Noble Gentleman*, VIII, 188. The OED defines *safeguard* (#8): "an outer skirt or petticoat worn by women to protect their dress when riding."
16. For just a few examples, see *Wit Without Money*, II, 166-67; *The Widow's Tears*, Revels, III. i. 0.s.d.; *A Woman Killed With Kindness*, II, 133; *Two Lamentable Tragedies*, TFT, D4ʳ, F1ʳ; *James* IV, MSR, l. 557; 1 *Edward* IV, I, 48

For potential meaning beyond the theatrical shorthand, the most interesting example is to be found in *Richard II*. Here, after discovering the plot against Henry IV, the Duke of York calls for his boots; "*His Man enters with his boots*"; and, after some stage business involving his servant and his Duchess, York puts on his boots (V. ii. 84-87). Although critics and directors usually treat this scene in terms of its potential for comedy, I have argued elsewhere[17] that it may form part of a pattern for the spectator's eye, especially if that spectator had seen Willoughby and Ross enter, booted, to show their support of Bolingbroke in II. iii (these two figures are described as "bloody with spurring, fiery red with haste"—57-58), and, after York's exit and re-entrance with his boots, if that spectator then saw Exton's arrival to murder Richard as the entrance of a group of booted figures (the stage direction reads: "*the murderers rush in*"—V. v. 104). I cannot prove that Willoughby, Ross, and Exton would have been wearing such boots in a production of *Richard II* in the 1590s, but, on one level, the stage shorthand would suit well the haste and the journeys involved and, on a deeper level, the three booted entrances would link for the eye three different choices or sets of choosers, each in haste to pick the rising sun of Bolingbroke over the falling star of Richard. Consideration of the larger group rather than the stage direction in one scene may thereby lead to a heightened awareness of analogous situations basic to this or other Shakespearean plays.

My last and largest group draws upon over fifty plays. Thus, one recurring stage direction calls for figures to enter "*as from their Chamber*" (*'Tis Pity She's a Whore*, Scolar, C3ᵥ); "*as from his chamber*" (*The Bashful Lover*, V. i. 71.s.d.); "*as from bed*" (*2 The Iron Age*, III, 381; *The Lover's Progress*, V, 128; *Thierry and Theodoret*, X, 30); "*as out of her bed*" (*The Coxcomb*, VIII, 325); "*as newly come out of Bed*" (*A Woman Killed with Kindness*, II, 141); and "*as newly wak'd from sleepe*" (*The English Traveller*, IV, 33). A playhouse manuscript, *Dick of Devonshire*, directs Henrico to enter "as newly risen" (MSR, l. 1286). Similarly, many figures are told to enter "unready": Prince John in *Match Me in London* (I. iii. 0.s.d.); Lucrece after the rape (*The Rape of Lucrece*, V, 226); a servant in *The Coxcomb* (VIII, 32); a group of surprised Greeks "halfe vnready, as newly started from their Beds" (*2 The Iron Age*, III, 413).

As with my previous groups, other stage directions then supply a

---

17. "Shakespeare's Patterns for the Viewer's Eye: Dramaturgy for the Open Stage," in *Shakespeare's "More Than Words Can Witness*," ed. Sidney Homan (Lewisburg, Pa., 1980), pp. 101-5.

variety of details to signal unreadiness or "as from bed." Consider first some morning scenes: enter *"trussing their points as new vp"* (*The Merry Devil of Edmonton*, TFT, E4ʳ); enter Moll *"lacing of her clothes"* (*The Puritan*, TFT, H2ʳ); *"enter Master* Honisuckle *in his night-cap trussing himselfe"* (*Westward Ho*, II. i. O.s.d.). In tenser situations, the depiction of unreadiness can be quite vivid: *"Enter at one dore* Alexandra *in her petticoate; at another* Aristobulus *the high Priest in his wastcoate or shirt, both amazedly"* (*Herod and Antipater*, STC 17401, I. i. O.s.d.); *"Alarum, with men and women halfe naked: Enter two Captaynes without dublets, with swords"* (*The History of King Leir*, MSR, ll. 2476-77; see also l. 2506); *"Enter* Widdow *vndrest, a sword in her hand, and* Bould *in his shirt, as started from bed"* (*Amends for Ladies*, STC 10852, F1ʳ). As in the example from *Leir*, a failure to "watch" properly that then leaves one vulnerable to one's enemies often is associated with unreadiness in clothing: in the sacking of Troy in *2 The Iron Age* (where much is made of "unready" and "naked" Trojans); in the capture of Edward IV in *3 Henry VI* (see especially IV. iii. 27.s.d.); and most clearly in *1 Henry VI* where, at Talbot's attack on Orleans, *"the French leap o'er the walls in their shirts"* and three French leaders appear *"half ready and half unready"* (II. i. 38.s.d.).

But references to points, trussing, shirts, night-caps, and general unreadiness are far outnumbered by the more than thirty plays with stage directions that call for nightgowns. In her often cited study, M. Channing Linthicum describes this Elizabethan garment as "an ankle-length gown with long sleeves and collar varying in size . . . worn for warmth both indoors and out." She then argues strenuously against those scholars who "have tried to prove that night-gowns were for night wear in one's chamber"; rather, to "show the error of this assumption" she cites "many accounts"[18] (actually three). Linthicum may well be right that off the stage in the "real world" a nightgown was not limited to a private chamber, much less a bedroom, but, unless the scholar is dealing with naturalistic drama, evidence from contemporary life cannot prove conclusively anything about on-stage activity, especially in a drama that draws heavily upon theatrical shorthand and stage metaphor. Thus, although Linthicum can cite a diary reference from Lady Anne Clifford in 1617 that "I went to Church in my rich night gown," the Shakespearean can counter with Margaret's comment to Hero that the Duchess of Milan's wedding gown was "but a nightgown in respect of yours" (*Much Ado*, III. iv.

---

18. *Costume in the Drama of Shakespeare and his Contemporaries* (Oxford, 1936), pp. 184-85.

17-18). Similarly, Linthicum's citation of Lady Jane Grey wearing a nightgown on the scaffold at her execution in *Sir Thomas Wyatt* does not take into account the potential symbolic value of the costume, a set of associations developed clearly in 2 *Edward IV* where the two little princes enter *"in their gowns and caps, vnbuttond, and vntrust"* (I, 153-54) and then, in their speeches, equate going to bed with going to their graves (since any good Christian should be prepared to die at any hour). Although I cannot offer a detailed description of the stage version of a nightgown, I can demonstrate a clear and consistent connection with night, morning, bed, unreadiness, or some combination thereof.

This ubiquitous garment could serve a variety of functions. On the simplest level, it provided a quick signal that placed the on-stage action at night or in the early morning (either in place of or along with the candles and torches also used to denote stage night or darkness). Thus, the opening stage direction of *Alphonsus Emperor of Germany* reads: *"Enter Alphonsus the Emperour in his night-gown, and his shirt, and a torch in his hand."*[19] Many examples can be cited of such theatrical shorthand: *"enter Gloster in his gowne, calling"* for a drowsy Porter (*Look About You*, TFT, C4ʳ); enter the count, in a morning scene, *"in his shirt and night gowne"* to spy upon his wife (*An Humourous Day's Mirth*, MSR, l. 1); enter the widow *"in her night-cloathes, as going to bed"* (*A Match at Midnight*, STC 21421, H2ʳ); enter Psyche *"in night-attire, with a Lampe and a Raysor"* to discover the identity of Cupid (*Love's Mistress*, V, 120). To escape pursuit in the middle of the night, enter Sir John Oldcastle *"in his gowne stealing"* (MSR, l. 2210); to set up a murderous tryst at night, enter the queen *"masked in her night-gowne"* (*The Bloody Banquet*, TFT, E1ᵛ); to pursue a seduction at night, enter the duke *"in a gown"* (*Rule a Wife, Have a Wife*, III, 229). After the brides have been stolen in *John a Kent*, the bridegrooms come forth in the morning *"in their nightgownes and kerchers on their heades"*; shortly thereafter, two figures enter *"vnbraste,"* then a third *"in his night gowne"*—all this from a playhouse manuscript (MSR, ll. 582, 596, 604). Occasionally, this stage nightgown could convey other associations (e.g., to help characterize the convalescent Dorothea in *James IV*, MSR, l. 1941 or *"My Gown? why, am I sick?"* in *Cupid's Revenge*, IX, 244), but a high percentage of the relevant stage directions signal the time (either night or early morning) along with connotations of unreadiness, furtiveness, surprise, or lust.

19. Ed. Herbert F. Schwarz (New York and London, 1913), p. 1.

Not surprisingly, the stage nightgown often turns up in a sexual or romantic context. Heywood, for one, provides several "morning-after" scenes, as in *The Golden Age* where, after an elaborate seduction that involves lights, a bed, and making unready, Jupiter re-enters with "*Danae in her night-gowne*" (III, 70). Similarly, in *The English Traveller* two lovers enter after a night together "*in a Night-gowne*" and "*in a night-tyre*,[20] *as comming from Bed*"; after an exchange of pleasantries ("a happy Morning now betide you Lady, / To equall the content of a sweet Night"), the wife is urged to "retire you / To your warme Sheets; I now to fill my owne, / That haue this Night bin empty" (IV, 70-71). Although no such signals are provided, I suspect that the same effect may have been found at the entrance of Antony and Cleopatra in IV. iv, where the queen urges "sleep a little" before she helps to arm Antony, and perhaps at the outset of *Troilus and Cressida*, IV. ii.

The "unreadiness" noted earlier in several historical plays can also be found in romantic situations. Thus, in *The Two Maids of Moreclacke*, Sir William calls forth his wife, who appears "*in her night gowne, and night attire*"; a few lines later, she brings in her would-be lover, "*vnready, in his night-cap garterles*" (TFT, E3ᵛ). In *A Woman Killed With Kindness*, after Wendoll and Anne have been surprised in bed off-stage, we see the seducer "*running ouer the stage in a Night-gowne*"; moments later, Anne enters "*in her smocke, Night-gowne, and night attire*" (II, 138, 139). The title figure of *The Insatiate Countess* departs in the middle of the night in pursuit of a new lover, leaving behind Roberto, who enters "*in his Night-gowne, and Cap*"; later, in the complex wife-swapping episode, the two husbands are brought in by the watch "*in their shirts and night-gownes*" (STC 17476, D3ᵛ, E2ʳ). In *The Great Duke of Florence*, the father of a strikingly beautiful daughter, roused from sleep by an emissary from the duke, enters "*in a night-Gown*" (II. ii. 43.s.d.). The emissary asks "pardon for disturbing / Your rest at this unseasonable houre" (II. iii. 19-20); quickly, that disturbance becomes a threat to both father and daughter.

Of particular interest to Shakespeareans are the appearances of the nightgown or unready dress in scenes dealing with troubled con-

---

20. For other references to "night attire" see *The Coxcomb*, VIII, 361; *The Fatal Contract*, H 1422, D4ᵛ; *Lust's Dominion*, II. iii. 91.s.d.; *The Two Maids of Moreclacke*, TFT, E3ᵛ; *Sophonisba*, I. ii. 0.s.d. For "night clothes" see *A Match at Midnight*, STC 21421, H2ʳ; *The Little French Lawyer*, III, 416; for nightcaps alone see *The Custom of the Country*, I, 363-64. Gowns along with slippers appear in *2 If You Know Not Me You Know Nobody*, I, 302, 309; *2 The Iron Age*, III, 385; *The Captain*, V, 296.

sciences. Thus, after Lord de Averne and Dennis have murdered Friar John in *The Captives*, the knight enters "halff vnredy"; he is then questioned by his lady about "these vnquiet sleepes" and tells Dennis that "strange thoughts sollicite mee." After being told to "awake and ryse in hast," Dennis enters "halff vnredy," complaining that "my Lord hathe doon a mischieffe / and nwe I must not sleepe ffor't" (MSR, ll. 2464, 2468, 2498, 2491, 2512, 2518-19). Remember, in the bad quarto of *Hamlet* the ghost is directed to enter in the closet scene not in the armour of Act I but "*in his night gowne*" (G2ᵛ), a potentially revealing distinction often ignored in modern editions, productions, and criticism. Less ambiguous or puzzling is the situation in *2 Henry IV* where the king enters "*in his nightgown*" (III. i. 0.s.d.) to deliver the soliloquy on troubled sleep that climaxes with "uneasy lies the head that wears a crown."

In at least three of his tragedies, Shakespeare may be using the stage nightgown to develop a rich network of associations. Thus, after a troubled night in Rome and just before hearing of Calphurnia's dream, Julius Caesar enters "*in his nightgown*" (II. ii. 0.s.d.). The Folio provides no specific signal that Brutus also was wearing such a gown in the previous scene, but the dialogue places heavy emphasis upon night and upon Brutus' troubled sleep. For example, he tells us that "since Cassius first did whet me against Caesar, / I have not slept" (II. i. 61-62), while Portia twice criticizes him for stealing from her bed (237-38, 264) in order "to walk unbracèd and suck up the humors / Of the dank morning" (262-63). Using other kinds of evidence, critics have linked Brutus and Caesar, whether in these two scenes or in general terms,[21] but parallel appearances in night-gowns could make the link obvious and emphatic. Such a link would then make more meaningful the aftermath of the quarrel scene when Brutus calls for his gown, Lucius enters "*with the gown,*" Brutus takes it (IV. iii. 231, 236.s.d., 239), and then Caesar's ghost appears to him while three figures (Lucius, Varro, and Claudius) lie asleep on stage. Brutus' inner turmoil, associated in part with a ghost that identifies itself as "thy evil spirit, Brutus" (282), is linked, here as earlier, with sleeplessness and perhaps with his own distinctive form of "unreadiness." As with the boots in *Richard II*, the nightgowns may thereby link these three scenes and, in various ways, enhance their metaphoric range.

The stage nightgown can also play a significant role in *Othello*. Thus,

---

21. See, for example, Norman Rabkin, *Shakespeare and the Common Understanding* (New York, 1967), pp.105-11.

in the 1622 Quarto Brabantio in the opening scene appears "*at a window*" and then enters to Roderigo "*in his night gowne*" accompanied by servants "*with Torches*" (B3ʳ). In a note in his New Arden edition, M. R. Ridley describes the light carried by Othello in the final scene (V. ii. 0.s.d.) as "no more than one of those 'code signs', like 'night-gowns', of which Elizabethan plays are full, as helps in indicating night-time" (p. 177). As already noted, such "code signs" *are* quite common, but Ridley's quick dismissal does not explain why Brabantio's nightgown should appear well into the progress of a scene that already has been established as taking place at night. Rather, what Shakespeare is setting up here is a Brabantio "*as newly wak'd from sleepe,*" with that awakening caused by a plot set up by Iago (with Roderigo as his agent) that leads to accusations against Desdemona and her lover, Othello. No equivalent stage directions survive from II. iii, but as a result of Cassio's brawling, Othello (rather than Brabantio) is awakened from sleep, again as part of a plot instigated by Iago and using Roderigo, a plot that soon leads to accusations against Desdemona and a supposed lover, Cassio. Neither quarto nor Folio stipulates that Othello is to enter here in a nightgown, but when Desdemona appears, Othello remarks: "Look if my gentle love be not raised up!"; then tells her: "All's well now, sweeting; come away to bed"; and concludes at his exit: "Come, Desdemona; 'tis the soldier's life / To have their balmy slumbers waked with strife" (240, 242, 247-48). Brabantio's sleep, interrupted and poisoned by Iago, has now become Othello's interrupted wedding night, again affected by Iago's pestilence, with the two moments perhaps linked by both the nightgown and, equally important, the associations that garment carries—here unreadiness, vulnerability.

The play's final sequence once more alludes to the nightgown. Thus, in the willow scene Desdemona asks Emilia for her "nightly wearing" (IV. iii. 15), and, moments later, Emilia asks: "Shall I go fetch your nightgown?" (Desdemona responds: "No, unpin me here"—33). For me, the key images in the murder scene are the bed and the light, not the nightgown, but for a third time the emphasis is upon interrupted sleep, this time Desdemona's by her husband owing to his tortured, poisoned sense of justice. A different sense of "unreadiness" is orchestrated here, for Othello wants to be sure that Desdemona has "prayed to-night" and has reconciled herself "to heaven and grace" so that he will not kill her "unprepared spirit" (V. ii. 25, 27, 31). As in *Julius Caesar*, strong verbal emphasis upon sleep and sleeplessness (see especially III. iii. 330-34, 338-43) is realized visually and theatrically in three rude awakenings, each a result of Iago's machinations, each linked perhaps by the presence of and associations with the stage nightgown.

What may be the most telling use of the stage nightgown has no stage directions at all as supporting evidence. Thus, after the murder of Duncan, Lady Macbeth instructs her husband: "Get on your nightgown, lest occasion call us / And show us to be watchers" (II. ii. 69-70). Presumably, when Macbeth reappears moments later, he is so attired (Macduff observes to Lennox that "our knocking has awaked him"—II. iii. 39). When the murder is discovered, Macduff awakes "the sleepers of the house" from "this downy sleep, death's counterfeit" (79, 72), thereby bringing onto the stage a group of obviously "unready" figures (Banquo, Ross, Malcolm, and Donalbain), whether in nightgowns or shirts or hastily donning garments as in my earlier examples. Banquo then calls upon the thanes to reassemble "when we have our naked frailties hid / That suffer in exposure" (122-23), with Macbeth concurring ("let's briefly put on manly readiness"—129). In this first nightgown sequence, the true unreadiness and interrupted sleep of the innocent is juxtaposed with the pretense maintained by the Macbeths ("false face must hide what the false heart doth know"—I. vii. 82).

In subsequent scenes, Shakespeare develops the implications of this murder with particular emphasis upon images of sleep, dreaming, and conscience that coalesce in the justly famous sleep-walking scene. Here, the gentlewoman describes how she has seen Lady Macbeth "rise from her bed" ånd then "throw her nightgown upon her" (V. i. 5-6); for the doctor, "this slumb'ry agitation" is "a great perturbation in nature, to receive at once the benefit of sleep and do the effects of watching" (9-11). The Folio stage direction then notes only that Lady Macbeth is to enter "with a taper" (16.s.d.), but the gentlewoman adds: "Lo you, here she comes! This is her very guise" (17). For me, the "guise" includes the nightgown just described for us. In the famous lines that follow, Lady Macbeth echoes her injunctions of Act II ("Wash your hands, put on your nightgown, look not so pale!"—57-58) and builds to a final speech that begins and ends with "To bed, to bed" (61, 63). Her assertions of strength and confidence (e.g., "what need we fear who knows it, when none can call our power to accompt?"—34-35) are belied by this "slumb'ry agitation," whether one ascribes her condition to internal guilt or some higher power or a combination of the two. This rich, complex moment builds upon and recalls some equally telling moments in Act II, so that the presence of the stage nightgown in both segments would reinforce key images and help to signal meaningful connections. Here

Shakespeare goes far beyond the conventional stage shorthand to develop his own distinctive links and images close to the heart of this tragedy.

In conclusion, let me confront several possible objections to my procedures and assumptions. First, consider T. J. King's argument that the principal evidence for reconstructing Elizabethan staging should come from "texts dependent on playhouse copy," while, conversely, "texts evidently not derived from the playhouse have no primary value as evidence for the study of staging." According to this formulation, stage directions in printed texts without playhouse authority "may represent the author's intentions not fully realized on stage."[22] Although I am sympathetic to parts of King's argument, I have made no effort to maintain such distinctions, but rather have let the wealth of examples take precedence over those instances with playhouse authority (of which there are many). Moreover, as one reviewer of King's book asked: "Is the staging projected by an experienced dramatist less reliable a guide to playhouse practice than actual prompt copy?"[23] Thus, in my "as from dinner" group, one example was drawn from a manuscript with playhouse annotations (*Woodstock*) while others came from a variety of experienced professional playwrights (Dekker, Heywood, Munday, Massinger, and Ford). In such situations, details may vary, but the general pattern remains fairly consistent in different scripts that span several decades. The stage historian cannot assume that such effects or techniques remained unchanged over long periods of time or were handled exactly the same way in different theatres, nor should he build any argument upon unique examples, especially from printed texts with questionable playhouse authority. But groups of stage directions from a variety of plays by experienced dramatists (and I have drawn heavily upon Dekker, Heywood, Fletcher, Massinger, and Shakespeare) strike me as important basic evidence—indeed, in many cases the only such evidence—for the study of Elizabethan staging.

A different kind of objection may arise to my use of "perhaps" and

22. *Shakespearean Staging, 1599-1642* (Cambridge, Mass., 1971), p. 8.
23. Bernard Beckerman in *Renaissance Drama*, N.S. 4 (1971), 243. Beckerman notes that King "merely assumes that demonstration of playhouse origin automatically endows a text with theatrical authority greater than that of all other texts," but, he asks, "does not an experienced dramatist embody in his manuscript the actual practices of the stage? The fact that so many authorial stage directions remain standing in prompt copies indicates that this is the case. Moreover, is not the text of a mature Shakespearean play, whether or not of playhouse origin, likely to reflect staging practice more accurately than the prompt manuscript of a relatively inexperienced author such as Henry Glapthorne?" (pp. 239-40). See also John Freehafer's review in *Shakespeare Studies*, 9 (1976), 337-43.

my various conjectures about nightgowns and boots in scenes where no such details are stipulated. Like Iago, I can offer no "ocular proof" for all my hypotheses, but I may be able to provide some "satisfaction" by resorting to "imputation and strong circumstances / Which lead directly to the door of truth" (III. iii. 360, 406-8). Consider some of the relevant scenes in plays that have survived in more than one version. Thus, in the manuscript of *Demetrius and Enanthe* (which R. C. Bald characterizes as "literary") the hero is directed to enter *"from hunting"* (MSR, l. 187), but the Folio version reads: *"Enter* Demetrius *with a Javelin"* (*The Humourous Lieutenant*, II, 285). Similarly, in the manuscript of *The Woman's Prize* (at the Folger Library) the opening stage direction calls for a group to enter *"as from a wedding"* but the Folio has the same group enter *"with Rosemary, as from a wedding"* (VIII, 2). The absence of a revealing detail in either manuscript does not necessarily mean the absence of the effect in the original production.[24] Again, in v. i. of *Romeo and Juliet* the second quarto (1599) provides only *"Enter* Romeos *man"* (K4^r), but the first or "bad" quarto (1597) reads: *"enter Balthasar his man booted"* (I3^r). Similarly, the hawk on Queen Margaret's fist appears in the 1594 quarto of *2 Henry VI* but not in the Folio; Brabantio's nightgown is found in the 1622 quarto of *Othello* but not in the 1623 Folio; and the ghost's nightgown in the closet scene is cited in the "bad" quarto but not in the second quarto or the Folio (Hamlet does refer to "my father, in his habit as he lived"—III. iv. 136). For Ophelia's appearance in IV. v, the second quarto provides only *"Enter Ophelia"* (K4^r); the Folio reads: *"Enter Ophelia distracted"* (l. 2766); and the first quarto reads: *"Enter Ofelia playing on a Lute, and her haire downe singing"* (G4^v). Scholars have advanced various arguments to explain these differences, but the very fact of such variation makes it at least reasonable to suspect the presence of such details in the original staging of those many plays that have no "bad" quartos or survive in only one version or, for whatever reason, have minimal stage directions.

Consider some relevant scenes from several experienced dramatists that lack any clear signals. Thus, in the Ralph Crane transcript of *The Witch* a servant called forth suddenly in the middle of the night pleads "give me leave to cloath myself" (MSR, l. 1666), but Middleton (or Crane) provides no specific indication of "unreadiness" or a nightgown. Similarly, in *The Tragedy of Valentinian* Lucina enters with her

---

24. For a detailed discussion of the differences in stage directions between Folio and manuscript versions of five Fletcher plays (*The Honest Man's Fortune, The Beggar's Bush, The Woman's Prize, The Humourous Lieutenant, Bonduca*), see R. C. Bald, *Bibliographical Studies in the Beaumont & Fletcher Folio of 1647* (Oxford, 1938), pp. 74-79.

ravisher, the Emperor (IV, 35), but Fletcher's stage directions and dialogue provide no references to hair or other details. Again, in *The Emperor of the East* a stage direction cites "*Huntsmen*" (IV. i. 63), and subsequent dialogue alludes to stags and hounds; then, when the hunt is over, Theodosius orders: "lay by / These accoutrements for the chase" (IV. iv. 7-8).Massinger here specifies no bows, spears, javelins, horns, or green costumes but rather leaves the on-stage implementation of "accoutrements for the chase" to the actors. In *The Great Duke of Florence*, Cozimo tells Sanazaro, who has just returned from a journey: "You have rode hard Sir, / And we thank you for it" (III. i. 180-81). Again, in *The Duke of Milan*, Sforza is told that "the Marquisse of Pescara, tyr'd with hast, / Hath businesse that concernes your life and fortunes, / And with speed to impart" (I. iii.220-22). Moments later, Pescara announces: "my hast forbids / All complement" (239-40); the message delivered, he is told "Pray take your rest" and responds: "Indeed, I haue trauaild hard" (264). Both passages correspond to situations in other plays where boots are specified, but Massinger provides no such signal. Nor does Shakespeare call for Leontes to wear a nightgown in II. iii although quite a few lines would support such a costume (see, for example, ll. 1, 31, 38-39). Are such omissions, then, significant, inadvertent, or irrelevant? My conclusion is that the absence of a specific stage direction need not preclude the presence of a detail or effect in the original production. Given the nature of the evidence, I see no way to pursue the reconstruction of the original staging without judicious use of "perhaps."

Certainly, these variations and silences do not justify the invention of whatever new stage directions please the investigator or critic. Still, some conjectures or hypotheses *are* given added force when a wealth of evidence from a wide range of plays demonstrates how specific effects often are linked to specific situations. In deciding what is "necessary" or "required" for a particular moment (e.g., a prison, tavern, tomb, or night scene), the modern scholar should proceed very carefully so as not to reason by a logic that may be at odds with the original evidence and theatrical practice. In contrast, my goal throughout this essay has been to look closely at what evidence we have as to what actually was provided for the spectator by the actors on the open stage and then, from that evidence, to determine what can be deduced about techniques and conventions. In a real sense, I did not go out looking for boots, nightgowns, and hair about the ears but rather, while I was reading through many, many plays, they found me. To fail to take such evidence into account is to run the risk of ignoring

something basic and distinctive that would have been readily understood by groundlings at the Globe, and, instead, to invent our own
"Elizabethan drama" that may satisfy a later sensibility but lack a firm
basis in the original evidence.

Unfortunately, my citations may be leaving an impression of an
Elizabethan stage cluttered with crumbs, napkins, boots, disorderly
hair, weapons, and nightgowns. In truth, nothing could be farther
from my point, for my inclination is to argue for less rather than
more detail on the open stage. Thus, the various effects I have been
describing require no sizeable properties. Rather, most could be
achieved with minor adjustments in costume (or wig) in ways that may
have been second nature to actor and spectator. As noted earlier, in
place of elaborate banquet or wedding or shipwreck or bedroom
scenes, many of my stage directions help to establish a sense of that
world just off-stage, never seen but there to be supplied by the
"imaginary forces" of the audience who implicitly are being asked to
"piece out our imperfections with your thoughts" or "eke out our
performance with your mind" (*Henry V*, Prologue, ll. 18, 23; III,
Chorus, l. 35). The key to such effects lies in some significant, visible
stage detail that is theatrically practical, that conveys some signal
deftly to the viewer's eye, and that, at least in the hands of a Shakespeare, has the potential for some larger meaning or pattern. Clearly,
large properties like tombs and scaffolds occasionally could be
introduced onto the Elizabethan stage; nonetheless, I would argue that
almost all of the scenes could have been staged with recourse only to
portable properties, appropriate costumes, and the "imaginary
forces" of the spectator.

Obviously, my group or series approach to stage directions can be
taken only so far. Evidence is often lacking or murky; many curious
stage directions appear to stand alone with no support from other
contexts; the strictures of King and others about the nature of the
evidence must be heeded. Still, students of Elizabethan images and
icons have shown how much can be gained from immersion in the
literary or learned tradition (e.g., emblem books, mythographers).
But need Alciatus and Ripa be the only sources for such a shared
language of images? Given the vitality of the developing Elizabethan
theatre and the inheritance from earlier popular forms like the moral
play, the modern scholarly detective should not be surprised to find
an evolving theatrical iconography, geared to the exigencies of this
particular theatre, with its open stage, its narrative flow, its practical
limits upon properties and stage effects, and its ever-present metaphoric or symbolic dimension. And where better to find clues for that

specifically theatrical imagery or stage iconography than in the evidence provided by the scattered, elusive, murky, but still potentially revealing stage directions? In the words of Falstaff, "a question to be asked."

The Psychopathology of Everyday Art[1]

RANDOM CLOUD

for Joe Barber
1913 - 1980

We had the meaning but missed the experience,
And approach to the experience restores the meaning
In a different form.

T. S. Eliot, *The Dry Savages*

PART ONE

On January 13, at the turn of the seventeenth century, William
Shakes*but no*—let me begin with George Shaw.

PART I

Shaw's *Press Cuttings* (first produced VOTES FOR WOMEN in 1909) opens
deep in the War Office, under siege by feminists, one of whom has
broken through army lines and chained herself to the doorscraper.

1. I wish to give my thanks to Erindale College and the University of Toronto for
granting me research leave in 1980-81 to work on problems of Shakespeare's text, and
also to the Social Sciences and Humanities Research Council of Canada, for its support
during the leave. I am grateful as well to Jerry McGann, for the opportunity to practise a
version of the essay before a captive audience at the California Institute of Technology
in April 1983; and to Tom Berger, in whose (voluntary) seminar on stage directions at
the meeting of the Shakespeare Association of America, Cambridge, Mass., April 1984,
the paper was circulated.

For permission to quote from the works of Shaw in this essay, I am immensely

VOTESFORWOMEN! An orderly arrives with a note from the militant protestor, and passes it to the incredulous General Mitchener, who opens it, and finds a key and a letter, "Dear Mitch . . ."—and signed not by the enemy, but by the Prime Minister himself!—unlock the woman's chains, and show her in. But no sooner in, than this panting suffraget begins to take off her skirt, to *reveal* herself, to reveal herself in *trousers*, to reveal herself as—*himself*, Prime Minister Balsquith, who has come in drag as the easiest means to enter his own office.

If *Press Cuttings* were a Renaissance play which modern editors had taken in hand—and Editing is not quite the Heroic Theme of my piece—they would typically have inserted between the title page and the opening stage direction their own list of *dramatis personae* (for plays properly must have them, mustn't they? and in that location?), in which we might read something like this:

DRAMATIS PERSONAE

PRIME MINISTER BALSQUITH, *first seen in women's clothing.*

And if the editorial stage directions tended to omniscience, we might find—

Enter Balsquith, disguised as the woman.

—his speeches prefixed by BALSQUITH.

But the naming in directions and prefixes that the real playwright (unlike my hypopathetical editor) actually offers for this role is quite different. As there is, typically in Shaw, no *dramatis personae* list, the first names occur in speech prefixes—

A VOICE FROM THE STREET.

THE VOICE OUTSIDE.

then in stage directions—

a panting Suffraget

The Suffraget

the latter repeated in speech prefix—

THE SUFFRAGET.

and finally

BALSQUITH.

indebted to the Society of Authors on behalf of the Estate of Bernard Shaw (previously unpublished Bernard Shaw material © 1984 by The Trustees of the British Museum, The Governors and Guardians of the National Gallery of Ireland and Royal Academy of Dramatic Art), and to Mrs. Roma Woodnut of the Society of Authors for her help in securing these releases.

I wish to thank also Felix Fonteyn and Steve Jaunzems, who took or processed many of the images. Warning to consumers: Reproductions are often cropped, and therefore do not necessarily show all the evidence on a page of the original document. They are, however, unretouched, though occasionally I have (obviously) underlined or circled parts of an image relevant to discussion. Photo transmission has often enhanced smudgy images. Indeed some faint marks have been enhanced right out of the picture. Reproductions are not to size.

—which continues to the end of the play. The names evolve toward a surprise (and durable) revelation of identity; but each of them aspires no higher than General Mitchener's current state of enlightenment—or than that of the reader or viewer on her first exposure.

These homily examples caution us about how we should think of names outside the dialogue, and of their structural relationship to the spoken names, which nomenclature is, after that Sublime Opening of the Undressing Suffraget, I must confess, the Ridiculous Topic of this lecture: *real* drag.

We might have supposed such unspoken names were centrifugal from the aesthetic vision of a play, pulling away from it toward the mechanics of staging—as if speech-prefix and stage-direction names served merely as signs to connect the actors with their speeches and their actions, as if such unspoken words were mere epiphenomena of the play, scaffolding to be dismantled when it could stand on its own. But this Shaw text shows that they can also be symbols that push readers back, centripetally, into the dramatic irony, making us experience it with shock, as we would in performance. A speech prefix can be, as it were, a self-dramatizing part of a script.[2]

If this lecture were to have a sense of proportion, I suppose I would have to emphasize that speech prefixes and stage directions are sub-generic strands—literary ones—within the dramatic textual artefact, and that dialogue is more important than they are, not only because of its relative bulk, but also because of their silence in production. But this obvious fact does not mean that, as he scripted, Shaw's design did not govern in things so small, or even that these dumb things are lost

2. When Henry Jewett produced *Press Cuttings* in Boston in 1920, he including in his program a letter from Shaw (dated 5 November 1919), which begins: "Dear Mr. Jewett. The change of names from Balsquith and Mitchener to Bones and Johnson was forced on me by the censorship here; so there is no reason why it should be adopted in America except the reason you mention: the sentiment about Kitchener. . . ." He continues by suggesting that for the American production "Balsquith" be allowed to stand in the text, but that "Mitchener" be changed to "George Ranger", to hint (very remotely for a Yankee audience) at Shaw's real target, the Duke of Cambridge.

Jewett's promptbook for this production is a typescript now in the Folger Shakespeare Library, during the typing of which most of Shaw's uses of "Mitchener" had been replaced by "Ranger". Several occurrences of "Mitchener" do survive, however, at least one of which (p. 35 [39]) is altered by pen to "Ranger". I said above that the variation of names can be part of an aesthetic plan. Here it seems to express an imperfect attempt by the author's delegate to alter the text to specification. The variation thus reflects layering of the composition and transmission of the text. The variation of names in this particular theatre document pushes the reader of it back, centripetally, not only, as before, into the drama of the script, but also into the political world it satirizes, and from which the censor arose to force Shaw to change his names—back, then, into the drama of the scripting.

necessarily when his play is produced. As Shaw continually argued against the idea that actors and readers were each best served by different kinds of texts,[3] it seems an overly acacademic exercise to attempt to isolate the purely literary from the purely dramatic or purely theatrical in Shaw's play texts. When he published his scripts (often after the first stagings of his plays), Shaw frequently buttressed them with a preface or an epilogue, which now generate critical contexts for the actor as well as the general reader; the fact that these essays can even continue the plot of the play, as in *Pygmalion*, vividly exemplifies the interanimation for Shaw of the dramatic and the literary. Furthermore, it was his practice actually to read his scripts to the actors, and before they had access to their own copies. For example, in his letter of 3 December 1923 to Lawrence Langner, whose Theatre Guild in New York was then rehearsing the first production of *Saint Joan*, Shaw wrote from London that he had just "read the play to Sybil Thorndike from the second set of proofs."[4] (I presume that this means that he would have to have read her at least *some* of his speech prefixes and directions.) Moreover, when rehearsals began, actors were not to learn their parts for a week, but to rehearse with book in hand, during which time such literary aspects of Shaw's dramatic texts as I have been referring to could influence them

---

3. "The fact is, the actor and the reader want exactly the same thing, vivid strokes of description, not the stage manager's memoranda of impertinent instructions in the art of acting from literary people who cannot act.... The safe rule is, write nothing in a play that you would not write in a novel; and remember that everything that the actor or the scene painter shows to the audience must be described—not technically specified, but imaginatively, vividly, humorously, in a word, artistically described—to the reader by the author." From Shaw's "How to Make Plays Readable," *The Author's Year Book and Guide for* 1904, ed. W. E. Price (New York, 1904), quoted from *Shaw on Theatre*, ed. E. J. West (New York, 1958), pp. 94, 95. For a general view of his direction, see Bernard F. Dukore, *Bernard Shaw, Director* (London, 1971).

4. Lawrence Langner, *G.B.S. and the Lunatic* (New York, 1963), p. 63: "I read the play to Sybil Thorndike from the second set of proofs; and the dialogue occupied exactly three hours and three minutes. Since then I have made another and more drastic revision which has, I think, got the last bits of dead wood out of the play, and have certainly saved the odd three minutes." Meanwhile an earlier state of the text was in rehearsal across the Atlantic. "When I heard that you were actually rehearsing from a copy which you knew to be an unrevised first proof [though Langner protested he did not know, as he took Shaw's autograph alterations to the proofs to constitute final revisions], I tore my hair. I should not have trusted you with it." This letter argues against rigid separation of the writing of the script and its theatrical realization, however much Shaw may have wished for it. (He forced Langner to stop rehearsals.) The fullest account to date of Shaw's development of the text up to its performance is to be found in Brian Tyson's insightful *The Story of Shaw's "Saint Joan"* (Kingston and Montreal, 1982).

on stage, and thus eventually produce their effects on the audience.[5] Obviously I am not suggesting that the audience of *Press Cuttings* would ever suspect, or, having suspected, be able to reconstruct accurately the varying speech-prefix designations from watching a performance of a play. At the moment I am trying to argue only for the likelihood in Shaw of "literary" influence on the actors. The same argument would perhaps be less contentious if I stated it in terms of Shaw's (inaudible) punctuation, which has a strong effect on actor and audience, though once the play is on the boards, the audience, and even the actor—or author—would not be able to reconstruct it with complete accuracy. The ultimate effect of the written text on the audience, and the importance of that effect, is quite a separate issue from the audience's knowing its origin. And, of course, the same argument is not contentious at all in terms of the title, a literary effect which is usually not voiced, but which can exert nevertheless a powerful force upon the audience's interpretation of the dialogue. "Like doth quit like, and *Measure* still for *Measure*."

Dramatic criticism is heavily influenced by the "teleology of drama," that is, that scripts are "for" production. To embrace a larger concern, I suggest the term "dramaturgic criticism," which, while scarcely denying the importance of enactment in drama, countenances the integrity of every state of a play, or a part of it, as we can discern it—to consider for the present only its manifestation in documents—in authorial notes, foul papers, prompt copies, revisions, adaptations, etc., and which focuses particularly on the transformations of a play (or the play of transformations) through successive drafts, or from written text to enactment—or back again, as in Jonson's literary refashioning of his plays for the press after they were staged. I can only

---

5. "The play should be read to the company, preferably by the author if he or she is a competent dramatic reader. . . . To the first rehearsals the director must come with the stage business thoroughly studied, and every entry . . . etc., is settled ready for instant dictation. . . . Properly such a plan [a prompt copy] is the business of the author; for stage directions are as integral to a play as spoken dialogue. . . . The players should be instructed not to study their parts at this stage, and to rehearse, book in hand, without any exercise of memory." ("Rules for Directors," *Theatre Arts* XXXIII [August 1949], quoted from *Shaw on Theatre*, pp. 280, 281.) In "On the Art of Rehearsal," in *The Arts League Annual* (London, 1922), Shaw speaks of the first rehearsal, when the director stands on the stage and handles and prompts the actors, "as they will, of course, be rather in the dark as to what it is all about, except what they may have gathered from your reading the play to them before rehearsal: nothing is a greater nuisance than an actor who is trying to remember his lines when he should be settling his positions and getting the hang of the play with his book in his hand. One or two acts twice over is enough for each preliminary rehearsal. When you have reached the end of this first stage, then call for 'perfect' rehearsals (that is, without books)."

introduce the term "dramaturgic criticism" here, depicting with a few broad strokes what may pertain to it as the lecture continues, and hope that my attention to literal detail may explode any merely literary or merely dramatic approach.

But first let me enlarge upon other functions served by Shaw's silent names. As we saw, when new figures appear in his plays they are often given vague names, which are replaced with more specific ones as information accrues in dialogue. Here is a typical example from his early play, *Pygmalion*, first produced in 1914.

> THE GENTLEMAN. I am myself a student of Indian dialects ; and—
> THE NOTE TAKER [*eagerly*] Are you? Do you know Colonel Pickering, the author of Spoken Sanscrit?
> THE GENTLEMAN. I am Colonel Pickering. Who are you?
> THE NOTE TAKER. Henry Higgins, author of Higgins's Universal Alphabet.
> PICKERING [*with enthusiasm*] I came from India to meet you.
> HIGGINS. I was going to India to meet you.

THE GENTLEMAN. introduces himself as "Colonel Pickering", and his next prefix is PICKERING. So with THE NOTETAKER., who introduces himself as "Henry Higgins": his next prefix is HIGGINS. Their new tags are used exclusively to the end of the play. This is common sense, no tricks; the fluctuation in naming ceases in a personal name.

But in *Buoyant Billions*, Shaw's last full-length play, written in 1947, although a specific name, "Junius", is the very first word of the dialogue. the subsequent speech prefix is not JUNIUS. but SON., and that of the other speaker is FATHER. So throughout the first scene.

> *A modern interior. A well furnished study. Morning light. A father discussing with his son. Father an elderly gentleman, evidently prosperous, but a man of business, thoroughly middle class. Son in his earliest twenties, smart, but artistically unconventional.*

> FATHER. Junius, my boy, you must make up your mind. I had a long talk with your mother about it last night. You have been tied to her apron string quite long enough. You have been on my hands much too long. Your six brothers all chose their professions when they were years younger than you. I have always expected more from you than from them. So has your mother.
> SON. Why?

Now, in an earlier draft, the son's name was "Ben".[6]

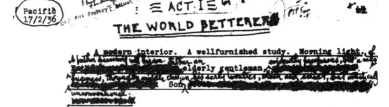

FATHER. Ben,my boy,you must make up your mind. I had a long talk
with your mother about it last night. You have been tied to her apron
string quite long enough. You have been on my hands much too long.
Your six brothers all chose their professions when they were years
younger than you. I have always expected more from you than from
them. So has your mother.

THE SON.   Why?

But, of course, the generic speech prefix—and this is its virture—did
not have to shift with Shaw's alteration of the name in dialogue.
Indeed, if one looks at the names "Junius" and "Ben" half etymologi-
cally, it seems that the change from one to the other stems not so
much from a new personalization of the character, as from a restating
of the notion already expressed by the prefix.

The second scene of this play begins with a stage direction that
refers to *"The Son"*, but his speech prefix is now HE. and that of his
nubile companion, SHE. We see that Shaw is again given to revising his

*The shore of a broad water studded with half-submerged trees in a tropical landscape, covered with
bush except for a clearance by the waterside, where there is a wooden house on posts, with a ladder
from the stoep or verandah to the ground. The roof is of corrugated iron, painted green. The Son,
dressed in flannel slacks, a tennis shirt, and a panama hat, is looking about him like a stranger. A young
woman, dressed for work in pyjama slacks and a pullover, comes out of the house and, from the top of
the steps, proceeds to make the stranger unwelcome.*

SHE. Now then. This clearance is private property. Whats your business?
HE. No business, dear lady. Treat me as a passing tramp.

6. British Library Addit. Ms. 50,641. My thanks to the British Library for permission
to quote from its mss., and to Douglas S. Webb, Head of Photographic Services
Administration, to photoquote from the mss.

speech-prefix names, but not, as in *Pygmalion*, in reaction to the dramatic revelation of personal identity. In this case, the change in prefixes indicates a change in the author's thematic preoccupations (with family and sexual role) on the level of the scene. This character's changing names are only local habitations. The now conventional critical illusion of "unity of dramatic character" is called into question by such a shift in Shaw's names, which highlights his plastic sense of type and role by episode. To maintain that illusion (against the text) requires, in Coleridge's phrase, a willing distention of belief. In any case, the practical point is the crucial one. If he is looking for unity, the actor playing SON./HE. must process and learn his role as *roles*— through the mediation of such fluctuating type names.

In the earliest surviving manuscripts of Greek drama a character's new speeches in a scene are introduced only by a *paragraphos*, an anonymous wavy line. In the modern tradition, however, having first named their characters, playwrights must rename them whenever they speak. A medium is thereby created in which authors *in their own words* must continually re-establish their fictional entities; and this medium can register the drifts and shifts of authorial attitude and interpretation in a play, just as if it were a novel. "I named them as they passed," said Adam, "and understood their nature."

Shaw on his working methods:

> I am not governed by principles. . . . I find myself possessed of a theme in the following manner. I am pushed by a natural need to set to work to write down the conversations that come into my head unaccountably. At first I hardly know the speakers, and cannot find names for them. Then they become more and more familiar, and I learn their names. . . . This is not being "guided by principles"; it is hallucination; and sane hallucination is what we call play or drama. I do not select my methods; they are imposed on me by a hundred considerations.[7]

Let us think what this statement means in relation to *Pygmalion*. We may have conceived that Shaw knew Higgins's name before he wrote the play, as if he began it with that Transcendent Paradigm, the *dramatis personae*, shimmering before him, ready to be declined as script; and that he tagged his speeches inmaterially with NOTETAKER. as a straight-forward literary device to symbolize the theatrical effect of Higgins's threatening anonymity in the opening scene. The present quotation suggests to the contrary, however, that Shaw might well have started the scene without himself knowing the protagonist's

7. "On the Principles that Govern the Dramatist," a letter to *The New York Times*, June 2, 1912, quoted from *Shaw on Theatre*, p. 116.

name, but that he worked up an answer when the plot required intro-
ductions. Thus, his use of the prefix NOTETAKER. may symbolize the
limitations not only in the audience's knowledge whenever the curtain
rises on *Pygmalion*, but in the author's knowledge as well, on that day
when first he put pen to paper. The fluctuating names may reveal to us
the author strayed-forwardly being initiated into his own creation.

Throwing principles to the winds, let us look at *Saint Joan* to explore
further some of the hundred considerations of Shaw's hallucinated
style. The introductory note to scene 4 speaks of "*A bullnecked English
chaplain*" and "*an imposing nobleman*".

SCENE IV

*A tent in the English camp. A bullnecked English chaplain
of 50 is sitting on a stool at a table, hard at work writing.
At the other side of the table an imposing nobleman, aged 46,
is seated in a handsome chair turning over the leaves of an
illuminated Book of Hours. The nobleman is enjoying himself:
the chaplain is struggling with suppressed wrath. There is an
unoccupied leather stool on the nobleman's left. The table is on
his right.*

THE NOBLEMAN. Now this is what I call workmanship.
There is nothing on earth more exquisite than a bonny book,
with well-placed columns of rich black writing in beautiful borders, and illuminated pictures cunningly inset. But
nowadays, instead of looking at books, people read them.
A book might as well be one of those orders for bacon and
bran that you are scribbling.

THE CHAPLAIN. I must say, my lord, you take our situation
very coolly. Very coolly indeed.

Their subsequent prefixes are THE CHAPLAIN. and THE NOBLEMAN., until
the entrance of Cauchon, to whom they introduce themselves: the
former as "Richard de Beauchamp, Earl of Warwick", whose prefix
thereafter is WARWICK., and the latter pretentiously as "John Bowyer
Spenser Neville de Stogumber"—but for all that his name does not
register in the subsequent prefixes (not shown here), which remain
THE CHAPLAIN.

*Cauchon, aged about 60, comes in. The page withdraws. The
two Englishmen rise.*

THE NOBLEMAN [*with effusive courtesy*] My dear Bishop,
how good of you to come! Allow me to introduce myself: Richard de Beauchamp, Earl of Warwick, at your
service.

CAUCHON. Your lordship's fame is well known to me. [→]

108

WARWICK. This reverend cleric is Master John de Stogumber.

THE CHAPLAIN [*glibly*] John Bowyer Spenser Neville de Stogumber, at your service, my lord: Bachelor of Theology, and Keeper of the Private Seal to His Eminence the Cardinal of Winchester.

WARWICK [*to Cauchon*] You call him the Cardinal of England, I believe. Our king's uncle.

CAUCHON. Messire John de Stogumber: I am always the very good friend of His Eminence. [*He extends his hand to the chaplain, who kisses his ring*].

Why, we may ask, is there not a coordinate change of names in both prefixes, as in the examples from *Pygmalion*? Of course, Shaw may simply not care to be consistent in this neglectible corner of the text. But let's look anyway. A clue may be provided in Shaw's Preface to *Saint Joan*, where he claims (in "A Void in the Elizabethan Drama") that the fault in Shakespeare's characters, even in the history plays, is that they are rootless egoists, whereas his own characters in *Saint Joan*, because they represent various social institutions, are therefore rooted in history. This idea suggests that Shaw initially may have called the Chaplain and the Nobleman by generic names not because they are not yet realized by them, and will remain vague until we learn their personal names, but because their historical identity and their thematic function in the drama can be realized only with generic terms.

We can see that the change in prefix from THE NOBLEMAN. to WARWICK., by the way, is quite different than a change from NOBLEMAN. to RICHARD. or DE BEAUCHAMP. would have been, these being more personal names—and Shaw is not out to personalize such a character completely: the change to WARWICK. has merely particularlized the nobleman within his class. Such a rationale suggests why there may not be a change in prefix for the Chaplain, for he is already precisely defined in his ecclesiastical class. If, for example, he had initially been termed "*clerk*" in the opening direction, and CLERK. in speech prefix, a refinement of his prefix might then have come to what it is now, CHAPLAIN. This explanation (obviously) does not say why his prefix does not become THE ENGLISH CHAPLAIN. (as he *is* first designated in the stage direction), as so much depends in this history play on incipient nationalism. You see that my attempts at explanation do not constitute a single, total allegory that permeates all the naming in stage directions and speech prefixes in a play. But I don't admit this as a fault. As Shaw said, "Instead of planning my plays, I let them grow as they came, and hardly ever wrote a page foreknowing what the next page would be."[8] This quotation suggests that the various allegorical tendencies in out-of-dialogue names work themselves out according to their own halfhazard logics during scripting, and that, barring finicky revision—the kind one does not associate with Shaw (or, to anticipate, with Shakespeare)—such inconsistencies of this scripting method can be conserved in successive drafts, to appear finally in and *as* the published text.

We are not yet done with Chaplain de Stogumber. In the Epilogue a

> *They listen. A long gentle knocking is heard.*
> CHARLES. Come in.
> *The door opens; and an old priest, white-haired, bent, with a silly but benevolent smile, comes in and trots over to Joan.*
> THE NEWCOMER. Excuse me, gentle lords and ladies. Do not let me disturb you. Only a poor old harmless English rector. Formerly chaplain to the cardinal: to my lord of Winchester. John de Stogumber, at your service. [*He looks at them inquiringly*] Did you say anything? I am a little deaf, unfortunately. Also a little—well, not always in my right mind, perhaps; but still, it is a small village with a few simple people. I suffice: I suffice: they love me there; and I am able to do a little good. I am well connected, you see; and they indulge me.
> JOAN. Poor old John! What brought thee to this state?
> DE STOGUMBER. I tell my folks they must be very careful. I say to them, "If you only saw what you think about you would think quite differently about it. It would give you a great shock. Oh, a great shock." And they all say "Yes, parson: we all know you are a kind man, and would

stage direction introduces "*an old priest, white-haired, bent, with a silly but benevolent smile*". The priest's speech, prefixed THE NEWCOMER., tells us that he was "formerly chaplain . . . John de Stogumber". The wordings of the direction, "*an old priest*", and of the prefix, THE NEW-COMER., serve to register the unrecognizability of this character at his reappearance. Whereas CHAPLAIN. was a name connected with his social and religious identity, NEWCOMER. merely locates him in the time and space and society of the Epilogue, where old and new, living and dead assemble. Once his family name, de Stogumber, is revealed again in dialogue, and we know our man, we might expect the prefix to revert to CHAPLAIN. But curiously it becomes DE STOGUMBER. for the first time in the play, and remains so. His days of climbing the ladder of ecclesiastical success are over; he is now a village priest to a few

8. "My Way with a Play," *Observer* (London), 29 September, 1946; reprinted in *British Thought*, 1947, and quoted here from *Shaw on Theatre*, p. 268.

simple people. His new tags accompany both a profound shift in his moral stature and a theatrical trick that temporarily renders his appearance in this scene (and his appearance alone) unfamiliar to the audience. Although we might be hard pressed to find allegorical significance in this particular change of names for this role, the general *fact* of their variation lends itself easily to allegorical readings. The point, I take it, is that his personal revelation during the execution (just before this Epilogue), his encounter with the spirit of his times, in which he was redeemed by Joan, the Christ who dies for him, has uprooted his vocation in the English army and established him in a new kind of church, one for which anything as specific as the old title (CHAPLAIN.) in speech prefix would now be inappropriate, one transcending the historical quarrel of French and English, and one for which the seemingly half-Norman half-Saxon sounding "de Stogumber" might be thought appropriate, and which at last registers as the prefix for his final speeches. He could also, of course, have been called PRIEST.[9] The mere change of prefix may be as symbolic as what it is changed to.

Again, as in *Pygmalion*, the fluctuating speech prefix comes to rest in a person's name. In this case, however, it does not arrive as soon as the dialogue or even the character himself reveals it. It arrives only after the meaning of his historical experience has come home to him or to us.

In any case, the changed prefix serves as a clue to the readers, the actor among them, that *something* has happened, something which may require a redirection of the role at this crux. I am not saying, of course, that the actor could not find clues, even sufficient clues, for such a reinterpretation without those in the prefixes—and for different reinterpretations than I have suggested. (I'm not *that* crazy. Yet.) But I do stress that the prefix changes are aesthetically engaged in symbolic aspects of the drama. And if you, like me, read from left to right, you first meet these symbolic aspects where Shaw left them: in the prefixes. It is the dialogue not the prefix that is redundant.

Dramaturgic criticism, by looking to process in creation rather than to hypostatized artefacts, steers us away from the editor's ideal single version—the so-called "definitive text"—to the author's actual multiple versions: an infinitive text.[10] When Shaw came to revise *Saint Joan* for the cinema in 1934-36, he seems to have used scissors

9. In Shaw's manuscript (British Library Addit. Ms. 45,923, p. 65) the prefix actually reads "The Priest."
10. These terms (and "infinite" text) are worked over in my "The Marriage of Good and Bad Quartos," *Shakespeare Quarterly*, 33, no. 4 (1982), pp. 421-31 (see p. 422).

and paste as much as a pen.[11] He eked out the role of the Chaplain by adding him to a new scene, that of Joan's execution; and what did he call him in speech prefixes now?—DE STOGUMBER—the name which he had formerly come to bear only at the *end* of Shaw's stage version.

JOAN is trying to stop; but the men-at-arms drag, and DE STO-GUMBER pushes, not continuously but with violent gestures.

JOAN
A cross. I want a cross. There is one in the church. You have no right to keep my Savior from me.

DE STOGUMBER
Witch. Sorceress. Strike her on her blaspheming mouth. To the fire with her.

But the prefixes in the original version of this scene, which now encloses this spliced-in episode, continue to read CHAPLAIN. It seems, then, we have a new explanation for shifting prefixes: they can reflect layering of the composition.

Shaw said, "As I correct a good deal, and dread the literary ghouls who dig up and publish all an author's mistakes and slips and blunders and redundancies, I ruthlessly destroy every trace of the successive polishings the book gets before I pass it for press."[12] Now, strictly between myself, I will confess to being that literary ghoul, if Shaw will confess not to having been the ruthless destroyer who buried the corpses of his successive polishings. Shaw's text, editorially unalterable till the next century, when his copyright runs out, forces all attentive readers to be such ghouls.

Let us see how this role of Chaplain de Stogumber is named in the promptbook of the first British production, which Shaw co-directed with Lewis Casson, who also performed this part (while Sybil Thorndike, his wife, played Joan).[13] The prompter's type-written

11. Two versions of the (unproduced) screenplay comprise British Library Addit. Ms. 50,634. See Shaw, *Saint Joan, A Screenplay*, ed. Bernard F. Dukore (Seattle and London, 1968), p. 116, from which I have quoted.
12. Quoted from a letter of 26 May 1944, now at the front of the British Library manuscript of *Saint Joan*, Addit. Ms. 45,923.
13. Reproductions from the promptbook in the Theatre Museum are with the kind permission of the Victoria and Albert Museum, temporary housing for the Theatre Museum, which is bound in several years to its own home in Covent Garden.

note pasted in the book refers to this role first as "Chaplain" to the upper left of the opening (printed) stage direction that identifies him as a "*chaplain*", and he continues with this prompt epithet throughout the scene.

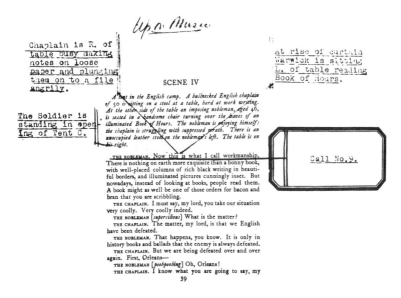

In the trial scene, however, he is referred to in the long stage direction as "*Chaplain de Stogumber*", and the speech following refers to him as "Master de Stogumber". And here the prompter's naming converts from the "Chaplain" we saw previously to "Stogumber"

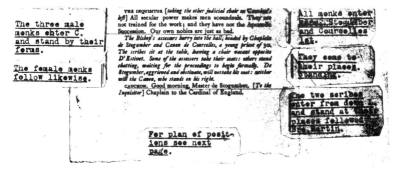

(top right), seemingly in response to the names in stage direction and dialogue, even though this procedure means the prompter breaks his established pattern, which is echoed still in the authorial speech prefixes (as would be apparent if we could see the next page).

Now, it is also possible that the prompter's new naming of this role responds to the vocabulary of Shaw's rehearsal notes,[14] which always name the role "Stogumber", never "Chaplain", "Priest" or "New-comer". Of course, the precise cause of these changes of name in the promptbook is beyond recovery. Their causality, however, is less important to me here than the fact of their arising in the first place (and the second, and third . . .), their continuation through revisions into the printed text, and the possibility of their literal and literary influence upon subsequent interpretation, including production.

It seems at this point that we have a new insight into these varying names. They can be understood as evidence of the practical steps through which dramatic scripts are not so much read, as "read off." The promptbook, offers evidence of the text arriving and departing.

Shifting names of another role in the play enlarge upon these notions. They call for different kinds of explanation than those offered for Warwick and the Chaplain. In scene 2 we are introduced (at the start of the long stage direction) to *"The Dauphin . . . really King Charles the Seventh since the death of his father, but as yet uncrowned."*

Shaw's prefixes in the rest of the scene are CHARLES., and the stage directions call him variously *"Dauphin"* or *"Charles"*, the names

14. British Library Addit. Ms. 50,644.

often occurring in runs. Two scenes later, when he has been crowned, his introductory stage direction calls him both "*King Charles*", and "*Charles*"; the prefix continues as CHARLES. Appropriately, we do not hear again of "Dauphin" in the printed text, either in dialogue or in directions. Such, however, is not the case in the promptbook annotations, which show a continual shifting of names, even calling him "Dauphin" after he is crowned, and "King" before.

The prompt note (lower right) refers to this map, where the role is

CHINON SCENE.

Position of Characters at the Dauphin's Entrance through the Curtains.

designated "Dauphin"; but the upper-right prompt note calls him "KING". In the next references, the prompt notes read "King" (right) and "Charles" (left). Now, "*Charles*" does happen to be the name in

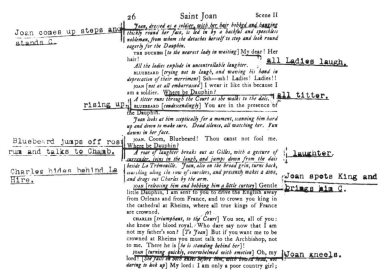

the stage direction beside the prompter's "<u>Charles</u>", and "king" is indeed a word in Joan's speech, preceding which the prompter has marked "<u>King</u>". Perhaps, then, the prompter's vocabulary is influenced variously by the local spoken and silent strands of the Shaw text he is annotating. But even if we grant such literal lines of influence, we cannot easily say why the prompter did not chose "Dauphin", which is Joan's most striking name for him, as she says it twice in dialect at the top of the page, "Where be Dauphin?". "Dauphin" is, however, the name he bears in the map of this moment,

<u>Chinen Scene.</u>

<u>The ultimate positions of crowd for Jeans entrance.</u>

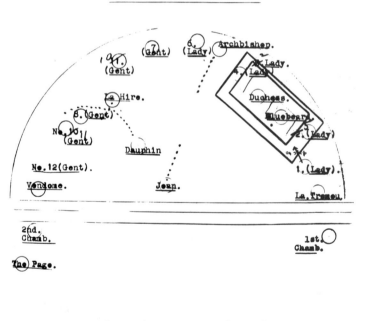

................Dauphink movement when Jean enters.

<u>Everybody this side of C.</u>
<u>exits O.P.</u>

<u>Everybody this side of</u>
<u>C. exits P.</u>

116

but three pages later we have "Charles" twice in prompt notation—

Scene II   Saint Joan   29

JOAN. Art afraid?
CHARLES. Yes: I am afraid. It's no use preaching to me
about it. It's all very well for these big men with their
armor that is too heavy for me, and their swords that I can
hardly lift, and their muscle and their shouting and their
bad tempers. They like fighting: most of them are making
fools of themselves all the time they are not fighting; but
I am quiet and sensible; and I dont want to kill people:
I only want to be left alone to enjoy myself in my own
way. I never asked to be a king: it was pushed on me.
So if you are going to say "Son of St Louis: gird on the
sword of your ancestors, and lead us to victory" you may
spare your breath to cool your porridge; for I cannot do it.
I am not built that way; and there is an end of it.
JOAN [*trenchant and masterful*] Blethers! We are all like
that to begin with. I shall put courage into thee.
CHARLES. But I dont want to have courage put into me.
I want to sleep in a comfortable bed, and not live in continual terror of being killed or wounded. Put courage into
the others, and let them have their bellyful of fighting;
but let me alone.
JOAN. It's no use, Charlie: thou must face what God
puts on thee. If thou fail to make thyself king, thoult be
a beggar: what else art fit for? Come! Let me see thee
sitting on the throne. I have looked forward to it.
CHARLES. What is the good of sitting on the throne when
the other fellows give all the orders? However! [*he sits
enthroned, a piteous figure*] here is the king for you! Look
your fill at the poor devil.
JOAN. Thourt not king yet, lad: thourt but Dauphin.
Be not led away by them around thee. Dressing up dont
fill empty noddle. I know the people: the real people
that make thy bread for thee; and I tell thee they count
no man king of France until the holy oil has been poured
on his hair, and himself consecrated and crowned in Rheims
Cathedral. And thou needs new clothes, Charlie. Why
does not Queen look after thee properly?

Charles X's in front of Joan to L.C.

Charles slowly goes up and sits on throne.

and then "Dauphin" again twice on the next page, where Joan's first
two speeches name him "Charlie".

30   Saint Joan   Scene II

CHARLES. We're too poor.' She wants all the money we
can spare to put on her own back. Besides, I like to see
her beautifully dressed; and I dont care what I wear myself: I should look ugly anyhow.
JOAN. There is some good in thee, Charlie; but it is not
yet a king's good.
CHARLES. We shall see. I am not such a fool as I look.
I have my eyes open; and I can tell you that one good
treaty is worth ten good fights. These fighting fellows
lose all on the treaties that they gain on the fights. If we
can only have a treaty, the English are sure to have the
worst of it, because they are better at fighting than at
thinking.
JOAN. If the English win, it is they that will make the
treaty; and then God help poor France! Thou must fight,
Charlie, whether thou will or no. I will go first to hearten
thee. We must take our courage in both hands: aye, and
pray for it with both hands too.
CHARLES [*descending from his throne and again crossing the
room to escape from her dominating urgency*] Oh do stop talking
about God and praying. I cant bear people who are always
praying. Isnt it bad enough to have to do it at the proper
times?
JOAN [*pitying him*] Thou poor child, thou hast never
prayed in thy life. I must teach thee from the beginning.
CHARLES. I am not a child: I am a grown man and a
father; and I will not be taught any more.
JOAN. Aye, you have a little son. He that will be Louis
the Eleventh when you die. Would you not fight for him?

close to Dauphin.

down right at bottom of steps. R.C.

down to top step. C.

over to Dauphin.

[→]

117

CHARLES. No: a horrid boy. He hates me. He hates everybody, selfish little beast! I dont want to be bothered with children. I dont want to be a father; and I dont want to be a son: especially a son of St Louis. I dont want to be any of these fine things you all have your heads full of: I want to be just what I am. Why cant you mind your own business, and let me mind mine?

JOAN [*again contemptuous*] Minding your own business is

Call No.6

After the coronation, in scene 5, Shaw's stage direction at the bottom of the page logically has enter "*King Charles*", but the prompter now calls him plain "Charles".

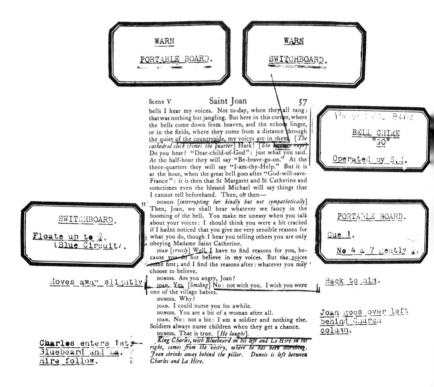

WARN

PORTABLE BOARD.

WARN

SWITCHBOARD.

Scene V   Saint Joan   57

bells I hear my voices. Not to-day, when they all rang: that was nothing but jangling. But here in this corner, where the bells come down from heaven, and the echoes linger, or in the fields, where they come from a distance through the quiet of the countryside, my voices are in them. [*The cathedral clock chimes the quarter*] Hark! [*She ____ rapt*] Do you hear? "Dear-child-of-God": just what you said. At the half-hour they will say "Be-brave-go-on." At the three-quarters they will say "I-am-thy-Help." But it is at the hour, when the great bell goes after "God-will-save-France": it is then that St Margaret and St Catherine and sometimes even the blessed Michael will say things that I cannot tell beforehand. Then, oh then—

DUNOIS [*interrupting her kindly but not sympathetically*] Then, Joan, we shall hear whatever we fancy in the booming of the bell. You make me uneasy when you talk about your voices: I should think you were a bit cracked if I hadnt noticed that you give me very sensible reasons for what you do, though I hear you telling others you are only obeying Madame Saint Catherine.

JOAN [*crossly*] Well, I have to find reasons for you, because you do not believe in my voices. But the voices come first; and I find the reasons after: whatever you may choose to believe.

DUNOIS. Are you angry, Joan?

JOAN. Yes. [*Smiling*] No: not with you. I wish you were one of the village babies.

DUNOIS. Why?

JOAN. I could nurse you for awhile.

DUNOIS. You are a bit of a woman after all.

JOAN. No: not a bit: I am a soldier and nothing else. Soldiers always nurse children when they get a chance.

DUNOIS. That is true. [*He laughs*].

King Charles, with Bluebeard on his left and La Hire on his right, comes from the vestry, where he has been disrobing. Joan shrinks away behind the pillar. Dunois is left between Charles and La Hire.

SWITCHBOARD.

Floats up to 3.
(Blue Circuit).

Moves away slightly

Charles enters 1st.
Bluebeard and La.
Hire follow.

Ps .... Blue

BELL CHIME
"GO"

Operated by S.M.

PORTABLE BOARD.

Cue 1.

No 4 & 7 gently up.

Back to dim.

Joan goes over left
behind Church
column.

On the top of the next page Dunois salutes him as "anointed King", and though the prompter does call him "King" (upper right), he reverts in the next note (left) to "Charles", perhaps in local reiteration

118

of Shaw's stage-direction name beside this prompt note, or of his speech prefix.

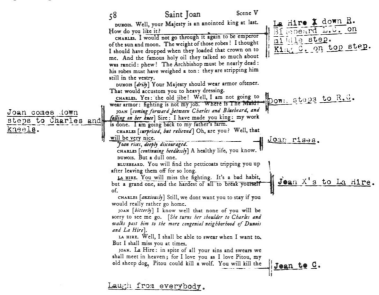

58   Saint Joan   Scene V

DUNOIS. Well, your Majesty is an anointed king at last. How do you like it?

CHARLES. I would not go through it again to be emperor of the sun and moon. The weight of those robes! I thought I should have dropped when they loaded that crown on to me. And the famous holy oil they talked so much about was rancid: phew! The Archbishop must be nearly dead: his robes must have weighed a ton: they are stripping him still in the vestry.

DUNOIS [drily] Your Majesty should wear armor oftener. That would accustom you to heavy dressing.

CHARLES. Yes: the old jibe! Well, I am not going to wear armor: fighting is not my job. Where is The Maid?

La Hire X down R.
Bluebeard L.C. on middle step.
King C. on top step.

Joan comes down steps to Charles and kneels.

JOAN [coming forward between Charles and Bluebeard, and falling on her knee] Sire: I have made you king: my work is done. I am going back to my father's farm.

CHARLES [surprised, but relieved] Oh, are you? Well, that will be very nice.

Down steps to R.C.

Joan rises, deeply discouraged.

CHARLES [continuing heedlessly] A healthy life, you know.

DUNOIS. But a dull one.

BLUEBEARD. You will find the petticoats tripping you up after leaving them off for so long.

LA HIRE. You will miss the fighting. It's a bad habit, but a grand one, and the hardest of all to break yourself of.

Joan rises.

Joan X's to La Hire.

CHARLES [anxiously] Still, we dont want you to stay if you would really rather go home.

JOAN [bitterly] I know well that none of you will be sorry to see me go. [She turns her shoulder to Charles and walks past him to the more congenial neighborhood of Dunois and La Hire].

LA HIRE. Well, I shall be able to swear when I want to. But I shall miss you at times.

JOAN. La Hire: in spite of all your sins and swears we shall meet in heaven; for I love you as I love Pitou, my old sheep dog, Pitou could kill a wolf. You will kill the

Joan to C.

Laugh from everybody.

Two pages on, the overbearing Archbishop informs Joan (line 3)

60   Saint Joan   Scene V

And you would stop while there are still Englishmen on this holy earth of dear France!

THE ARCHBISHOP [sternly] Maid: the king addressed himself to me, not to you. You forget yourself. You very often forget yourself.

Dauphin up 2nd. step C.

JOAN [unabashed, and rather roughly] Then speak, you; and tell him that it is not God's will that he should take his hand from the plough.

Joan puts her hand on Dauphin's arm. He brushes it aside.

THE ARCHBISHOP. If I am not so glib with the name of God as you are, it is because I interpret His will with the authority of the Church and of my sacred office. When you first came you respected it, and would not have dared to speak as you are now speaking. You came clothed with the virtue of humility; and because God blessed your enterprises accordingly, you have stained yourself with the sin of pride. The old Greek tragedy is rising among us. It is the chastisement of hubris.

CHARLES. Yes: she thinks she knows better than everyone else.

JOAN [distressed, but naïvely incapable of seeing the effect she is producing] But I do know better than any of you seem to. And I am not proud: I never speak unless I know I am right.

BLUEBEARD \ [exclaiming \ { Ha ha!
CHARLES / together] { Just so.

THE ARCHBISHOP. How do you know you are right?

JOAN. I always know. My voices—

Charles down steps to Arch. L.C.

CHARLES. Oh, your voices, your voices. Why dont the voices come to me? I am king, not you.

119

that "the king" addresses him, not her. But the prompter's name for him is now "Dauphin" (twice at the top), and then "Charles" (toward the bottom of the page).

Such malapromptism is neither abnormal, nor unique to this document. Let me turn to a prepublication typescript of the play, now in the New York Public Library; a clean copy, it seems to be one of the texts rehearsed from for the premier production.[15] Here we see what are most likely unregularized prefixes from Shaw's manuscript carried over into printer's proof and thence into a typist's fair copy.

```
              BLUEBEARD X's up to L. to below
              Archbishop)
a religious man, Archbishop. Give the saint a chance.
Let us arrange when she comes that I shall be the
Dauphin, and see whether she will find me out.

                         Charles
              (Turning - delighted)
Yes: I agree to that. If she cannot find the blood
royal ⊥ will have nothing to do with her.

                    The Archbishop
It is for the Church to make saints: let De Baudricourt
mind his own business, and not dare usurp the function
of his priest.
              (
                         Dauphin
But -
     .
                    The Archbishop
I say the girl shall not be admitted.

                         Dauphin
I say she shall ⸗

                    The Archbishop
I speak in the Church's name.
              (DAUPHIN X's up toward Archbish-
              op. ARCHBISHOP lifts hand to stop
              him)
              (To Dauphin)
Do you dare say that she shall?
```

15. Reproduction from the New York promptbook is with the permission of the Billy Rose Theatre Collection, the New York Public Library at Lincoln Center, Astor, Lenox and Tilden Foundation. My thanks to Dorothy L. Swerdlow, Director of the Billy Rose Collection.

I had assumed that this typescript derived from Shaw's "unrevised first proofs" with, nevertheless, his manuscript revisions (see note 4), though according to my own argument, its variation in naming could just as well be typical of unrevised proof. I don't know. Again.

They register the same kind of alteration as was generated (or re-generated) by the English prompter working subsequently with the printed text, in which the non-dialogue naming had been largely normalized. The character speaks first under "Charles" (top), though he was just referred to as "Dauphin"; only later does he speak under "Dauphin". Later still, when seated on the throne to satisfy Joan's desire for regal show, he is plain "Charles" again in the prefix

> Joan
> It's no use, Charlie: thou must face what God puts
> on thee. If thou fail to make thyself king, thoult be
> a beggar: what else art fit for? Come! Let me see
> thee sitting on the throne.
>> (Takes Charles' right hand and
>> pulls him up, swinging him toward
>> throne)
> I have looked forward to that.
>
> Charles
>> (Stops - looks back at her)
> What is the good of sitting on the throne when the
> other fellows give all the orders? However! -
>> (Goes up and sits in L. of 2 throne
>> chairs. He sits enthroned, a pit-
>> eous figure with his candy in right
>> hand sticking up from his knee)
> here is the king for you ! Look your fill at the poor
> devil.
>
> Joan
> Thourt not king yet, lad: thourt but Dauphin. Be not
> led away by them around thee.
>> (Up to King stands L.)
> Dressing up don't fill empty noddle. I know the people
> the real people that make thy bread for thee; and I tell
> thee they count no man king of France until the holy oil

(middle), after she has called him "Charlie"; but when she says specifically that he is not king yet, only Dauphin, he is paradoxically referred to as "King" in the stage direction which immediately follows (four lines from the bottom).

Shaw's actual manuscripts are no better. In his rehearsal notes for the first English production, he seems to have varied his names over time, originally calling the role "King" before the coronation, but later "Dauphin" in the Epilogue.[16]

---

16. I have looked too at the promptbook of the 1981 production of *Saint Joan* at the Shaw Festival at Niagara-on-the-Lake, and I find two prompters' hands, one designating the role "D" for Dauphin throughout (though this is confusable with "D" for Dunois),

What might dramaturgic critischism gather from this noumenclature, this nomenclutter? (A question to be asked.) The following may suggest *kinds* of explanations. (My aim is rather to excite wonder than to secure agreement.) First we must allow for Randomness in the prompter (and in the author). But having made allowances, and so having backed off from watertight allegorical interpretation, we need still to ask how it is that some roles are variously named, and others not. What is it about a particular character that promotes variant naming?

Now, the play is focused, obviously, on Joan the outsider and on her conflicts with medieval institutions at a particular crisis in their historical evolution, institutions in terms of which she had to manoeuvre, and on which she eventually foundered. Thus, we should not look to the institution of monarchy for a personal hero; and the big event in Charles's life, his coronation, is understandably conducted offstage. Since it is rendered as emotionally inconsequential, we can readily comprehend why "Dauphin" and "King" might become confused—especially as we meet him after his father's death, but shortly before his own coronation. As a king, moreover, Charles is never his own man, appearing childish against La Trémouille, feminine beside Joan. We can see, too, in purely practical terms, that Shaw's and the annotator's anachronistic uses of "Dauphin" are quite tolerable in a production script, as they evidently lead to no confusion in designating the role: whatever variety of meanings "Dauphin" and "King" may denote symbolically, they function unambiguously as signs.[17]

Shaw was also concerned to frustrate the romantic expectations of his audience, to make them forget sex and violence and concentrate on ideas. "I could get drama enough out of the economics of slum poverty. I scorned the police news and crude sexual adventures with which my competitors could not dispense."[18] Of his cleistogamous heroine Shaw had written to Langner that the "girlish" Joan of "act" one was to be "quite definitely masculine" by "act" two. If Charles had been conceived as a romantic lead rather than a sexual foil, I think

and the other often but irregularly altering the former, designating it "C" for Charles throughout.

Margaret Webster's book (now in the Library of Congress) for the Theatre Guild's revival of 1951 shares the same problem: On page 82, in the first scene when these two characters are together, a map shows "Dun" and "Dau"—the prompt names used till then. Both are crossed out and replaced by "Dun" and "Ch" respectively. "Ch" or "Charl" seem to be consistently used thereafter for the latter role.

17. This is not to say that the *abbreviation* of "Dauphin" is unambiguous. See the preceding note.

18. Shaw, "My Way with a Play," p. 269.

that we might not expect such shifting of his names (for nothing rivets the attention on personal identity quite like a sexual rush). But, as Shaw had written to Langner two months earlier about the difficulty of casting a "comedian" in this role, Charles has to be both "a credible zany" (a theatrical type, we may observe) and "a credible scion of the house of Valois" (an historical type).[19] Now, there may be no neat way to correlate the *three* names from the text — Charles, King and Dauphin — specifically with the *two* roles—zany and scion, but we can at least connect their multiplicity, and argue that the variation of names in the promptbook and also in the author's rehearsal notes owes something to Shaw's lifelong program to explode romance. The various denotations may be the result of that detonation.

A secondary, but still useful conclusion is that the variety of names seems at times to be explicable in terms of whether the annotator was responding to different sub-generic strands of the play—speech prefixes, stage directions or dialogue, or even to the physical locations of names in the layout of the page. The usefulness of phrasing the observation like this is that it allows for literary (as opposed to theatrical) effects to act upon those engaged in production. Thus, the literary in the dramatic, which plays an important role in Shaw's crafting his plays, may register its effect in the nomenclature of the prompter. Again, the phrasing suggests that the literary is not inconsequential as the play moves out of the author's study and onto the boards.

Let me turn to another variously-named character. In the first scene Joan exhibits her tendency to call others by nickname. Her dubbing the soldier Bertrand de Poulengey (who is her social superior) by the unmasculine-sounding "Polly" greatly shocks the straight de Baudricourt, whose sympathy she is trying to win. The prompt naming of this role had initially followed Shaw's prefix, POULENGEY. But now,

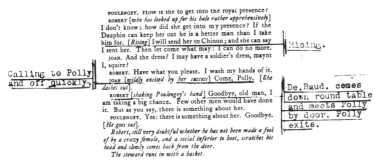

19. Shaw's letter to Langner of 1 February 1924 is in British Library Addit. Ms. 50,539, p. 139; that of 3 December 1923 is on p. 127.

when Joan begins to win de Baudricourt over, and the nickname "Polly" rings out again and again in dialogue, the prompter eventually picks it up. This change of naming suggests that he was taking his cue from Joan. The general meaning of such an idea is that what we might regard as a purely practical matter of the prompter's tagging a direction is subsumed in a symbolic identification—*Joan's* identification—of that role. The prompter's notes (like Shaw's names in stage direction and speech prefix) are not merely directions to invoke a dramatic experience which is entirely separate from them; they also derive from that dramatic experience. Chicken and egg.

Curiously, even Shaw's shorthand draft of this scene begins the prefix for Poulengey's last speech (p. 9) as "Pol"; but this is crossed out and "Poullengey" written instead. Evidently, the prompter's instincts were Shaw's own, and duplicated his innermoist thoughts.[20]

Now for another character. In his stage directions in the manuscript of this play, Shaw introduced Gilles de Rais, an historical person; that his distinctive feature of a blue beard dominates the initial dialogue of Scene 2 may explain why Shaw soon went back and altered his non-dialogue name to "Bluebeard," and used it (with only occasional reversion) thereafter. The printed text (opposite) is not too different from the manuscript's[21] (a slice of which is shown below), and will guide us through the Pitfall shorthand. (Mark well my words. They are

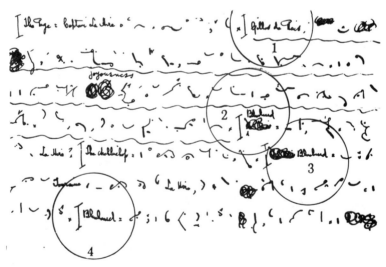

20. The Niagara-on-the-Lake book designates this role variously as "Polly" and "POL" initially, later as "POUL" and "PU."
21. British Library Addit. Ms. 50,629, p. 10.

(1) *Gilles de Rais, a young man of 25, very smart and self-possessed, and sporting the extravagance of a little curled beard dyed blue at a clean-shaven court, comes in. He is determined to make himself agreeable, but lacks natural joyousness, and is not really pleasant. In fact when he defies the Church some eleven years later he is accused of trying to extract pleasure from horrible cruelties, and hanged. So far, however, there is no shadow of the gallows on him. He advances gaily to the Archbishop. The page withdraws.*

(2) BLUEBEARD. Your faithful lamb, Archbishop. Good day, my lord. Do you know what has happened to La Hire?

LA TRÉMOUILLE. He has sworn himself into a fit, perhaps.

(3) BLUEBEARD. No: just the opposite. Foul Mouthed Frank, the only man in Touraine who could beat him at swearing, was told by a soldier that he shouldnt use such language when he was at the point of death.

THE ARCHBISHOP. Nor at any other point. But was Foul Mouthed Frank on the point of death?

(4) BLUEBEARD. Yes: he has just fallen into a well and been

of your eternal Salvation.) Here are the first three successive speech prefixes and speeches for this character, that show the texture of Shaw's first and second thoughts. He is introduced by his name, at number 1, at the start of the stage direction (underlined in the manuscript). At 2 the alteration of the prefix from "de Rais" to his nickname seems to have come after the speech had started, and so is written above the deletion. At 3 it came after the first go at the prefix but before the speech, and so could be written between them. And at 4 there is only the new prefix. This progression may be taken— "graphically" is the word—to bear out Shaw's statement, that he wrote down whatever speeches came into his head, and only subsequently discovered the speaker's name

I would like now to return briefly to the printed text of *Pygmalion* to illustrate some kinds of variation of names not shown in *Saint Joan*. In the first published version of the play the heroine's names in speech prefix change in the second scene from THE FLOWER GIRL. to LIZA for one speech, back to THE FLOWER GIRL. for one speech and then to LIZA. for many more, to THE JAPANESE LADY. for one, and then to LIZA. again for the rest of the play. The first of these changes can be seen here.

THE FLOWER GIRL. Ah-ah-ah-ow-ow-oò! [*She stands, half rebellious, half bewildered*].

PICKERING [*very courteous*] Wont you sit down?

LIZA [*coyly*] Dont mind if I do. [*She sits down. Pickering returns to the hearthrug*].   [→]

125

HIGGINS. Whats your name?
THE FLOWER GIRL. <u>Liza Doolittle.</u>
HIGGINS [*declaiming gravely*]

> Eliza, Elizabeth, Betsy and Bess,
> They went to the woods to get a bird's nes':

PICKERING. They found a nest with four eggs in it:
HIGGINS. They took one apiece, and left three in it.

They laugh heartily at their own wit.

122   Pygmalion   Act II

<u>LIZA.</u> Oh, dont be silly.

The introduction of her personal name—LIZA—in prefix, just before
she is asked it, suggests layering of text: that this speech was written
after the surrounding FLOWER GIRL. speeches, when Shaw already had
"found a name" for her. The LIZA-prefixed speech originated in fact
as a handwritten marginal addition to a pre-publication proof of the
text which Shaw annotated for use in the theatre.

16   Pygmalion   Act II

MRS PEARCE [*quietly*] Sit down, girl. Do as youre told.
[*She turns the chair near the hearthrug towards Higgins and
stands behind it, waiting for the girl to sit down*].
THE FLOWER GIRL. Ah-ah-ah-ow-ow-oo! [*She sits down,
half intimidated, half bewildered*].
HIGGINS. Whats your name?
THE FLOWER GIRL. Liza Doolittle.
HIGGINS [*declaiming gravely*].

> Eliza, Elizabeth, Betsy and Bess,
> They went to the woods to get a bird's nes':

PICKERING. They found a nest with four eggs in it:
HIGGINS. They took one apiece, and left three in it.

They laugh heartily at their own wit.
LIZA [*coyly*] Oh, dont be silly.

Now, something interesting happens here when the heroine finally
states her name. Higgins simply will not take it literally. With help
from Pickering he declaims gravely the old nursery rhyme, "Eliza,
Elizabeth, Betsy and Bess,"[22] and completely omits her own name for

22. Iona and Peter Opie, *The Oxford Dictionary of Nursery Rhymes*, corrected ed.
(Oxford, 1973), no. 151, p. 158.

herself, Liza, by which, in fact, he never addresses or refers to her in the play. This behaviour aggressively raises the issue of multiple names in the dialogue itself, and suggests that our growing list of interpretations of variations of silent names ought to be coordinated with it. ("JOAN [*chattily*] They always call me Jenny in Lorraine. Here in France I am Joan. The soldiers call me The Maid"—though in Shaw's movie script the English soldier calls her "Judy." And when Ladvenu mis)guides her shaking hand through the letters "J.E.H.A.N.E.", she signs an X. Shaw?—he calls the play *Saint Joan.*) Higgins and Pickering both always address their Galatea as "Eliza", displaying the formality and class attitude which it is the point of this play to anatomize.

There are, however, two others who do call the heroine by her own name for herself. One is her father, later in this scene. The other is not so much *in* the dramatic fiction, as *about* it: Shaw himself, as we see in the speech prefixes, which never use ELIZA.—and also, more notably, as we see in this typical example, in the stage directions for the rest of this scene.

> HIGGINS. Pledge of good faith, Eliza. I eat one half: you eat the other. [*Liza opens her mouth to retort: he pops the half chocolate into it*]. You shall have boxes of them, barrels of them, every day. You shall live on them. Eh?
> LIZA [*who has disposed of the chocolate after being nearly choked by it*] I wouldnt have ate it, only I'm too ladylike to take it out of my mouth.

Doolittle in dialogue and Shaw in stage direction are not consistent, however, as both also call her "Eliza". Shaw's stage-direction name for her becomes "*Eliza*" permanently after this scene, even though that name never appears as her prefix. The LIZA. prefixes and the later *Eliza* directions seem to conjure up the heroine simultaneously from different angles of vision, like a cubist painting. Through purely internal evidence they may suggest, and give the critic a toe-hold on, the author's ambivalence towards his heroine.

When Shaw came to draft additions to the play for the movie script, he added passages like this in manuscript,[23]

23. A photograph of the full paste-up page can be seen in Shaw, *An Autobiography*, ed. Stanley Weintraub, Vol. 2, (New York, 1970), between pp. 148 and 149. I am grateful to Penguin Books and to Constable and Company for permission to photoquote from their editions of Shaw.

FREDDY [*springing out of a taxicab*] Got one at last. Hallo! [*To the girl*] Where are the two ladies that were here?

THE FLOWER GIRL. They walked to the bus when the rain stopped.

FREDDY. And left me with a cab on my hands! Damnation!

THE FLOWER GIRL [*with grandeur*] Never mind, young man. I'm going home in a taxi. [*She sails off to the cab. The driver puts his hand behind him and holds the door firmly shut against her. Quite understanding his mistrust, she shews him her handful of money*]. ~~Eighteenpence~~ A taxi fare aint no object to me, Charlie. [*He grins and opens the door*]. ~~Angel Court, Drury Lane, round the corner of Micklejohn's oil shop. Let's see how fast you can make her hop it [She gets in and pulls the door to with a slam as the taxicab starts].~~ ~~FREDDY. Well, I'm dashed!~~

Here. What about the basket?

THE TAXIMAN. Give it here. Tuppence extra.

ELIZA. No: I dont want nobody to see it. [*She crushes it into the cab and gets in, continuing the conversation through the window*], Goodbye, Freddy.

FREDDY [*dazedly raising his hat*] Goodbye

TAXIMAN. Where to?

ELIZA. Bucknam Pellis [Buckingham Palace].

in which he now used the ELIZA. prefix; but this usage was altered before publication, to be consistent with the LIZA. prefixes of the printed text, even though what is the norm in this early part of the play is, in fact, THE FLOWER GIRL.

FREDDY. And left me with a cab on my hands! Damnation!

THE FLOWER GIRL [*with grandeur*] Never mind, young man. I'm going home in a taxi. [*She sails off to the cab. The driver puts his hand behind him and holds the door firmly shut against her. Quite understanding his mistrust, she shews him her handful of money*]. A taxi fare aint no object to me, Charlie. [*He grins and opens the door*]. Here. What about the basket?

THE TAXIMAN. Give it here. Tuppence extra.

LIZA. No: I dont want nobody to see it. [*She crushes it into the cab and gets in, continuing the conversation through the window*] Goodbye, Freddy.

FREDDY [*dazedly raising his hat*] Goodbye.

TAXIMAN. Where to?

LIZA. Bucknam Pellis [Buckingham Palace].

But Shaw's normalizing extended no further, and he did not alter the oddities of silent naming in the printed text that I have just sketched;

and so the premature LIZA between FLOWER GIRL. prefixes and also the discrepancy *within* the stage-direction names and *between* those names and the prefix names ("Liza" versus "Eliza") all appeared in the new publication, which therefore bore—as current editions still do, and as tomorrow's shall continue to bear (it is the Law)—clear evidence of multiple layers of composition, of Shaw's visions and revisions.

The variations of the non-dialogue names in all these examples seem to derive from many causes, from pedestrian artfulness to sublime inattention. If we could clearly determine which causes effected which variations, editors might feel that they could create an edition for art's sake and relegate some of the readings to psychologists. Happily, however, art and life are too complex to be so separated. Whatever the origin of this variation in naming, Shaw was adamant that no part of his text should be wrectified by the well-meaning editor or producer. What and how his variation of names all means is ever to be discovered: the text is all before us. My main point here is to draw attention to the potential for fluidity in naming in any given document of a play, and to demonstrate also the flow throughout the successive transformations of it from earliest script to latest revision, from author through theatrical personnel.

—and even to the audience: for, as a publicity stunt, Beerbohm Tree, the first Higgins and also the manager of the first production, had suggested to the editor of the *Daily Express* that he invite a real London flower-girl to come to a performance of *Pygmalion*, and give her opinions of it to the press.[24]

> Well, I never had sich a night in all me natural. Everybody a-looking at me and a-photographing me and a-shaking me hand, and all because I said as how I'd go and see how they played a flower-girl in this play. You see, I never thought as how I'd be so conspic ... well, you know what I mean. I thought I'd just sit in the queue, and then go and sit somewhere in the corner, see the play and then tell the bloke what I thought of it. Well, when we got into the theatre I found meself right in front of the pit. Then, when the nobs come in, all wearing evening dress, I got red in the face for they all turned round and stared at me. I could see some o' them was reading the paper with me picture in it and all, and when they saw the picture, they all turned round to have a squint at the real thing.
> It was alright when the curtain went up, I reely enjoyed meself then, and when I heard the language, it was quite home-like. I never thought as

24. Quoted from Richard Huggett, *The Truth About Pygmalion* (London, 1969), pp. 143-46.

how I'd hear sich words on the stage. I shall have a word or two to say about this before I've done. Now about Liza Doolittle, the flower-girl: I thought Mrs Patricia Campbell who played her was just *luvly*—but she was not altogether what you might call true ter life. As for Bernard Shaw, well, he thinks a blooming sight too much of himself, he does. There was one line in the first act which shows just how conceited he must be. It was when the Professor was talking about the flower-girl, when she was miserable at not being able to sell her flowers. "The woman", says he, "who can utter such disgusting sounds does not deserve to live anywhere." When I heard this I could not help shouting 'RATS' and people in the pits says 'HUSH. 'Hush yourself,' says I, 'he's got no right to say a thing like that."

Now, I didn't like the bit when the prof. makes his housekeeper take away the flower-girl's clothes and burn them. It's as much as to say flower-girl's are lousy. I thought Mrs Patricia Campbell talked a bit rough. I asked people in the pit if I talked as rough as her, and they said NO, not arf as rough as her. I thought it was funny when she got into the taxi wiv her basket. Of course, flower-girls don't make a habit of getting into taxis, but you know, when you've had a good day, you feels sporty. I didn't like the last bit when Eliza's supposed to fall in love with the Prof. He wanted her to go back to him, yet he didn't say he loved her. It wasn't one thing nor another. And then Sir Herbert waves his arms round her, above her and all over her, but he didn't kiss her or hug her. Doesn't Mr Shaw believe in kissing or hugging?

And now a bit about the language. There was one word in particular which Mrs Patricia Campbell said when she was supposed ter be a lidy. The editor says I must not repeat it, but it begins with a B and ends with a Y. WELL!! No self-respecting flowergirl would say such a word when she was on her best behaviour and speaking in a drawing-room. And when another young lidy said it after her, well, it sounded simply horrible . . . I wish he'd found a better title. Who's ter know *Pygmalion* is anyfing ter do wiv flower-girls? It would have been better it he gave it a good rousing name like they have for the Lyceum dramas. He might have called it *From Flower Girl to Duchess*. We should have known what it was about then. Mister Shaw can have this tip from me, free, gratis and fer nuffin.

This old Girl begins by calling the heroine "Liza Doolittle, the flower-girl"—but, like the author of the stage directions, shifts to Eliza when referring disparagingly to "the last bit when Eliza's supposed to fall in love with the Prof." Her proposed title for the play is *From Flower Girl to Duchess*, and she evidently conceives of the heroine in the Duchess phase as an Eliza. When his copyright expires, it will likely be deemed then, as it is now, the job of sinserious editors to clean up the inconsistency of a ploywright's non-dialogue naming. But so to tidy up the text seems indistinguishable from emaculating it, from plucking out the heart of a mystery, a mystery known to play-wrights, prompters, and flower-girls.

Shaw—but perhaps I should return to Shakespear, having, I hope, shown in a variety of Shavian documents, early and late, less and more formal, more "literary" or more "dramatic", a modern master of the theatre, who insisted that he knew what he was doing with his text, and that we should not tamper with it.

PART 2

THE EDITOR PROBLEM

in

SHAKESPEAR

by

Sir Greg Walters

Propriety was thus appalled,
That the self was not the same.

Shakespeare, *The Poenix and Turtle*

To compare editions of a Shakespear play from the sixteenth through the present century—not that Grand Inquisitors encourage you to do this—makes vivid the many abiding and the many transient Editorial Distortions in our traditional views of Shawkespearean dramaturgy. But the one I will single out in this lecture is that the variation in non-dialogue naming in his texts, which greatly resembles Shaw's, and which must be in many cases the old boy's, has been subeliminated from the glossy texts used in the school and in almost all Shakspearian scholarship—which because they are out of copy-right have been copy-wronged by editors. Shakespear's artifice has been swallowed up in the Artofficial, and all his hallucinations hidden from us—except where vestiges of them here and there may survive in a footnote. A *footnote!*—where our encounter with Shakespeare's whole is inevitably through a gloss darkly. Editors in the manger! And the laity of this dog-eat-dogma world: sheepishly we look up, and are not fed.

(That was a way of putting it, not very periphrastic, satisfactory perhaps, certainly tongue-in-chic; but one which leaves still the intolerable wrestle with words and meanings.) McKerrow (to start again) seems to have been the first to argue that the shifting of non-dialogue names in the earliest printed versions of some of Shakspeare's texts is an indication that the printers' copies had been foul papers; for such variation, though natural to early stages of composition ("At first I hardly know the speakers, and cannot find names for them."), would have been normalized in the fair copy of each text needed for production.[25] "Needed for production." Hmmm, suspicious. For the cleaning up of Shakesper in these matters has been, since it began systematically with Ed. Rowe at the start of the eighteenth century, a pre-eminently *Editorial* function, co-ordinate with the general rationalization and regulation then descending in Procrustean fashion upon English—as most obviously in contemporary spelling and punctuation—and creating a gulf between it and the retrospectively mythillogical world of Elizabethan English. Suspicious, then, because McKerrow's theory can be seen merely to serve to justify the editorial orthodoxy, which had taken shape without recourse to any *dramaturgic* theory. But *now* the need was felt to base editing upon theory and upon historical fact: Shakespeare's complicity was needed in the editing of his plays. Suddenly (it was the twentieth century) nothing has changed; Greg's *Fiat Lex* inaugurates our method-conscious era:

RULE I

The aim of a critical edition should be to present the text, so far as the evidence permits, in the form in which we may suppose that it would have stood in a fair copy, made by the author himself, of the work as he finally intended it.[26]

25. R. B. McKerrow, "A Suggestion Regarding Shakespeare's Manuscripts," *Review of English Studies*, XI (1935), 459-65; and later in his *Prolegomena for the Oxford Shakespeare*, Oxford, 1939, pp. 9 (n.1), 19-20, 56-57. Fredson Bowers, "Foul Papers, Compositor B, and the Speech-Prefixes of *All's Well that Ends Well*," *Studies in Bibliography*, 32 (1979), 60-81, refers to McKerrow's RES essay (curiously by a different title, "The Elizabethan Printer and Dramatic Manuscripts") and says, "The significance of these variable prefixes as evidence for foul-papers copy as against a transcript was first pointed out by R. B. McKerrow. . . . His interpretation has never been *seriously* [italics mine] challenged," p. 61, n. 4.

26. W. W. Greg, *The Editorial Problem in Shakespeare: A Survey of the Foundations of the Text*. The Clark Lectures, 1939, 3rd ed. (Oxford, 1954), p. x. Greg footnotes a passage from McKerrow which is almost identical in phrasing, but which is not styled RULE; it appears in *Prolegomena*, p. 6. McKerrow is eloquent on the unattainability of an ideal Shakespeare edition, partly because he distrusts the notion of a written final form for Renaissance dramatists, though he is more sanguine about contemporary writers: "We must not expect to find a definitive text in the sense in which the published version of the plays of a modern dramatist is definitive." (He did not know, of course, of the controversial state of Pinter's or Stoppard's texts.)

But we have seen enough of Shaw and his producers, and will soon see enough of Shakespear and his, to disabuse ourselves of the notion that a fair copy with all non-dialogue names normalized is required (or even tolerated) in the theatre. Of course, McKerrow's deduction that foul-paper copy can explain the variations of non-dialogue names in Shakespere's printed texts was and remains a brilliant critical insight. However, if the Renaissance printer used a promptbook as copy, even if the prompter had originally received fair copy from the author, we could still expect that the prompter's additions and alterations to the text could have "fouled" it. The distinction between foul-copy-draft and fair-copy-promptbook origins for Shakspeare's printed texts counts heavily with modern editors. But the distinctions cannot be made on McKerrow's evidence of varying names alone.

This similarity of pre-theatrical scripts to actual promptbooks neatly short circuits the potential difference between the evidences of the artist's early and his final intent, which difference is the main source of voltage that drives current through editors in Greg's tradition, and that animates them to create ideal from actual texts. "The editors world is golden," Sidney said, "the poete delieueres onlie a brazen."

One of the oldest Shakespear theatre documents is the first quarto of 2 Henry 4.[27]

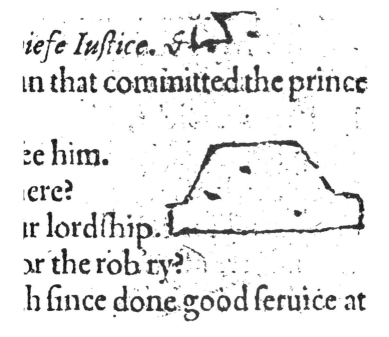

I am not sure whether it is an actual promptbook, but it does bear theatrical markings, as in this, the first stage map of a Shakespere production. Several seemingly seventeenth-century hands have briefly indicated exits throughout; there are occasional embellishments, as in this note that Falstaff enters singing, and in added punctuation.

Qui. Why thats well said, a good heart's worth gold : loe here comes sir Iohn.

enter sir Iohn:

sir Iohn When Arthur first in court, empty the iourdan and was a worthy King : how now mistris Doll?

host. Sicke of a calme, yea good faith.

Falst. So is all her sect, and they be once in a calme they are sicke.

What is of concern are the names used by these annotators to fill out their directions. Here the printed direction (top right) reads "*Enter Harry*", but the next speech prefix for this role reads "*Prince*".

King Set me the crowne vpon my pillow here.

Clar. His eie is hollow, and he changes much.

War. Lesse noyse, lesse noyse.　　　*Enter Harry*

Prince Who saw the duke of Clarence?

Clar. I am here brother, ful of heauinesse.

Prince How now, raine within doores, and none abroad? How doth the King?

Hum. Exceeding ill.

Prince Heard he the good newes yet? tell it him.

Hum. He altred much vpon the hearing it,

Prince If he be sicke with ioy, heele recouer without physicke.

War. Not so much noyse my Lords, sweete prince, speake lowe, the King your father is dispofde to sleepe.

Clu. Let vs withdraw into the other roome.

War. Wilt please your Grace to go along with vs? *Exeunt*

Prince No, I wil sit and watch heere by the King.

Why doth the Crowne lie there vpon his pillow,

Being so troublesome a bedfellow?

O polisht perturbation! golden care!

27. Listed as number 1 for this play in Charles H. Shattuck, *The Shakespeare Promptbooks*, (Urbana and London, 1965), p. 141. The promptbook is in the Huntington Library. My thanks to the Librarian, Daniel H. Woodward, who has kindly permitted the reproduction of these images.

Co-operative Ventures: English Manuscript Playbooks, 1590-1630, the work of Bill Long

The handwritten direction (bottom right) uses the prefix name, and reads "Exeunt manet <u>Prince</u>". In the layout of the printed page the variations in non-dialogue naming are localized, and the theatrical annotator, who added directions, evidently was satisfied with the prefix name (which is closer in time, though not in space), even if his choice of it introduces inconsistency in the stage-direction naming between print and handwriting. We have seen this phenomenon at work in the names "Charles", "Dauphin", and "King" in the *Saint Joan* promptbook.

In the following passage there are two different characters identified by the speech prefix "*Iohn*". At the top left it is Falstaff, who

is also the "sir Iohn" in dialogue (top right). But with the printed stage direction (just below), we find *"Enter Iustice and prince Iohn"*, whereupon the role designated previously by the *"Iohn"* prefix acquires the new name, *"Fal."* (mid left)—and *"Iohn"* comes thereupon to designate the speech of the prince (bottom left). At the bottom right the annotator wrote the direction "manet Iustice & Iohn", which is ambiguous, as either John Falstaff or Prince Iohn could answer the call to stay. Again it seems that for his own stage direction the annotator took his "Iohn" locally from the prefix rather

forthcoming from AMS Press, New York, will provide an exhaustive study of the irregularities and inconsistencies in the notation of contemporary promptbooks—or, to purge the anachronism, as he suggests, "*playbooks.*"

than from the remote stage direction that entered prince John, and that having clarified the text, he was content to leave it ambiguous.

A last example from 5.2 is particularly interesting. The printed stage direction gives the name "*Sincklo*", which also appears in the speech prefixes. This is not, however, or at least not only, the name

Pʃt. Let vultures vile ſeize on his lungs alſo : where is the life that late I led, ſay they, why here it is, welcome theſe pleſant dayes. *exit.* *omn* ℞ ſ

Enter Sincklo and three or foure officers. ℐƒoſƶɛ₅ . ℞ʋ ḥoʃℓ

Hoʃt. No, thou arrant knaue, I would to God that I might die, that I might haue thee hang'd, thou haſt drawn my ſhoulder out of ioynt.

Sincklo The Conſtables haue deliuered her ouer to mee, and ſhee ſhall haue whipping cheere I warrant her, there hath beene a man or two kild about her.

Whoore Nut-hooke, Nut-hooke, you lie, come on, Ile tell thee what, thou damnd tripe viſagde raſcall, and the child I go with, do miſcarry, thou wert better thou hadſt ſtrook thy mother, thou paper-facde villaine.

Hoʃt. O the Lord, that ſir Iohn were come! I would make

of a fictitious character in the play (one of the "Beadles" or an "Officer", as the Folio direction and prefixes name him), but of a real actor in Shakespeare's company.[28] His name appears very frequently in contemporary texts. He was the King's Men's thin man, and his predictable effect on stage may have led to his being cast by the author during scripting, so that his name survives even in what are regarded as foul-paper derivatives, which therefore bear no other suggestions of staging. Modern editors are concerned not to intermangle dramatic fiction and the means of staging it, though there is every reason to believe that Shake-speare's dramaturgy mixed them, that he could have been responsible for the name and for the casting, or even that Sincklo was the inspiration for aspects of the scene. (In this way editors and their all-perversive normalizing ensure that Shakespere is not of his age, but for all time.) Now, the manuscript annotator of 2 *Henry 4* was not, I presume, connected with a production with Sincklo in it, yet he did not alter the quarto name to one of those in the Folio, as editors do even when using the quarto as their

28. See Allison Gaw, "John Sincklo as one of Shakespeare's Actors," *Anglia*, 49 (1925), 289-303.

copytext. Whatever the origin of the name "Sincklo"—in Shakspeare's scripting or in the staging of the King's Men—it functions unequivocally as a sign to designate the role.

The character whom the annotator designated "Whoer" in this same episode was presumably named from the speech prefix, "*Whoore*" (or from the catch-word, not shown here), for she is not called "whore" in the dialogue of this scene (and is so termed only once in the play: "*Poynes* Lets beate him before his whore" (E1ᵛ; 2.4.257)). Elsewhere in the non-dialogue naming of the quarto she is "*Doll*", *Dorothy*" and "*Tersheete*". Unlike modern editors, the seventeenth-century annotator showed no sense of generalization of her role name, but for her as for others simply used a name that was close to hand. His interpretation of the text (as revealed by his writing directions on it) was strongly mediated by its physical layout.

What does this all mean? I think it means that when the early annotators worked on specific theatrical problems, they often solved them successfully by drawing upon local textual resources, dialogue or non-dialogue. This means that their behaviour resembles that of the modern annotators we have witnessed already in the *Saint Joan* promptbooks. And it means, if the printed variations of naming in the quarto of *2 Henry 4* were Shakespear's, as at least some of them must be, that these early annotators adapted to Shakespear's hallucinated style. If four hundred years ago Shakspeare wrote with impractical variations in his signing of roles; and if contemporary production used the impractical practically, as it were; and if Shaw and his producers do the same in our own century, why must our Shakspear texts be edited to "normalize" the variation? Are they so edited in the name of art or practicality? If art, then not Shawespeer's (or Shak's). If practicality, then not that of theatrical production, old or new. In whose *name* do editors undertake their busyness?

[   ]

(This last section of my paper, on *Richard 2*, might best be titled by the hero's self-uncharacterization, "The King is not himself," and the epigraph could be "thus play I in one person many roles.")

From a Machiavellian point of view the history plays are concerned with power and with the rise and fall of kings. Although a monarch's fall may be precisely timed in a political sense, we often find, when we look into the early quartos and folios, as of this play, that the actual title, "King", can continue to be employed in prefixes and directions *after* the fall. And conversely, the regal title may begin to disappear from prefixes and directions *before* the fall. This coming and going of the title suggests that Machiavellian analysis was not upper-most in the dramatist's mind as he wrote. In general it suggests an authorial focus less on the political than on the psychic or moral stature of the hero; specifically it suggests a response of the writer (or of the observer) to the hero moment by moment.

Let us trace examples of this phenomenon in the first quarto (1597). At the start of *Richard 2* the first speech prefix is *"King Richard."*; thereafter we find *"King."*.

ENTER KING RICHARD, IOHN
OF GAVNT, WITH OTHER
Nobles and attendants.

King Richard.

Vld Iohn of Gaunt time honoured Lancaſter,
Haſt thou according to thy oath and bande
Brought hither Henrie Herford thy bolde ſonne,
Here to make good the boiſtrous late appeale.
Which then our leyſure would not let vs heare
Againſt the Duke of Norfolke, Thomas Moubray?
Gaunt. I haue my Leige
King. Tell me moreouer haſt thou ſounded him,
If he appeale the Duke on ancient malice,
Or worthily as a good ſubieƈt ſhould
On ſome knowne ground of treacherie in him.

His antagonist is first named *"Bullingbrooke"* in stage direction and *"Bulling."* in prefix (though the king addresses him as "Cousin of Hereford").

Enter Bullingbrooke and Mowbray,

Bulling. Manie yeares of happie daies befall,
My gratious ſoueraigne my moſt louing liege.
A 2   *Mow.*

When he appears formally as *"appellant in armour"*, he is named *"Duke of Hereford"* in stage direction, a title echoing the immediately preceding dialogue, but the speech prefix continues "*Bul.*", though his name for himself is "Harry of Herford, Lancaster and Darbie".

Mow My name is Thomas Mowbray Duke of Norfolke,
Who hither come ingaged by my oath,
(Which God defende a Knight fhould violate)
Both to defend my loyalty and truth,
To God,my King,and my fucceeding iffue,
Againft the Duke of Herford that appeales me.
And by the grace of God,and this mine arme,
To proue him in defending of my felfe,
A traitour to my God,my King,and me,
And as I truely fight,defend me heauen.

*The trumpets found. Enter Duke of Hereford
appellant in armour.*
King Marfhall aske yonder Knight in armes,
            B 2   Both

The Tragedie of
Both who he is,and why he commeth hither,
Thus plated in habiliments of warre,
And formally according to our lawe,
Depofe him in the iuftice of his caufe.
Mar. What is thy name? and wherfore comft thou hither?
Before king Richard in his royall lifts,
Againft whom comes thou? and whats thy quarrell?
Speake like a true Knight, fo defend thee heauen.
Bul. Harry of Herford,Lancafter and Darbie
Am I, who ready here do ftand in Armes
To proue by Gods grace,and my bodies valour
In lifts, on *Thomas Mowbray* Duke of Norffolke,
That he is a traitour foule and dangerous,

"*Appellant in armour*" and "*Duke of Hereford*", like the vocabulary of the dialogue here, are strongly reminiscent of Hall's *Union of the two Noble and Illustre Families of Lancaster and York* as recycled through Holinshed's *Chronicles*, 1587, one of Shakespeare's sources. (One feels that Shakespeare's naming is influenced by the physical layout as well as by the content of his source.) When Bullingbroke leads his force against the monarch at Flint Castle, he calls him "King

139

Richard'', but the stage direction for the first time terms him plain
"*Richard*"—and at this auspicious point in his decline, strong, kingly
name though "Richard" be, it seems to register the fatal transformation of his political power. Equivocally, the prefix remains
unchanged—"*King*".

The Tragedie of
My water's on the earth, and not on him.
March on, and marke King Richard how he lookes.

The trumpets found, Richard appeareth on the walls.
Bull. See fee King Richard doth himfelfe appeare,
As doth the blufhing difcontented Sunne,
From out the fierie portall of the Eaft,
When he perceiues the enuious cloudes are bent
To dimme his glorie, and to ftaine the tracke
Of his bright paffage to the Occident.
Yorke Yet lookes he like a King, beholde his eye,
As bright as is the Eagles, lightens forth
Controlling maieftie; alacke alacke for woe,
That any harme fhould ftaine fo faire a fhew.
King We are amazde, and thus long haue we ftoode,
To watch the fearefull bending of thy knee,
Becaufe we thought our felfe thy lawful King:
And if wee be, howe dare thy ioynts forget
To pay their awefull duety to our prefence?
If we be not, fhew vs the hand of God
That hath difmift vs from our Stewardfhip,

The scene that will most interest us now must be that of the deposition. It was not in the first quarto; when it first appeared, in the fourth
(1608), the stage direction read "*Enter king Richard*"— but the speech
prefix read merely, "*Rich.*"

Bull. Lords, you that are heere, are vnder our areft,
Procure your Sureties for your dayes of anfwere;
Litle are we beholding to your loue,
And litle looke for at your helping hands.
Enter king Richard.
Rich. Alacke why am I fent for to a King,
Before I haue fhooke off the regall thoughts
Wherewith I raignd; I hardly yet haue learnt
To infinuate, flatter, bow, and bend my limbes?

When the text appeared in the first folio, it showed, unlike the quarto, "*Richard*" in direction, but, like the quarto, "*Rich.*" in prefix.

> *Bull.* Lords, you that here are vnder our Arreſt,
> Procure your Sureties for your Dayes of Anſwer:
> Little are we beholding to your Loue,
> And little look'd for at your helping Hands.
>
> *Enter Richard and Yorke.*
> *Rich.* Alack, why am I ſent for to a King,
> Before I haue ſhooke off the Regall thoughts
> Wherewith I reign'd? I hardly yet haue learn'd
> To inſinuate, flatter, bowe, and bend my Knee.

(The folio uses "*King*" prefixes only in the first scene.) A neater equivocation (or jumble of evidence) could not be asked for.

Now back to the first quarto. When Richard subsequently is led away to prison at Pomfret, he encounters his wife, still (as always) called "*Queene*" in stage direction and in speech prefix.

> *The Tragedie of*
>
> Heere let vs reſt, if this rebellious earth,
> Haue any reſting for her true Kings Queene.   (*Enter Ric.*
> But ſoft, but ſee, or rather doe not ſee,
> My faire Roſe wither, yet looke vp, behold,
> That you in pittie may diſſolue to deaw,
> And waſh him freſh againe with true loue teares.
> Ah thou the modle where olde Troy did ſtand!
> Thou mappe of honour, thou King Richards tombe,
> And not King Richard: thou moſt beauteous Inne,
> Why ſhould hard fauourd greife be lodged in thee,
> When triumph is become an alehouſe gueſt?
> *Rich.* ioyne not with greife faire woman, doe not ſo,
> To make my end too ſudden, learne good ſoule,
> To thinke our former ſtate a happie dreame,
> From which awakt the trueth of what we are
> Shewes vs but this; I am ſworne brother (ſweet)
> To grim neceſſitie, and he and I,
> Will keepe a league till death. Hie thee to Fraunce,
> And cloiſter thee in ſome religious houſe,
> Our holy liues muſt win a new worlds crowne,
> VVhich our prophane houres heere haue throwne downe.

[→]

141

Quee. what is my Richard both in ſhape and minde
Transformd and weakned? hath Bullingbrooke,
Depoſde thine intellect? hath he been in thy hart?
The Lyon dying thruſteth foorth his pawe,
And woundes the earth if nothing elſe with rage,
To be ore-powr'd, and wilt thou pupill-like
Take the correction, mildly kiſſe the rod,
And fawne on Rage with baſe humilitie,
VVhich art a Lion and the king of beaſts.
  King. a King of beaſts indeed, ıf aught but beaſts,
I had been ſtill a happie King of men.
Good (ſometimes Queene) prepare thee hence for France,
Thinke I am dead, and that euen here thou takeſt
As from my death bed thy laſt liuing leaue;
In winters tedious nights ſit by the fire,
with good old folkes, and let them tell the tales,
Of woefull ages long agoe betidde:

And

In a political sense, of course, she is no more Queen than he is King—
as we note from Richard's address to her, "Good (sometimes
Queene)" (six lines from the bottom); but in a dramatic sense she is
every inch a queen, and exhorts him to be more than what he now
seems to be, "King Richards tombe" (line 8). In this quarto the hero
enters again as "*Ric.*", upper right, and his prefix is "*Rich.*"—the first
such coincidence of this name in prefix and direction in this quarto;
but the prefix turns shortly to "*King*", perhaps in response to the
Queen's address to him as "a Lion and the king of beasts" (nine lines
from the bottom), which immediately precedes the new prefix, and
which the hero reiterates at the start of his speech—or perhaps from
the Majesty of his heart, which has no relationship to his political
Power (unless it be inversely proportional), but which is apparent as
he responds to his wife's call, and begins, like the dying Lion she
exhorts him to be, to thrust forth his paw. Perhaps the *King.* prefix can
recrown him here only because his adversary is not before him on
stage to force the political issue to our attention. But however we try to
explain it, we must not explain it away (for it *is* the text).

When he comes to soliloquize before his murder, he again both
enters and speaks under the name "*Richard*". Note that before this

entrance Exton refers to Bolingbroke as his king; but more significantly, his reference to Richard is also as king.

> *Exton* And fpeaking it, he wifhtly lookt on me,
> As who fhould fay, I would thou wert the man,
> That would diuorce this terrour from my heart,
> Meaning the king at Pomfret. Come lets go,
> I am the kings friend, and will rid his foe.
>   *Enter Richard alone*
> *Rich.* I haue beene ftudying how I may compare
> This prifon where I liue, vnto the world:

In the next image the Keeper speaks of Henry by this title, but
Richard's retort pointedly calls him mere "Henry of Lancaster",
which was his name even before he styled himself (against the King's
law) "Duke of Lancaster", let alone "King". The questions of identity
are being worked out in the terminology of both dialogue and non-
dialogue.

> *Keeper* My Lord I dare not, fir Pierce of Exton,
> Who lately came from the King commaunds the contrary
> *Rich.* The diuell take Henry of Lancafter, and thee,
> Patience is ftale, and I am wearie of it.
> *Keeper* Help,help,help.
>   *The murderers rufh in.*
> *Rich.* How now,what meanes Death in this rude affault?
> Villaine, thy owne hand yeelds thy deaths inftrument,
> Go thou and fill another roome in hell.
>   *Here Exton ftrikes him downe.*
> *Rich.* That hand fhall burne in neuer quenching fire,
> That ftaggers thus my perfon : Exton,thy fierce hand
> Hath with the kings bloud ftaind the kings owne land.
> Mount mount my foule,thy feate is vp on high,
> Whilft my groffe flefh finckes downeward here to die,
> *Exton* As full of valure as of royall bloud:

Although the usurper had been crowned "King Henry" and had
spoken under that name before Richard's death, his next and last
appearance (5.3) is ushered in with the stage-direction name of
"*Bullingbroke*", as though his kingship were no more firmly established than Richard's was at Flint Castle. Paradoxically, however, now
that his rival is dead, his prefix is plain "*King.*" rather than "*King
Henry*", as it was when he had just been crowned. Now, Richard's

majesty and the slipperiness of Henry's kingship are scarcely critical
novelties, nor are they discernible through the non-dialogue names
alone. I'm still not that crazy. And that is not the issue; for artistic
communication often contains redundancy. My point· is that to
eliminate any of it is to alter the structure of aesthetic meaning.

It is not unlikely that the variations of title and name in stage
direction and speech prefix reflect to some degree the layering of the
composition of the text; in essaying to read them as allegory of the
dialogue, I have tried to show that they can function well enough on
that level too. But editing is about not leaving well enough alone. In
normalizing the titles and names it finds in its copytext, the New
Penguin edition (to take the nearest to hand) makes an exact demarca-
tion of where the hero loses "King". When summoned before Bolingbroke's court in the modern edition's 4.1, he is named only "Richard"
in direction and in prefix, and the title "King" never reappears. Meanwhile the antagonist continues as "Bolingbroke" in directions and
prefixes; but in his next appearance the editor introduces him like
this—"*Enter Bolingbroke, now King Henry*"—and his prefix changes to
KING HENRY, and so to the end. The modern edition does not reflect
the coming and going of the regal title in the copytext, as in his last
entrance in Q as "*Bolingbroke*", not as "*King*".[29] The editor's allegory of political change has forced itself on the text.

The unobtrusive editorial tour de force may at first glance seem
comnonsense—enough so not to quibble with—but not after we see

29. As is done in a few earlier editions, the New Penguin editor also changes the stage-
direction and speech-prefix name of the Queen to "Queen Isabella". This change is not
sanctioned by anything in the Q text, either in or out of dialogue. Instead it depends on
history—or, more accurately, on an editorial association of history with the fictional
meeting dramatized in the play. This *was* the name of Richard's second queen, but as she
was a mere girl at the time of her husband's death, Shakespeare seems imaginatively to
have infused her with the maturity of the late Anne of Bohemia, as Daniel had done, in
his *Civile Wars*, 1595. Now, we saw that the editor specifically marked the transfer of
political power from Richard, by removing the epithet "King" from the non-dialogue
naming at the start of the deposition scene. It may strike us, then, that the editor's
having given Richard's wife a personal name (along with the title that Shake-speare gave
her) sets him up to strip away her QUEEN when she meets him after the deposition, and
still leave her with *something*, ISABELLA, for a prefix; and thereby to make symmetrical his
allegory: an Isabella for a Richard. But no, she continues to be QUEEN ISABELLA. And so
the editor's alteration of Shakespear's naming of his characters allegorizes regal power
for the reader, but does not allegorize consistently. He is as bad as Shakespeare—in a
regular sort of way.

There is an unlikely chance, of course, that Shakespeare did not call her "Isabella"
because he did not know the name of Richard's wife at the time of the deposition, or did
not know that he married twice, though Holinshed (who calls the new bride "yong
Isabel", but "The Queen" after she is crowned) is clear on both issues, and though
Daniel calls her "Queen Isabel" (and refers to her husband as the King during their

how other editors juggle the names, for not all of them give this solution to the alleged problem. In some editions the speech-prefix designations of the antagonists are *Richard* and *Bolingbroke* throughout. But others offer *King Richard* and *Bolingbroke* throughout. Thi sedition curtails Richard's *King* before the deposition scene, that after. Often, *Bolingbroke* becomes *King Henry* in 5.3 in his first appearance after this scene; but sometimes this title is subsequently shortened (as it is in Q) to mere *King* after Richard has been murdered. Here is an edition that not only has *King Richard* throughout, but also changes *Bolingbroke* to *King Henry* at the usual place; and so has two simultaneous *Kings* toward the end of the play. (England's tragedy is that it has two kings.) It thus presents a complete contrast to the New Penguin edition, where there is never more than one *King*, and, at one point, the deposition in 4.1, no *King* (England's tragedy is that it has no king.)—and so goes beyond the evidence of Q, which finally stops Richard's *King* in 5.1 before it starts Henry's in 5.3.

From the Machiavellian perspective the editor's two simultaneous *Kings* may seem risible in a monarchy, like the prefixes "Hen. 4." and "Hen. 5." in *The Famous Victories of Henry V* (1598) when the King and the uncrowned Prince speak with each other passionately as father and son. But from a medieval and renaissance perspective the simultaneous *Kings* may indeed be apt. I'll take a moment to defend this editorial normalization here, not because I believe in editors' prosaic licence, but to argue that, if one's change is as reasonable as an other's but they issue in contradictory allegories, it is best to leave the original alone—to put up with the paradoxical single text from which partial consistencies in separate editions can be derived.

(*Counsel rise*)

The Tour de Farce

The defence, My Lord, could begin with internal evidence, for we saw a moment ago that Exton speaks of both Richard and Henry as kings, and that each cousin deems himself a king. But the external evidence—the more unfamiliar—may be more compelling. I'm think-

meeting); or because, though he likely knew there were two marriages, Shakespere sought by the general title, "Queen", to avoid the embarrassment or the irrelevance of specifying by personal name the dead one or the child, when he was after a type. And there is a good chance that Shakspear's continuing to call her *"Queene"* after the deposition, and his also calling the hero first *"Richard"* and then, after her regal challenge to him, *"King"*, registers Shakespeare's own allegorical interpretation—even *direction*—of the play. In some aspects his allegory seems as inconsistent as the editor's, in an irregular sort of way. Shakefpeare is, however, the one we came to read.

ing of one of Shakespear's sources, where we can see how Holinshed and his redactors in the 1587 edition styled these adversaries. Some proofsheets from this work survive and show that naming received its share of corrections—if that is quite the right term for it, as here, at the end of the history of Edward III, who was Richard's grandfather and immediate predecessor. (Exhibits A, B, etc.)

Thus farre Edward the third, sonne to Edward the second, and Philip the faire.

The corrector calls for the addition of

"Isabel y̆ the daughter [. . .]

(the end of the line is trimmed off) before *"Philip the faire"*, but the final version prints *"queene Isabell"* instead of *"Philip the faire"*. (There was likely another stage of proof that cleared up the confusion of Edward's wife and his mother.)

Thus farre Edward the third, sonne to Edward the second and queene Isabell.

Slightly lower on the page the section on Richard 2 begins; we note that the corrector was attentive to the types that identify his father as "Edward prince of wales", but let stand the marginal note (lower right) that calls "prince" Richard "K[ing] Richard."

Richard the ſecond, the ſecond
ſonne to Edward prince of wales.

 Richard, the ſecond of that name, and ſonne to prince Edward, called the blacke prince, the ſonne of king Edward the third, a child of the age of eleuen yeares, began to reigne ouer the realme of England the tenth daie tith daie of June, in the yeare of the world 5344, of our Lord 1377, after the conqueſt 310, about the two and thirtith yeare of the emperour Charles the fourth, and in the fourteenth yeare of Charles the fift king of France, and about the ſeuenth yeare of the reigne of Robert the ſecond king of Scotland: he was named Richard of Burdeaux, bicauſe he was borne at Burdeaux in Gaſcoigne, whileſt his father ruled there. The daie before it was vnderſtood, that his grandfather king Edward was departed this life, being the one and twentith of June (on which daie neuertheleſſe he deceaſſed) the citizens of London hauing certeine knowledge that he could not eſcape his ſickneſſe, ſent certeine aldermen vnto Kingſton, where the prince with his mother the prin-ceſſe then laie, to declare vnto the ſaid prince their reſolute good wils, to accept him for their lawfull king and gouernour, immediatlie after it ſhould pleaſe God to call to his mercie his grandfather, being now paſt hope of recouerie of health. Whereſuppon they beſught

eg. 1.
'7

Thom. Walſ.

The London-ers ſent to R. Richerd, commending themſelues to his fauour be-cauſe of death of K. Edward.

B. q 4.

146

The self-articulation of the text in sub-generic strands of narrative and gloss is structurally reminiscent of those strands in drama—of dialogue and prefix. (Indeed, Holinshed does use marginal notes elsewhere as speech tags.[30]) And, as before, the differentiation of naming in the text opens up a dialectical approach to character.

As we read on over the bottom of the Holinshed page, we see that the discrepancy of "Prince" and "King" is actually taken up in the narrative.

147

As his predecessor's death came earlier than expected, Richard entertained London's delegation to its future King as their Prince of Wales, though he had unwittingly already become their sovereign. Richard's kingship was equivocal from beginning to end.

Indeed, from the moment of Prince Richard's birth, when he was not then, because of his older brother, the heir apparent, Holinshed's glosses always call him "King". More to the immediate point, his narrative and gloss call him "King" after his deposition, even after Henry's coronation.

Now back to Fakespeare. Though all the various editorial stylings of speech prefix do distort Shakspeare's quarto text, this editor's arbitrary styling of two simultaneous *Kings*, though it may seem odd in this court, My Lord, given its constitutional absurdity—er, not the court's, My Lord, the simultaneous *Kings*'—does curiously jibe with Shakspeare's source, and may be intuitively pre-Machiavellian. It may be the editor's way of specifying the tragic paradox. It may simply be arbitrary. It may be absurd. It may be risible, even laughable (or funny). It may simply be as ridiculous as it seems, for it remains but a partial interpretation of the earliest text, which it rumours, and not the whole text itself.

In contrast to Holinshed's gloss on Richard's birth, his adversary's goes unrecorded; as he climbs the ladder of success, he appears before us—now Hereford, now Derby (the spelling of which the corrector alters from "Darby"), now Lancaster, now King—his unprophetically updated marginal glosses keeping generally steady pace with his progress in rank: A VOICE FROM THE STREET, THE VOICE OUTSIDE, *A Suffraget, The Suffraget:* BALSQUITH! (For Holinshed, some are born Kings, some have kingship thrust upon them.)

In Holinshed's narrative and gloss the subtleties of the various fixes on Bolingbroke as Hereford he Darby approaches Lancaster and King gains the throne offer fascinating study in cubist (oh, I used that

---

30. I am indebted to Randy MacLeod for pointing out the structural similarities of subgeneric strands in the play and its source. Prof. MacLeod is preparing a bibliographic study of the proofsheets, in the collection of the Huntington Library.

For glosses as speech tags, see "The order of the araigne-/mente of Sir Nicholas Throcke-/morton Knight, in The Guild Hall of London the seuententh day of April, 1554. expressed in a Dialogue for the better vnderstanding of e-/uery mans parte" in the Queen Mary section of Holinshed's *Chronicles*, Vol. 3, (1587) pp. 1737-41. I call them tags rather than *prefixes* because, for the right-hand columns on each double-columned page, they appear in the margin to the right of the first line of the speech. My thanks again to the Huntington's Librarian, Daniel H. Woodward, for permission to photoquote from Holinshed.

before)—in *dynamic* perspective, then, which I'll have to pass over here for the main point, and so conclude. *(Pause. Then comes to point)*. When the Shakespeare editor drops Richard's *King* he allegorizes fickle politics; when Holinshed retains it he recognizes abiding royalty, a kingliness that cannot be stripped off like a crown. The general point in Holinshed or in Shakespear seems not to be kingliness as our secular and constitutional age conceives it. To listen to King/Richard refer to the thousand angels that lacky him or to his comparison of Himself with Christ is to hear the interpenetrating notes of politics and theology that we associate with the Divine Right of Kings—an idea current not only before Shakspeare's birth but also after his death, though it is alien to ours. We live in an age when editors may (properly) pride themselves on the fidelity of their texts. But, specifically, for editors to reorganize the trustwordy nomenclature of Shakespeare's non-dialogue names, as if they were mere paragraphia, is to disorganize art. It is an activity especially inappropriate in an Einsteinian age, which has triumphantly comprehended the interaction of the frame of reference with the object observed.

Q.E.D., my Lord. *Quod eros demonsterandom.*

(Sudden applause. Def. rests)

FINIS.

As it happens, the New Penguin edition was the basis of the prompt-book for John Barton's controversial production in the mid 1970s, in which Pasco and Richardson alternated the roles of Richard and Henry.[31] Barton added very theatrical opening and closing scenes, which brought Shakespear on stage in a mask based on the Droeshout icon. In the first scene he carried the promptbook for the ensuing production, and Pasco and Richardson in rehearsal costumes held the crown between them in a freeze, until Shakespeare chose one actor to play king for that performance; now in regal robes, he read his opening line from Shake-speare's book, and so assumed his

---

31. This production is discussed at length in Stanley Wells, *Royal Shakespeare: Four Major Productions at Stratford-upon-Avon* (Manchester University Press, 1977), pp. 54-81. I am indebted to John Barton, the director of this production, and to the Governors of the Royal Shakespeare Theatre, and to Penguin Books, holders of the copyrights to the illustrations, which they have kindly allowed to be reproduced here. I wish to thank as well Dr. Levi Fox, Director of the Shakespeare Centre Stratford-upon-Avon, where the book is housed, for his help in securing permission of the director and the Governors.

character.[32] When I spoke of Shaw, it was clear that he and his books had to leave the stage to the actors before the curtain rose on opening night. In this *Richard 2*, however, the presence of the author with his book, and of the actors unadorned by their roles, force the question of dramaturgic criticism for the performance from the outset. In the deposition scene, for example, when Bolingbroke and Richard grasp the crown between them, and debate who will "play the king," the audience must recall the prefigurement, actors standing before Shakespeare and vying for the crown; and so it is particularly attuned to the notion of the interchangeability of these two roles and to the idea that these characters' modes of behaviour are precisely that, roles.

Usually to look at a promptbook we have to go backstage. Now we'll just leap over the footlights. Come on. In this promptbook—Oh, thank you, Sir (We are now looking over His Majesty's shoulder.)—it is striking how artists in the theatre dehomogenize and denormalize the edited text, and restore it to a state of artistic chaos analogous to that of the editor's sources in the quartos and folio, and of Shakespeare's in Holinshed. By attending particularly to the names written into the promptbook, we will glimpse some of the practical language that mediates script and performance.

What first struck me about the Barton book is that it did away with the editorial numbering of acts and scenes. Such numbing is not to be found in the copytext, Q1, but is lifted almost intact from the Folio. The promptbook numbers and letters all the scenes or episodes in continuous sequence (with a notable exception to be mentioned in a moment); it also gives these new units names. The following list of numbers, letters and names is gathered from their scattered locations in the promptbook. Almost identical information is found coherently as tabs at the side of the book. (A later Barton promptbook, for the London run at the Aldwych, is like the Stratford book in both these structural respects.)

32. Most of these details are from the designer's account of the production: Timothy O'Brien, "Designing a Shakespeare Play: *Richard II*," *Shakespeare Jahrbuch* (West), (1974), pp. 111-20, p. 116. The detail of rehearsal costumes is Wells's (pp. 75-76); he regarded the book carried by Shakespeare as "a book resembling his First Folio" (p. 75); O'Brien calls it "the promptbook," which is also Peter Thomson's term in his review, "Shakespeare's Straight and Crooked: A Review of the 1973 Season at Stratford," *Shakespeare Survey*, 27 (1974), 143-54, 152. Whatever it *looks* like, of course, it *functions* as the promptbook—though I don't for a moment suppose that it really was one for anything more than the first line, if even for that. It may have been an anti-promptbook: there is a wicked tradition of impractical jokes in the theatre—of writing fake messages in letters and books that are used as props. (You can surely imagine some choice ones.)

New Penguin	Stratford Promptbook	
1.1	sc.1	Opening.
1.2	sc 2.	D of Glouc.
1.3	3	Lists
	a)	Tournament.
	3b.	Banishment.
	3c.	Farewell.
1.4	4.	Caterpillars.
2.1	5.	Death of Gaunt. a) 2 brothers.
	5b.	
		Exposure.
	5c.	York & Richard.
	5d.	
		The Barons.
2.2		1st Garden a) The Queen.
	6b.	Rebellion.
	6c	
		Politicians.
2.3	7.	Bollingbroke's Return.
	a)	
	1b.	Lords
		in Arms.
	7c	Bol. & York
2.4	8.	Welsh Captain.
3.1	9.	Bristol.
3.2	10.	Return from Ireland.
3.3	11.	Flint Castle. a) Approaches.
	b)	Battlements.
	c)	Base Court.

[. . . . . INTERVAL . . . .]

3.4	12.	2nd Garden a) 3 Ladies.
	b	3 Gardeners
	c)	Gardeners & the Queen.
4.1	13.	Deposition a) Gage throwing.
	b)	Carlisle
	c	Deposition.
	d	Abbot of
		Westminster

151

5.1	14.	Tower a) lament.
	b)	K & Queen. [Aldwych =
		R & Queen]
5.2	15	3rd Garden a) York at home
	b)	Aumerle.
5.3 [F=5.3]	16	Bolingbroke's study. a) Hal.
	b)	Kneeling.
5.4 [F=5.3]	16c)	Exton.
5.5 [F=5.4]	17	Pomfret castle
	a)	Soliloquy.
	17 b)	Groom.
	17 c	Murder.
5.6 [F=5.5])	sc. 18.	
		Last.

Barton's first and concluding scenes are named ordinally, "Opening" (discussed above) and "Last," (discussed below); but the intermediate divisions of Shakspeare's text are given thematic names. Many of these duplicate vocabulary from the dialogue: "Lists" (3), "Banishment" (3b), "Farewell" (3c), "Caterpillars" (4). But some are not found in Shakespere: "Tournament" (3/a)), "Exposure" (5b), "The Barons" (5d), "Politicians" (6c), "Deposition" (13), "Bolingbroke's study. a) Hal" (16), "Soliloquy" (17/a))— and these terms written onto the promptbook suggest specifically the attitudes and the means of production. The editor took care to number nineteen scenes within five acts, but the director restructures half of these scenes into episodes, each with its own name; and he ignores act divisions. (His interval falls in the middle of the Folio's (and the editor's) Act 3.) And on one occasion the editor's distinct scenes, 5.3 and 5.4, are combined as one new scene, number sixteen. (One *old* scene, in fact, as they count as one scene in the Folio.) The promptbook titles mention "Richard" (5c) while he is still King, and "Bolingbroke" (16) after he has become King Henry. And we hear of "K & Queen" when the deposed monarch is on his way to Pomfret (14/b)). This moment, of course, was the occasion in Q when the *"King"* speech prefix reasserted itself after the entrance direction and prefix had referred to mere *"Richard"*.[33] As the promptbook never refers to the Queen as "Isabella", the editor's "historicizing" seems to go for

---

33. When the promptbook was prepared for Barton's Aldwych revival, however, it read "R & Queen" here, and so dropped the "K".

naught. (The name did make its way to the audience, however, in the cast list in the program, which was drawn up, I imagine, from the editorial *dramatis personae*.)

One of the lessons of all this is that the editorial care to separate and number the scenes and acts organizes the dramatic text in a way foreign to its author and first printers, and which may be so to producers of the play, both in Shakspear's day and in ours. The same can be said with regard to the precise naming and changing of titles that busies editors. Like Shakespear, the players have fluid means of reference, which are not merely inconsistent (though they may be so), but which can also measure the pulse of the work of art.

This pulsometry can best be suggested by a quick tour through the promptbook. (I mean quick, so hold on to your stethoscope.) Here on page 78 is a typical example of shifting names in which it is hard

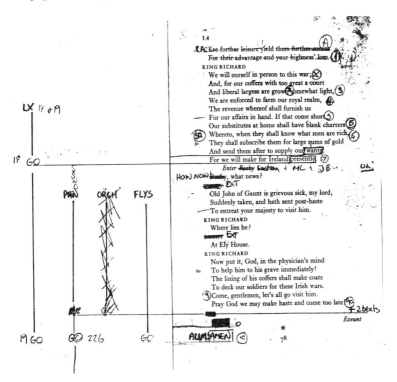

to detect a symbolic meaning. The printed prefixes read KING RICHARD — but on the facing notes we see a consistent shift from "K." (in notes

(X) IR DS is closed)

(A) DP takes helmet   (1½) IR stands

: IR

(1) K. (takes helmet, placks
IR   Plume & gives it back to WG.

(2) King opens crest.

(3) Shuts chest.) DP

(4) Move in. -Bushy takes book to K.   ) DS , rise?

(5) Rich tears page out of bk.   (5a) Opens book Bushy

(5a) Dictates to Bushy.

(6) Rich sits.) (7) DP

(7) Ext MC enter UR. JB ent. L Pros. ed.
                                    IR exits

(9) Move DS.   RA   LM   EX.   AU   ME
    MC & JB etc to chest to L Pros

(11) Rich ex E Pros.

(12) AU follow to R. Pros.
     Bushy leaves bk DC.

1 and 4) to "Rich" (in 5 and 9a). The role is otherwise designated
"R"—or "IR" or "DP" (the initials of Barton's Richards).

Page 119 ends one line before the interval, and the prompter has
carried the last speech back from overleaf to the bottom of this page.
Again he does not use the editor's KING RICHARD— but "RICHARD"
instead. This occasion *is* auspicious, as the editor will himself drop
KING from all of Richard's subsequent speeches. The (deleted) exit
cues also call him "Rich[ard]", but the two lighting cues call him
"K[ing]".[34]

---

34. In these promptnotes there may be several hands at work over an extended period.
As my thesis concerns the confusion of naming in the document, I will not attempt an
analysis of the hands, instructive as that would prove (if it could be done thoroughly) in
ascribing patterns of consistency and variation over time and over text to each annotator. For convenience I speak of the prompter in the singular, and differentiate him (for
want of evidence) from the director.

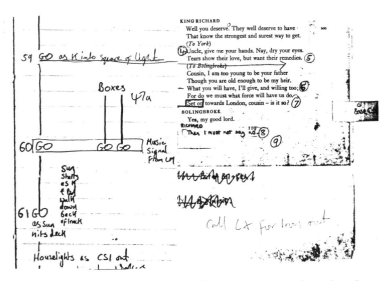

By page 130 we have come to the deposition scene, where the editor has ceased to use the KING— but "K's entrance" is written beside

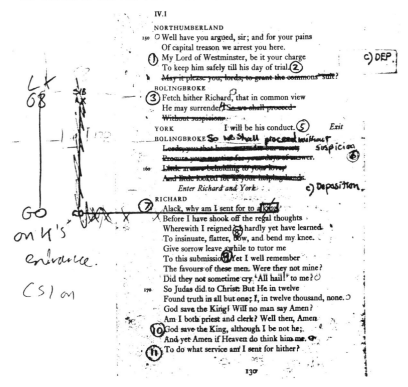

RICHARD's first lines, and the relevant prompt notes facing this page (numbers 7-11) also refer only to "K.". On the next page comes the

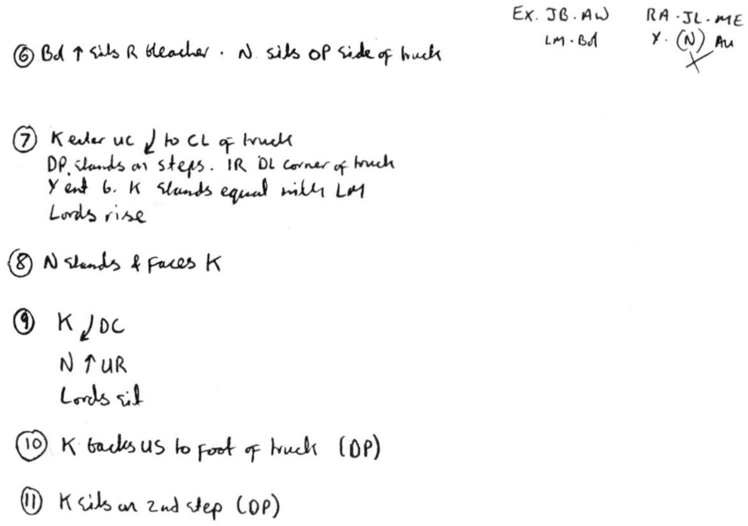

Ex. JB · AW RA · JL · ME
LM · Bd   Y · (N) Au
                    X

⑥ Bd ↑ sits R bleacher · N sits OP side of truck

⑦ K enter uc ↙ to CL of truck
DP. stands on steps. IR DL corner of truck
Y ent 6. K stands equal with LM
Lords rise

⑧ N stands & faces K

⑨ K ↙ DC
N ↑ UR
Lords sit

⑩ K backs US to foot of truck (DP)

⑪ K sits on 2nd step (OP)

moment when the adversaries hold the crown between them, at number 5. At number 6 the King (at least Pasco's King) lets go and

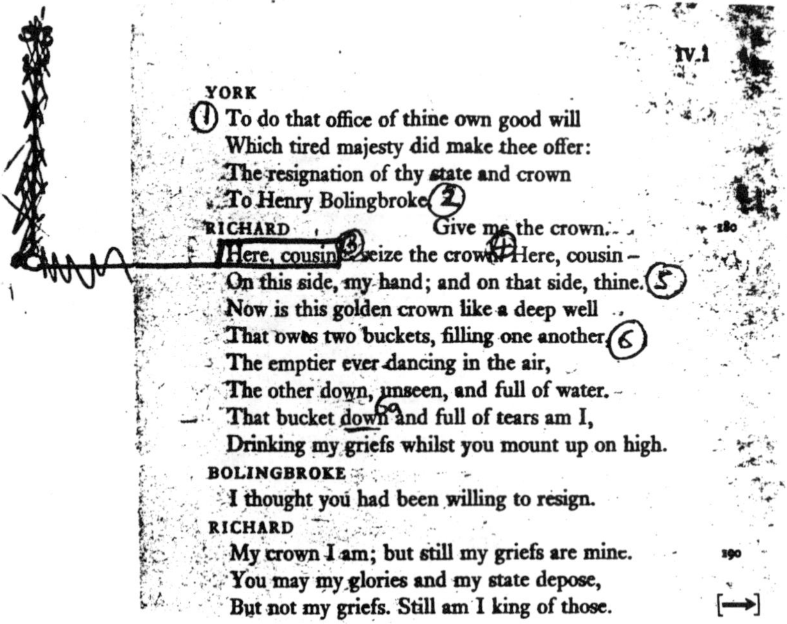

IV.1

YORK
① To do that office of thine own good will
Which tired majesty did make thee offer:
The resignation of thy state and crown
To Henry Bolingbroke ②

RICHARD   Give me the crown. ③
Here, cousin ③ seize the crown ④ Here, cousin –
On this side, my hand; and on that side, thine. ⑤
Now is this golden crown like a deep well
That owes two buckets, filling one another ⑥
The emptier ever dancing in the air,
The other down, unseen, and full of water.
That bucket down and full of tears am I,
Drinking my griefs whilst you mount up on high.

BOLINGBROKE
I thought you had been willing to resign.

RICHARD
My crown I am; but still my griefs are mine.   190
You may my glories and my state depose,
But not my griefs. Still am I king of those.   [→]

BOLINGBROKE
Part of your cares you give me with your crown.

RICHARD
Your cares set up do not pluck my cares down. (66)
My care is loss of care by old care done;
Your care is gain of care by new care won.
The cares I give, I have, though given away.
They 'tend the crown, yet still with me they stay.

BOLINGBROKE
Are you contented to resign the crown?

RICHARD (7)
Ay, no. No, ay; for I must nothing be,   200
Therefore no no, for I resign to thee. (8)

131

kneels, though he is still called "K.", as he is in all preceding references
on this page. But when he stands again, and takes back the crown from
Bolingbroke (number 7) and makes *him* kneel, his prompt name shifts
to mere "Rich".

① Y onto truck behind throne.

② K stands (DP) ↑ up steps. Gets crown.

③ Bol stands & slowly DS.
   N stands UL of truck.

④ K & DC leads Bol down.
   N to C w bleachers   Lm takes cloak from N C
   LM "

⑤ K puts Bol's hand on crown.

⑥ K lets go crown (DP)

⑥ₐ K kneels (1R) +

⑥ᵦ K stands (1R)

              (cloak)
              LM   N
              [Y]
              Bol. K.

⑦ Rich takes crown back

⑧ Rich gestures Bol to kneel DC
   Bol kneels facing US.
   8d.) K

157

If we are looking for symbolic meaning in shifts of name, this may seem paradoxical—that he should submit as "king", but reclaim his crown as "Richard". And, indeed, it is paradoxical; but it may also be right to recall that his text lines (overleaf) are

> Now mark me how I will undo myself.
> I give this heavy weight from off my head.

—and so he rises only to uncrown himself formally, to be monarch of his own deposition. The prompter may be symbolizing a change in status just as the editor and Shakespeare had done—only in a different place and with less conscious intent. (To keep ourselves guessing, though, we should note that the maps at 7 and 8 call him "K".)

Here on page 138 is the episode named "King & Queen", for which the prompt notes are decisively "King".

① Richardson kneels. Takes mirror off

② Pasco kneels.

③ Head onto lap.

④ Ross + Will pull King's arms.

⑤ Qu holds King's waist

You'll recall that the first quarto reinstituted the "*King*" prefix in this dignified but powerless encounter of King and Queen. The editor, however, has decided to signal the fall from power, and uses only RICHARD.

What of his rival? On page 145 the director has interjected some lines from *2 Henry 4*, and named the episode "Bolingbroke's study."[35]

35. Thomson's review, p. 154, states that the program pointed out that 500 lines in *Richard 2* were cut and 20 lines imported from *2 Henry 4* to give extra body to the role of Bolingbroke. Wells states: "the suggestion of equivalence between Richard and Bolingbroke which Mr. Barton's production undoubtedly gave required the importation of lines from *2 Henry IV* and the transference of an important passage in *Richard II* to Bolingbroke from another character" (p. 75).

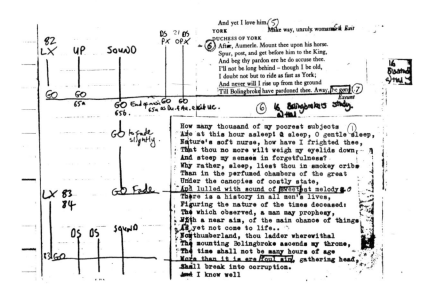

The term "Bolingbroke" is not appropriate to *2 Henry 4*; it likely derives from *Richard 2*—either from the last line of the preceding scene, for he is not completely "King" to the Duchess of York, or from the recollection of Richard's prophecy (five lines from bottom) or selectively from the editor's stage direction (which is obscured here): "*Enter Bolingbroke, now King Henry, with Harry Percy and other lords*." The promptbook annotator seems not to have cared for the editor's synthesis of Q ("*Enter the King with his nobles.*") and F ("*Enter Bullingbrooke, Percie, and other Lords.*"), though he may have derived his "Bolingbroke" from the editor's direction.

When the dialogue continues overleaf, the "Bol:" prefix is used, which, again, cannot derive from *2 Henry 4*. When the hand- and typewritten passage stop, the KING HENRY prefix resumes.

In the middle of this page we see that the prefix PERCY (in its first use only) has been crossed out, and "Hots" substituted for it. At the bottom of the illustration the end of King Henry's speech is assigned to HOTS:, and this is the only name for this character in the prompt notation. Now, "Hotspur" is indeed another name for this Percy, but it is not a name that occurs in *Richard 2*; it is found instead in the *Henry 4* plays, from the second of which the typewritten text pasted in at the top of the page derives. The use of it here in prefix and in dialogue runs counter to the editor's name in direction and in prefix, one example of which is allowed to stand (1. 16). (In the Aldwych book neither

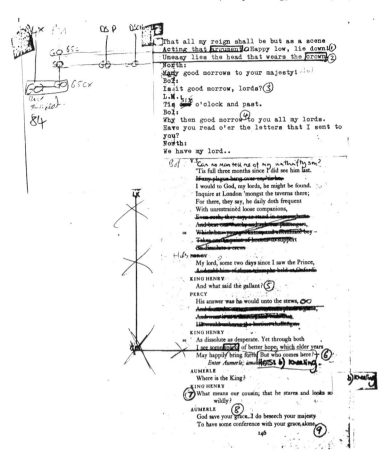

That all my reign shall be but as a scene
Acting that argument. Happy low, lie down! (1)
Uneasy lies the head that wears the crown. (2)
North:
Many good morrows to your majesty!
Bol:
Is it good morrow, lords? (3)
L.M.:
Tis one o'clock and past.
Bol:
Why then good morrow to you all my lords. (4)
Have you read o'er the letters that I sent to
you?
North:
We have my lord..

Bol. Can no man tell me of my unthrifty son?
'Tis full three months since I did see him last.
If any plague hang over us, 'tis he.
I would to God, my lords, he might be found.
Inquire at London 'mongst the taverns there;
For there, they say, he daily doth frequent
With unrestrained loose companions,
Even such they say as stand in narrow lanes
And beat our watch and rob our passengers,
Which he, young wanton and effeminate boy –
Takes on the point of honour to support
So dissolute a crew.

My lord, some two days since I saw the Prince,
And told him of those triumphs held at Oxford.

KING HENRY
And what said the gallant? (5)
PERCY
His answer was he would unto the stews, OO
And from the common'st creature pluck a glove,
And wear it as a favour; and with that
He would unhorse the lustiest challenger.

KING HENRY
As dissolute as desperate. Yet through both
I see some sparks of better hope; which elder years
May happily bring forth. But who comes here? (6)
Enter Aumerle; and HOTS b) kneeling.

AUMERLE
Where is the King?
KING HENRY
(7) What means our cousin; that he stares and looks so
wildly?
AUMERLE
(8) God save your grace. I do beseech your majesty
To have some conference with your grace, alone. (9)
146

printed prefix is altered—though HOTS is still used to reassign the
sentence at the end of King Henry's dialogue.) The prompt notes for
this page are quite clear. The monarch is refered to only by "Bol" or
by actors' initials—never by "King", though later in this scene, while
we still find "Bol." in promptnotes, there is a "K" in a map. Also in

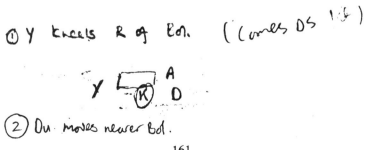

this scene Barton has "Bol" echo one of the Duchess's lines ("That sets the word itself against the word."), though as before the editor's prefix (where the typewriting ends) is KING HENRY (and the map refers only to "Bol").

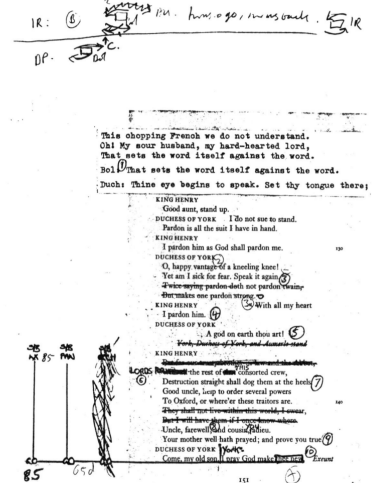

In this production the role of the Groom who visits the jailed Richard in 5.5 (F=5.4), and who is ironically saluted by him as "noble peer", was assigned inventively to Richard's antagonist—a noble peer indeed. The two cousins met in prison, and in a ritualistic scene looked at each other through the frame of the mirror that Richard had smashed during the deposition scene. In the prompter's terminology they look at each other not as King and King, nor as Richard and Henry, nor as Richard and King Henry . . . , but rather as King and Bolingbroke.

Like the coronation of Charles in *Saint Joan*, that of Bulingbroke in *Richard 2* is an off-stage event. We register them both as facts, but not as emotions. But the decoronation of Richard, by contrast, is the emotional centre of the play, and though it removes him from the English throne, it may crown him paradoxically as king of our hearts, or, as he says, king of his griefs. The prompter's terminology in Barton's staging of the "Groom." scene seems to reflect this relative estimation of the two cousins' kingliness, and one may feel it is truer to the fluid contrasts of the two roles that are reflected by the varying prefixes of the quarto than are the editorial normalizations.

On page 154 we see the GROOM prefix crossed out, and that of BOL: (not KING) substituted.

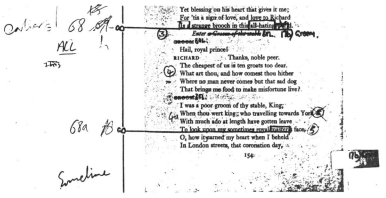

"Bol" is also used in the facing prompt note #3, where significantly "K" means "King Richard". Here and on the next pages of notes

"Rich" and sometimes "K" designate the one character; but "K" never denotes the other. And when finally (on page 156) the hero is lifted in the air and murdered, "K" appears twice, just to the left of his last speech (one-third from bottom) "GO as K to highest point" and (below it, to the left) "GO Keening out as K Down". Barton's Richard is a king, if not to the end, at least at the end.

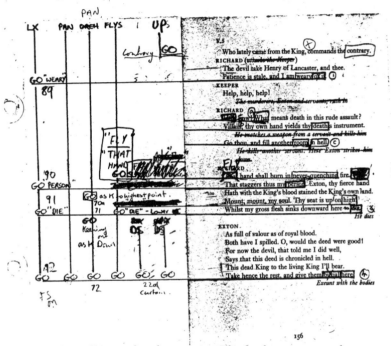

But what of his rival and successor? The final scene interpolates text from *1 Henry 4*. Perhaps the prefix, "Henry:", added in typescript at the top of page 157, betrays the edition used. In any case, it runs against New Penguin usage: KING HENRY. Now, the first four lines of the first speech are actually from the beginning of this scene, as we would see if we could lift up the typewritten paper; but the subsequent three lines of this speech (and the next speech of York's) are from *2 Henry 4*. When the typewritten passage ends, the first printed line visible is the last in the original opening speech of the scene in *Richard 2*, a speech assigned to KING HENRY. As that prefix is obscured by the paste-up, a new prefix was called for, and we find the handwritten "BOL:", with no attempt to smooth it into the typescript "Henry:" above, or the printed KING HENRY below. (In the middle of the page (just after number 3) we also see more of "Hots" in direction and

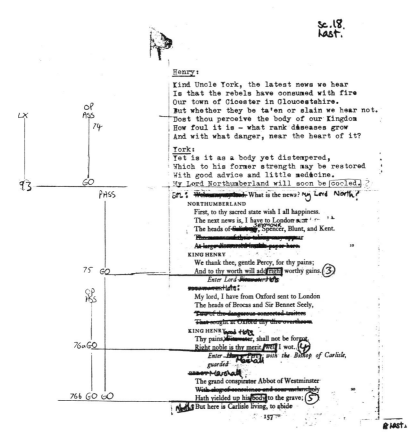

prefixes, and in the dialogue added to King Henry's speech (number 4). Again, Hotspur is not a character so named in the quartos, folios or the New Penguin edition of *Richard 2*, which all refer to him as "Percy".)

On the verso of the final leaf we witness another ritual episode, "Crowning Sequence" (eight lines down), of the director's invention,

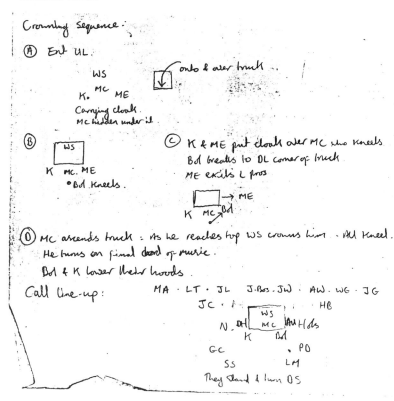

Crowning sequence:

(A) Ent UL.

WS
K. MC ME
Carrying cloak.
MC hidden under it.

onto & over truck

(B)
WS
K MC. ME
• Bol kneels.

(C) K & ME put cloak over MC who kneels
Bol breaks to DL corner of truck
ME exits L pros

WS
K MC Bol → ME

(D) MC ascends truck: As he reaches top WS crowns him. All kneel.
He turns on final chord of music.
Bol & K lower their hoods.

Call line-up: MA · LT · JL   J.Bos. JW · AW· WG · JG
JC · M   HB
N. DH WS MC AW H(ols
K Bol
GC   • PO
SS   LM
They stand & turn OS

and added to scene "Last." "WS" (in the box by "B") indicates
Shakspere, who crowns—not King Richard, not King Henry—but
King Death, as the audience discovers to its surprise. ("MC" are the
initials of the actor who plays this King of Kings.) The only point I
wish to make about the annotations here is that they are of a piece with
the scene in which "Bolingbroke" took the role of the Groom, and the
dying Richard was called "King" in the prompt notes. Similarly, in the
prompt notes for the interment (top of the ms page), we hear only
of "Bol", not of "King Henry". In the crowning of Death, "K" is
reserved for Richard, and "Bol" is the name of his rival, a distinction
that persists even into the call line-up at the bottom of the page. This
all suggests to me that when the antagonists are on the stage together
the one may be named "King Richard", "King", or "Richard", but
the other is always "Bolingbroke" and never "King" or "King
Henry". In the varying names of both the quarto and this production
the sun king outshines his usurper. Quite against the logic which
activates the editorial normalizations, the King of this play is para-

doxically himself and not himself; his double nature has a double name.

But whatever potential for allegorical meaning I may see in the shifting prompt names, I wish to stress, in closing, their existence before their essence. They are there, they are part of the theatre text, and they are like the shifting names in the early textual authorities, and quite unlike the orderly edited version, on which the prompter has written and pasted to create (and restore) fertile confusion. The varying names graphically show layering in the scripting and shifts in directorial interpretation, not only in the sense of the evolution of the production in rehearsal, but also of the episodic discontinuities in the work as it was performed.

Most importantly, Barton's promptbook is confused and incomplete and inconsistent in the ways a practical promptbook is not in theory supposed to be. If such a book had gone to the printers on January 13 at the turn of the seventeenth century, and if modern scholars were given the printed quarto to analyse, would they not assure us that what underlay the printed version was in part either foul papers (because of the speech-prefix irregularities), or a memorial reconstruction (because of its corrupted and transposed lines and its borrowings from other plays)? I doubt if anyone would think it derived from a promptbook, because, as we are told, promptbooks must, for practical reasons, be neat and consistent, must aim toward the kind of text in Greg's RULE I. Compared to Barton's promptbook, however, Shakespeare's quarto text is as clean if not cleaner. This fact suggests that the manuscript behind that quarto (from which its variant names seem to have derived) could easily have served as a promptbook; and that if it did, its authorial inconsistencies may have made their mark on the players or expressed their wavering sense of the King who was not quite himself. We've come full circle, and it's time to get off.

I began with Shaw because he is one of our greatest dramatic writers, because there is an abundance of textual and contextual evidence about him and his works, and especially because we are not allowed by law to take a patronizing attitude towards his text. Its variant naming out of the dialogue mirrors uncannily those anarchic aspects of early Shakespeer printings which our editorical tradition has been systematically purging and normalizing since Rowe in 1709. This form of editorial behaviour sets an aesthetic but unartistic Standard above art, and is part of a perverse tendency that perfects Shakspeare's text by

righting and rewriting it for him. In so doing it contrasts the dramaturgic to the Dramatic and to its editorial enshrinement. It disengages
artefacts from their creation and their recreation, and so, reifying
them, opens an abyss between normal and esthetic experience. Which
side are *you* on?

I intend (she said modestly) that "The Psychopathology of Every-
day Art" should put editors of Renaissance plays—and not only of
Renaissance plays—in the position of having to justify every one of
their normalizations of non-dialogue names, a position which does not
look very tenable, does it?—not least because it would force editors to
reveal that their acadumbic aesthetics flies in the face of Shakespere's
art and of the arts of his sources and of those who stage his plays.

> When I began to write,
> William was a divinity and a bore.
> Now he is a fellow creature.
> —George Shaw[36]

Iamque opus exaggeravi

---

36. From Shaw's "last review as a regular drama critic." Quoted from Edwin Wilson's
introduction to *Shaw on Shakespeare: An Anthology of Bernard Shaw's Writings on the
Plays and Production of Shakespeare* (New York, 1961), p. xvii.

"I Know You All": Possible Assaults upon and Invitations to the Audience by Shakespeare's Characters

HERBERT S. WEIL, Jr.

Some readers may feel troubled by my title. Are we confusing Shakespeare who wrote at the turn of the seventeenth century with Peter Handke who in the late 1960s wrote a short play that he called *Offending the Audience*?[1] No doubt there is a long way from *As You Like it* or *All's Well That Ends Well* to *Offending the Audience* and I have no desire to carry out the threat posed by Handke's title. Perhaps we can best escape offence if we quickly face some of the limitations of argument and of evidence intrinsic to my subject.

If we consider speeches by Shakespeare's characters that *may* (but need not) be delivered so as to address directly the individual spectator, we face at least two potential dangers. At one extreme, we risk restating the obvious when we look at such oft-studied conventions as the soliloquy, the aside, or the epilogue, when we observe a request for applause or imaginative sympathy, for tolerance or forgiveness. At the other extreme, we admittedly risk an anachronistic overemphasis through post-modern critical focus upon the creative role of the reader and the spectator. Now that we have frequent MLA lectures and seminars, Princeton and Johns Hopkins University Press anthologies, one, for example, with a lengthy 26-page annotated bibliography, and long historical surveys of the reader-spectator, we

---

1. Translated by Michael Roloff in *Kaspar and Other Plays* (New York, 1969).

are today less likely to miss even unobtrusive examples.[2] When many of our students feel at ease with the conventions of film and television, but have never seen a competent stage production, actors and directors may too readily seek theatrical analogues for the close-up with the expressive gesture of eye or mouth—or the intrusive miking of voice.

But these dangers and the potential exaggerations and misuses of even the examples here proposed surely need not cause us to ignore Shakespeare's exploration of the relations between character, actor, and audience—what Sheldon Zitner has described as speaking to the audience "over the heads of other characters."[3] The addition of the word "possible" to my overly long title indicates both that we will focus upon examples which cannot be supported with absolute certainty and that we will *not* consider in any detail speeches which, beyond any doubt, do address the spectator directly. Brief mention of several explicit examples, however, should help us to define our subject here by contrast. We shall forego the oft-disputed lines of Lear's fool: "She that's a maid now, and laughs at my departure, Shall not be a maid long, unless things be cut shorter." (I. v. 45-6.).[4]

Nor will we explore the epilogues and other final speeches in which Puck, Rosalind, Pandarus, the King of France, and Prospero clearly do speak to us, the actor often stepping out of character to do so. And although a literal reading might permit discussion of Feste's final song, I reluctantly drop that too, because, while the clown does not tell us how to act, the juxtaposition of his song with the final speeches clearly invites us to relate the vision and mood of Feste's world (which is so like our own) to the world of Illyria. There can be few responsive spectators who fail to accept that invitation and make *some* connection between the two worlds.

Before we examine particular speeches, it should be helpful with such a broad, sometimes hypothetical, and often imprecise subject if I indicate two points of departure for this paper. The first, by analogy, will suggest the sorts of theory and evidence that seem appropriate; the second will explore the single controversial speech which provided the initial impetus for this paper and which should help point toward both

2. See for example, Susan R. Suleiman and Inge Crosman, eds. *The Reader in The Text: Essays on Audience and Interpretation* (Princeton, 1980) and Jane P. Tompkins, *Reader-Response Criticism: From Formalism To Post-Structuralism* (Baltimore, 1980).
3. In a manuscript for our word Shakespeare Congress Seminar (1981), which later published as "Wooden O'S in Plastic Boxes: Shakespeare on Television," *UTQ* (Fall 1981), pp. 1-12.
4. All quotations from Shakespeare's works come from the Pelican *William Shakespeare: The Complete Works*, ed. A. Harbage (Baltimore, 1969).

the possibilities and the very limited certainty which we can hope to establish. First, Richard David in his lively, provocative British Academy Lecture in 1961, "Shakespeare and the Players," as he approached his conclusion, discussed Shakespeare's heroines and second "female" parts.[5] He modestly began, "Here let me warn you that I am doffing my sober historian's gown and intend for five minutes only to wallow in conjecture." David then distinguishes three players of female parts in the original company. The comedies of "the 1590's . . . share a very recognizable type of heroine, sprightly buoyant, but with a deep underlying seriousness—Portia, Beatrice, Rosalind. . . . Not only are these three a single type, but they manifest an increasing sophistication of the 'line.' " He argues that Portia's exchanges with Nerissa are "a conscious display of fireworks, and her serious scenes are to be played as absolutely straight as if the actor could not compass grave and gay together." Beatrice's wit is more unforced, the passion more direct and deep. But Rosalind "can plunge from gay to grave and back again in the twinkling of an eye . . . [with a quality] of self-ridicule almost, but without any alienation of the audience's emotional sympathy, that is quite outside the compass of any but a very skilled, and a very confident actor."

Furthermore, the "heroine has a regular foil, small ('a little scrubbed boy') and pert: Nerissa, Margaret, Celia. In two of the comedies, a third prentice appears as a very dark girl: Jessica, Phebe . . . while Hero is surely a beginner's part." David argues convincingly that Shakespeare's writing employs an increasing complexity largely because he can later take advantage of the growing skills of the boys for whom he created the roles.

Such hypotheses may never be demonstrable with absolute certainty, but they have opened new possibilities for many of my students and for me. We can only infer what Shakespeare might have written differently had he had less competent performers in his company. David attempts no full explanation but he does provide us with insight about aspects of the writer's problems that many had ignored or undervalued. My examples that follow should serve in a similar way if they help demonstrate possible or probable effects of staging in Shakespeare's day and in ours that can help make more rich the relationship between playwright and audience, and consequently more active the participation of the alert, sensitive spectator in the situation and the problems of the character.

5. This lecture is conveniently reprinted in Peter Alexander ed., *Studies in Shakespeare: British Academy Lectures* (Oxford, 1964), p. 51.

My second point of departure comes from the vigorous dissent aroused by the final paragraph of a talk that was delivered at the International Shakespeare Conference of 1978 in Stratford-upon-Avon.[6] The phrase in my title "I know you all" of course opens Hal's first soliloquy and has almost invariably been taken to refer to Hal's drinking companions. In the final paragraph of this talk on "Expectation and Surprise", I briefly turned to this speech and argued that it should surprise us not only as a reversal of many personal traits in Hal as he had been presented to us throughout his first scene, but also as a direct statement to each of us present in the audience. While the surprise at the structural sequence simply reapplied a critical commonplace, my tentatively proposed and barely supported suggestion for a *possible* staging of the soliloquy raised important questions that could not then be answered. It therefore seems worthwhile to explore and develop some of the relevant assumptions that many of us make and the conventions that we often accept.

In the context of that conference, the subject of which was "Construction in Shakespeare," and of my own subject, "Expectation and Surprise," I wanted an example that would *not* follow too obviously from my immediately preceding ones. But this example needed to provide a possible and historically legitimate if unusual staging which would offer new perspectives to the scholars in the audiences, all of whom knew the play reasonably well.

Here is the disputed concluding paragraph:

> I eagerly await an actor and a production that will take full advantage of the thrust stage. After Hal's companions have left by rear and side exits, (and last not Falstaff, but Poins)—Hal will step forward and will address us in the audience. We all think we know the speech well. We expect Hal's promise and his rejection of his drinking fellows. But the true Shakespearean surprise comes not through accident or through idiosyncratic original interpretation —but through a more full realization of the lines and the character expressed by them. No doubt most of Shakespeare's earlier audiences, too, came primarily to see Falstaff, to escape their cares, and to be entertained. It is those audiences—and ours—who are Hal's "foul and ugly mists" when he steps forward and speaks not to Falstaff—but to us:
>
> > I know you all, and will awhile uphold
> > The unyoked humor of your idleness.
> > Yet herein will I imitate the sun,
> > Who doth permit the base contagious clouds
> > To smother up his beauty from the world, . . .

6. A slightly revised and condensed version of this lecture was published in *Shakespeare Survey 34* (Cambridge, 1981), 39-50.

There seemed no doubt among the commentators that the conclusion of this scene *could* be staged effectively in this way, but some
argued that this would be an historical aberration. Yet it seems more
likely that the normal way for the sixteenth-century actor to deliver
these lines would be *to* the audience. In a theatre that we now praise
for its flexibility and for its intimacy between actor and audience, the
actor would be unlikely to deliver the lines to the exit or exits where
Poins (and earlier Falstaff) had left the stage. A vague gesture *away
from* the audience in the theatre would only diffuse the force of a
powerful, intense, and complex sequence of images and statements.
And even if, by gesture of head or body, the actor could make every
spectator aware that he spoke *only to* the "you all" who had left the
stage, I think it far from certain that this is the sole interpretation that
a contemporary reading or hearing of the text would bear.

Many seem to assume that when Hal steps forward alone and says
"I know you *all*," the "all" includes Falstaff, Bardolph, Peto, Mistress
Quickly, and the other companions that the King deplores. Yet it is
worth noting that none of these *except Falstaff* has appeared on stage.
(And only in passing have some of the others been mentioned.)
Shakespeare's initial audiences were not made up of scholars who
knew the whole text well. The audience in the theatre would be
familiar only with that which had taken place in the first two scenes,
perhaps supplemented by that which has been very clearly predicted
or which is part of popular legend or familiar history.

Some of those who are minimally or distantly knowledgeable about
Henry IV mistakenly recall that Hal's soliloquy concludes the scene
in which we have met the whole group of cronies (or subplot characters). But this is no large scene in the Boar's Head Tavern. Since
Theobald, it has been set in the Prince's apartment. More significant,
we never have more than three characters on stage. Until Poins enters
at line 105, Hal and Falstaff are alone; after Falstaff leaves at line 155,
Poins remains with the Prince for a duologue until line 189, when Hal
stands alone for his soliloquy. Who, then, are addressed in "I know
you all"? In the only other scene we have watched, no one speaks
except the King and Westmoreland though others in the court party
are present. It does seem far-fetched to treat the King and his followers
as "the base contagious clouds" that smother up the sun or those
whose "unyoked humor of idleness" Hal promises to "uphold." This
leaves only Poins and Falstaff of characters who have appeared on
stage to represent the "you all." However strange the yoking of these
two, and however ambiguous are the position, role, and character of
Poins, he seems hardly likely to stand clearly for the very characters—
Bardolph, Peto, and Gadshill—whose names we have heard but

quickly as part of the jest that he plans to execute. Perhaps the mistaken memories and impressions of readers may come partially because of the nature of the dialogue that the soliloquy follows. For quite natural reasons, those lines that immediately precede the soliloquy and set the context for it have received relatively little attention. After Falstaff's departure at line 149, when he may or may not hear the Prince's "Farewell, the latter spring! Farewell, all-hallown summer!", Hal's whole personality seems suddenly to change. In this sequence, left alone with Poins, Hal becomes very dull. He becomes almost a straight man to Poins, worrying about the danger of their disguises being discovered and even asking for reassurance lest Falstaff's group "will be too hard for us." Gone are all the wit, energy, and vigour he has just shown with Falstaff. Here, still in his first scene, when our impressions, sympathies, and expectations are being established, Shakespeare's Hal sacrifices his individuality, his personality, his wit and energy, for the sake of exposition. Perhaps it is little wonder that John Barton in his 1969 version for Theatre-go-Round thought it necessary to insert an opening scene from *The Famous Victories* to tilt the sympathies of the audience toward Hal.

In this context, the transformation of Hal bursts forth all the more emphatically the moment he speaks when alone. In other words, even if "I know you all" is *not* taken in a manner to implicate us in the audience, much the same point is being made in a muted less decisive way. We must still decide which characters in the play are involved and why the seemingly 'inept "all" should be used here.

If we do grant it probable that Hal challenges the audience in the theatre with his "I know you all," this knowledge creates no major conflict. It primarily reinforces clearly existing relationships because it lumps us with characters of past and future—surely Falstaff, almost certainly Poins, perhaps intermittently the King, just possibly those sub-plot or comic characters who have not yet appeared. Each of these at this time seems to be conceived and presented essentially for his relationship to the speaker, Hal.

It would be most valuable if we had careful records about the ways in which Hal has been played, about the intonation of key lines in his speech. Two possibilities are often proposed: one makes Hal a near impersonal choral figure, the speech a non-naturalistic, non-psychological pointer to the audience. Other actors have played Hal as indecisive, as relatively weak, improvising his strategy as he works his way through the speech.[7] But if the confidence that Hal asserts is played to hide his deeper doubts, is this a "modern" falsification?

7. See, for example, Daniel Seltzer, "Prince Hall and Tragic Style," in *Shakespeare Survey* 30 (Cambridge, 1977), pp. 22-24.

Neither of these approaches seems to capture the essential contrast between Hal with Poins and Hal alone. Nor does either permit the complexity and the mingling of characteristics that many of us consider integral. Hal may be discovering himself as the play progresses, but surely the tones conveyed by the surface of this speech present him as already sure of himself and decisive in his value judgments. Even so, this soliloquy stresses the ways in which Hal promises to behave, and the audience is left to infer his essential character through image and symbol. We receive no precision, no depth, no detailed understanding of his character. The extremely strong and confident opening phrase "I know you all" immediately gives way to the transitory and misleading "and will awhile uphold the unyoked humor of your idleness," and then quickly to promises to imitate "the sun . . . [so] that when he please again to be *himself* . . . He may be more wondered at."

The relationships of Hal to the audience are quite ambiguous, particularly when we think of the repeated word "men": "By so much shall I falsify men's hopes" and in the climactic line, "Redeeming time when men think least I will." Are we to feel privileged in contrast to the generic "men" in each of these lines because we are taken into Hal's confidence? Or should we accept our participation as "men" as part of the human condition rather than somehow excluding ourselves from the "you all"? If Hal is trying to invite the spectator to join the company of those he knows, what does this do to our interests and our sympathies?

If the speech promises reform, redemption, and leadership, it primarily remains self-analysis in which the self is defined by manipulation of political expectations and values. The concept of virtue that remains is much like that of Cressida in the soliloquy placed identically at the end of that character's first scene.

III

The structure, presentation, and expository reversals of the scene for Cressida and that for Hal bear striking resemblances: each character first appears in the second scene of the play and each in a soliloquy which concludes that scene promptly establishes a strikingly different character from the one we have been watching and listening to. But at first glance, the content, tone, perspective, and character revelation in Cressida's soliloquy seem thoroughly unlike those in Hal's. Act I, scene ii, of *Troilus and Cressida* creates a series of stage groupings remarkably like those in the parallel scene of *I Henry IV* that we have been considering—if we limit our discussion to the characters who speak rather than include the silent Trojan officers and soldiers who cross the stage and thereby evoke comment. Initially Cressida is alone with her "man," as Hal was with Falstaff. Pandarus enters to make up a trio, as did Poins. After the brief lines with Troilus' boy, Cressida and Pandarus talk, as did Hal and Poins. And finally, Cressida remains alone on stage, as did Hal. Although Pandarus' role as a manipulator seems much like that of Poins, the similarities between the staging of the two scenes might seem to end here if we accept the usual stage direction in modern texts. But, of course, the line that precedes Cressida's soliloquy, "By the same token, you are a bawd!" can readily be played either so that the departing Pandarus does or does not hear it. If he does not, or if we treat the line as part of Cressida's speech, the insult presents a more gross and blunt parallel to Hal's opening. But when Cressida is unquestionably alone, she first simply tells the audience the facts of what Pandarus is doing. Her third and fourth lines, "But more in Troilus thousandfold I see/Than in the glass of Pandar's praise may be," create the reversal from the Cressida we have been watching, but they express clearly and directly the character's judgment as only she can know it when she takes us into her private feelings. But in lines 5 to 8, the explanation for "Yet hold I off," the actor establishes a major departure while the declarative confident tone of statement remains. So bitter are these lines in their conceptions of personal value that it seems hard to imagine what Cressida means by "more in Troilus thousandfold I see." Such critical assertions, allegedly universal, as "Things won are done," and "Men prize the thing ungained more than it is" make explicit the denial of any real value or any real virtue—the attitude that was far less overt in Hal's soliloquy. When Cressida concludes by telling us that her eyes will hide her love, she may or may not convince us. But, unlike Hal, she at this time clearly is making no frontal assault upon our beliefs as they affect the internal action of the play. Shakespeare's boy actor retains important options as to the manner in which he speaks the central lines. He is addressing us in the audience; he is not groping for words to define the beliefs of the character. He must present an extremely jaded and bitter, if poignant and sympathetic, character, one who may have acquired this view from her own faithless experience or who may be adopting a mask based upon second-hand descriptions. In any case, the distinctions that I have been making about how we are to relate the narrative descriptions of Pandarus' and Troilus' "enterprise" with Cressida's ensuing generalized denial of any continuing joy, triumph, or essence remain implicit in the text. Shakespeare, the actor, and the character leave the spectator to establish or to ignore the relationship between the narrative and the moral/epistemological general claims. The relations of spectator to character remain much more problematic than they were to Hal because they are based mainly upon open invitations to apply general statements about sex, woman, joy, and transitory values. The spectator may simply accept the world-view argued by Cressida; but it is quite possible that he may react against such extreme cynicism and attempt to balance the world-view expressed. If so, the assault against his more idealistic or affirmative beliefs will evoke compensating expectations.

Clearly, in responding to the soliloquies of Hal and of Cressida, any spectator must participate to some extent because very poignant general statements are made as if they grow from the immediate situation and action when in reality there is an imaginative leap left for us to make. I am suggesting that both speeches share certain qualities; that each encourages us to engage ourselves with, or to react against, the bitter perspective that is asserted. I have also argued that Hal's speech suggests, but does not require, a further step in participation, because it challenges and implicates its hearer more directly. Perhaps this conjectural distinction will become more clear if we compare two soliloquies in *Much Ado About Nothing*.

IV

Let us consider the carefully juxtaposed scenes in which the wits Benedick and Beatrice are gulled into admitting their love for each other. Each overhears friends praising his or her beloved while pretending that first Benedick and then Beatrice is not present. The staging may be tricky because some very traditional conventions are both employed and subverted. First Don Pedro and Claudio, then in the next scene Hero and Ursula, must clearly distinguish for us the lines that Benedick or Beatrice need to overhear from those asides which they must not. But this complex series of changing expository techniques has worked well in most of the very different productions that I have attended. And the moving from aside to overheard speech will help make the audience in the theatre particularly alert not only to shades of discrimination that cannot yet be appreciated by the on-stage audience (even though that audience in the two linked scenes is made up of the hero and heroine who are easily the most perceptive characters in the play), but also to shades of reference and implication when these two speak in soliloquy.

Although Beatrice's soliloquy in Act III, scene 1, comes later, it presents a much simpler, more accessible example—one in ways similar (in its summing up) to Cressida's but quite opposed to hers in relying upon others. Unlike the immediately preceding gulling which started with Benedick alone on the stage—and which was interrupted repeatedly by his comments to the audience—Act III begins with Hero telling Margaret, "Run thee to the parlour" to find the absent Beatrice. Very quickly, in fact before Hero can finish her next speech, we hear and see: "For look where Beatrice, like a lapwing, runs / Close by the ground, to hear our conference."

But Beatrice never speaks until the others leave, when she comes forward and gives the soliloquy that concludes the scene. In this 10-line rhyming speech, Beatrice is unusually straightforward (fore-shadowing the fine repartee with Margaret who is able to profess apprehension or wit because the enamoured Beatrice has left it). Beatrice capitulates so promptly and fully that there seems very little for the spectator to interpret or add. By her second quatrain, "And, Benedick, love on; I will requite thee, / Taming my wild heart to thy loving hand," the spectator is lulled into simply accepting a fait accompli. Yet, interestingly enough, for a drama in which so much of the action—and especially the climactic church scene in the next act—interweaves with false report and personal/sexual reputation, Beatrice makes a surprising juxtaposition in her first quatrain:

> What fire is in my ears? Can this be true?
> Stand I condemned for pride and scorn so much?
> Contempt, farewell! and maiden pride, adieu!

To accept literally the leap from the three questions in the first two lines to the terse decision for action would surely be to reason much too literally. Beatrice does not relinquish her maiden pride, her scorn, and her wit simply because society "condemns" her, even though in her penultimate line she returns to explain, "For others say thou dost deserve..." The boy actor was left to establish a sub-text in the character of Beatrice that would convince us of depth, complexity, subtlety—an ability to love quite beyond that expressed in this rather conventional epiphany. The spectator here is left little to do except to notice how inadequate are the reasons the heroine gives for her sudden drastic change in behaviour.

I wonder how much these generalizations should apply to Benedick's corresponding epiphany, even in the memories of an audience of scholars who know the play very well indeed. Act II, scene iii proves much more fully developed than Act III, scene i, [for it] is closer to those scenes from other genres such as *Richard III* and *Hamlet* where we repeatedly enter the hero's mind and watch how his thoughts and his feelings change. The scene opens with Benedick alone for only one word, moves into a very brief near-mechanical exchange in which Benedick calls his boy, quickly to send him away again—a dialogue almost identical with the one in *Measure for Measure* that Frank O'Connor argued no man of the theatre would ever write.[8] Then comes a long prose soliloquy in which Benedick searches for the truth about the nature of love and of his companion, Claudio, "He was wont to speak plain and to the purpose like an honest man... And now he is turned orthography." For Benedick, the earlier Claudio seems much more interesting than he has ever appeared to the audience. With great virtuosity and flexibility, with rapid changes of tone and rhythm, the speaker engages us. Clearly, his comments about Claudio's fall into orthography foreshadow his own. But far from hybris or pompous egoism is such a sequence as this: "May I be so converted and see with these eyes? / I cannot tell; I think not."

There will be few with any romantic susceptibility in any audience, I think, who will not identify with Benedick in some of his confusions and fluctuations (long before his "Man is a giddy thing, and this is my conclusion"). Now in his series of quick short statements and questions, a good actor will engage the spectator to recognize in a general sense that he shares the human condition with Bendick and especially his weaknesses—even when we know much more than he does about the present and future of the particular action that helps form the core of the play. I include these general summary comments because they prepare us for Benedick's two speeches *while* the gulling goes on, "Is it possible? Sits the wind in that direction?" and "I should think this a gull, but that the white-bearded fellow speaks it: knavery cannot, sure, hide himself in such reverence." Although not usually printed as asides, they surely serve as addresses to himself by the actor who speaks and gestures on a different plane from those who dupe him. Clearly we have no knavery involved so that the logic in Benedick's character analysis of Leonato proves irrelevant.

We have been very well prepared for Benedick's two long soliloquies, briefly interrupted by a dialogue with Beatrice, that conclude the scene. These I want to look at closely because of a controversial recent production directed by John Barton, starring Donald Sinden and Judi Dench for the RSC in 1976. While Judi Dench's performance gained near-universal acclaim, Sinden's was perhaps the most debated in any recent influential production of a Shakespearean

---

8. *Shakespeare's Progress* (New York, 1960), p. 155.

comedy. In a session that year of the International Shakespeare Conference in Stratford-upon-Avon, Daniel Seltzer attacked Barton, asking substantially, "How do you combine the most unselfish actress on the English stage with her leading man who always hams and tries to steal every scene he can?"[9] In sharp contrast, Richard David praised Sinden, especially for the aspects we are considering:

> Sinden is one of those masterful actors who can visibly control an audience. He can raise a laugh or (more difficult) quell it with equal decisiveness. In the scenes where Benedick is solus, he played to the gallery, becoming broader and coarser as the season progressed. Given an actor as boldly extrovert as this, given that the writer of the part invites this sort of treatment, given that the direct, uninhibited reaction of audience to stage is one essential ingredient of theatre, the performance was not objectionable.... It was much to his credit that, good actor that he is, he would drop this boisterousness the moment Beatrice entered and soliloquy became dialogue, tuning his style to something much more intimate and unemphatic that meshed with Judi Dench's more introverted mode of playing.[10]

One personal note: Sinden's performance on the same night Seltzer found him so unsatisfactory skilfully won over many non-professionals in the audience, including my children, then thirteen and nine. So my own detached scholarly objectivity may well be even less reliable than usual.

This particular production should be relevant to scholars attending to Elizabethan staging because David convincingly, if not conclusively, argues:

> For each of five seasons until 1976, the Royal Shakespeare Theatre has made a steady progression towards a new stage.... The directors have explicitly denied any intention to reproduce the actual Elizabethan stage for which the plays were designed.... But it would seem that in producing these plays the directors have found their peculiar demands as to staging becoming more and more insistent and that as a result the Stratford stage has approximated more and more to the Elizabethan. It is now probably as close to that of the Globe as one can get under modern conditions.[11]

One reason that I have dwelt upon the preparation for Benedick's soliloquies (and the contrasting minimal preparation for Beatrice's) is that without this contrast many lines of the speeches themselves would fit far less appealing characters. Sinden brought to Benedick

9. This discussion has not been published.
10. *Shakespeare in the Theatre* (Cambridge, 1978), p. 10.
11. Ibid., p. 215.

much of the Malvolio he had played during a long run, a decision that I thought would be terribly reductive, but which in the event, did not prove so. And many of the lines that Benedick speaks *to* the audience might well come from Bertram in *All's Well That End's Well.*

When Benedick steps forward just after Claudio, Leonato, and Don Pedro exit (and after we have watched him listen silently for over one hundred lines), his first line confidently challenges us: "This can be no trick." Of course Benedick speaks to himself, but Sinden showed how smoothly parts of the speech can be directed to us, to convince us. On the surface, of course, we react against the ignorance, the gulling—the mistaken effrontery. Yet, unlike the gulling of Malvolio, that of Benedick is a trick that will lead the lovers to each other, to reveal the truth of the feelings they have been hiding. Unlike Malvolio and Bertram who primarily expose their own selfishness, Benedick, even when at his most disadvantageous rhetorical relation with the audience in the theatre, must win us over. Unlike our relation to Bertram, where our sympathies rest uneasily with our expectations, that with Benedick almost invariably achieves a new harmony. Not only do we by now expect a successful romantic resolution, we desire it and respect its rightness. From these soliloquies by Benedick we can see some of the ways in which he succeeds despite his mistaken premises. "This can be no trick" is followed by statements showing admiration for the virtues and the sincerity of Pedro, Leonato, Claudio, and especially Hero. Then Benedick suddenly leaps to, "Love me! why it must be requited!" Even so sensitive a critic as George Hunter misleadingly emphasizes what he calls the comic hybris of Benedick.[12] When Benedick is duped, he speaks both to himself and to the audience in a long series of declarative statements that rely upon the accuracy and good will of those who, in one obvious sense, are deceiving him: "They have this truth. . . . They seem to pity the lady . . . They say . . . They say. . . ." Benedick explicitly responds to their censure, "I must not seem proud!" Naturally he struggles with his sudden "transformation" from the misogynist, the railer at woman; and this leads to the nonsensical, non-causal argument, "When I said I should be a bachelor, I did not think I should live till I were married." The actor not only mends his "detractions," he modestly calls Beatrice "wise, but for loving me; by my troth, it is

---

12. *Shakespeare: The Late Comedies* (London, 1962, rev. 1969), p. 27; The phrase "comic hubris" refers specifically to Benedick's soliloquy, earlier in II, iii (9-32). Hunter stresses the "need to change," but one questions how much Benedick has changed within a few moments of the same scene.

no addition to her wit." Yet in mid-sentence, he is capable of superb comic reversal and recovery: "nor no great argument of her folly, for I will be horribly in love with her." The staging by Barton in which Sinden repeatedly alternates between addressing himself and responsive members of the audience, both those seated behind the stage and those out front, demonstrated how much we could participate with him—with his mistakes as well as his good humour and exuberance. A character and a mood were established so that Benedick can readily survive both his absurd responses to Beatrice when she comes to fetch him for dinner and his Malvolio-like naively romantic, false explication of her simple words.

It may not be necessary to stage the scene in this way, nor for each spectator to respond fully to the actor's invitation to participate imaginatively. An alert and sensitive spectator will perceive how different from Bertram (for example) is the Benedick who before Beatrice speaks had begged Don Pedro earlier in Act II: "Will your Grace command me any service to the world's end? I will go on the slightest errand now to the Antipodes ... rather than hold three words' conference with this harpy." But by encouraging our participation in the blunders, the comic hyperbole, and the bravado of Benedick, Shakespeare uses us to help create a much richer comic hero than, say, Orlando, Orsino, Lysander, Demetrius, or Bassanio.

V

Unlike these scenes in which our imaginative participation makes us feel *with* the characters—even though we may recognize that they are mistaken—Shakespeare often uses our responses primarily so that we reject their statements or beliefs. Rather than conclude by discussing far too briefly the varied soliloquies and asides of Hamlet, Iago, or Richard III, or the less familiar but challenging ones in *All's Well That Ends Well*, I would like to turn briefly to an aside and an exchange from Act II of *Measure for Measure*. In Isabella's couplet and in Escalus' suit to Angelo, we may find two sharply contrasting appeals to our sympathies. Although some scholars think of Isabella's lines as pointers to the original audience of an essential change from earlier versions of the play, she speaks to herself as in soliloquy: "Then, Isabel, live chaste, and, brother, die: / More than our brother is our chastity."

(II. iv. 184-5).

In the other speech, responding to Angelo's scene-opening lines, "We must not make a scarecrow of the law, . . ." Escalus urges:

> Let but your honour know,
> Whom I believe to be most strait in virtue,
> That, in the working of your own affections,
> Had time cohered with place or place with wishing,
> Or that the resolute acting of your blood
> Could have attained th' effect of your own purpose,
> Whether you had not some time in your life
> Erred in this point which now you censure him,
> And pulled the law upon you.   (II. i. 8-16)

Perhaps surprisingly, I think that the actor should deliver the lines so that we listening in the audience will engage ourselves more fully in response to the lines in dialogue by a minor character than in response to the vivid climactic statement by the heroine at her moment of decision. Isabella's couplet is explicit; it expresses her decision and its expected effect. The actor challenges the spectator even though the character addresses herself. This seems true even though in recent years many have recognized that Isabella's choice accords with traditional church doctrine and some ardent feminists find similarities in contemporary situations. Yet to sympathize fully with Isabella demands either a complete sacrifice of any naturalistic characterization or a projection of the spectator's moral struggles upon the heroine. Even though many excellent scholars have discussed the moral conflict, the inner turmoil that the heroine allegedly undergoes, theatrically the most clear aspect of her decision is that she, unlike her prototypes in Whetstone and Cinthio, never for a moment considers any other course of action. The challenge to the spectator then does not demand what he or she would do in a similar situation, as one might normally expect. We rather are asked to respond to a choice that has been very quickly made. Clearly each spectator will respond forcefully in some way. But even if Shakespeare's boy actor or our contemporary actress clearly spoke to inform the audience while overtly addressing himself or herself, most of us will reject the invitation that we go along with the heroine.

By the end of the next scene—as all know after their initial exposure—Isabella's choice will have very little to do with what happens. We will apply our response to her decision and the way it is expressed with many other elements in deciding what we think of her character.

183

Escalus' speech, a clear simple practical argument for mercy, challenges us in a quite different way. Because the speech, so completely straightforward, is made to the only other character on stage, we would not for a moment expect the actor to address us directly in order to make overt our participation in the situation he poses for Angelo. Yet in this play, and particularly in the intense problematic debates of its second quarter, these lines stand out. Unlike the hyperboles, the extreme situations, and the dilemmas that pervade this act, these lines speak so surely to the near universal condition of human temptation, that many spectators will apply to themselves the appeal made to Angelo. When the deputy so swiftly rejects any possibility that he might be unable to resist temptation, many in the audience will perceive his inability to relate the ideal to the practical, the perfect to the minimally flawed. And the spectator may well ponder the possibility of this deputy's governing efficiently or with justice in any situation in which the ideal is not fully operative. To some extent, this example differs from all the earlier ones, each of which should be—or might be—spoken directly to the audience in the theatre. They are spoken by the leading actor, the leading boy actor or the villain. These are among the more experienced, more sublte players, those most flexible, most capable of quick clear changes of tone, of rhythm, of direction. But Escalus' lines, like Hal's with which we began, show how deeply ingrained in Shakespeare's ways of thinking and of writing are the posing of possibilities, of options for the spectator—which he may apply to his own experience or which, on a conscious level at least, he may limit to the fictive action and characters in the play.

VI

In each of my examples we feel, I hope, that the choice by director and actor to have the character speak *to* the spectator can prove theatrically effective. The reader, late in the twentieth century, can readily recognize and respond to such appeals. I do not argue that such communication across the footlights is the only appropriate way of playing these speeches. Even to argue that such invitations should prove the best way of playing any of the more complex examples which appeal to us in many different ways and which function in different ways would require far more extended demonstration than I have attempted here. Perhaps the most fruitful discussions will grow from the individual director as he works out his production or the editor as he evolves his edition.

In considering these speeches when Shakespeare through his actor addresses the spectator and encourages him to participate imaginatively in the experience of the character — and at times to go beyond this in applying the words and feelings to his own experience — I have never attempted to describe or explain how that application should develop. To tell the spectator just what he or she should come to think or feel seems to me to risk a terrible reductivensss, whether the model be psychological, ideological or theological. Escalus' speech and Isabella's couplet may in fact evoke in some of us responses that too readily congratulate ourselves as virtuous in opposition to the narrow-minded rigidity or inflated self-confidence of the heroine or the deputy. But such reductiveness would be most un-Shakespearean. Facile formulas, whether of structural pattern or simple didactic statement, share the weaknesses of superficial claims for thematic unity so prominent in the criticism of the 1950s and 1960s. Instead, the speakers of Shakespeare's lines plant disturbing possibilities which we cannot immediately ponder too precisely or feel with full complexity, for that would cause us to violate the flow of the action. We would become in effect stop-action mechanical devices freezing the present and future of the play—as did the Trevor Nunn production of *The Winter's Tale* in 1969 at Stratford-upon-Avon when the audience shared visually Leontes' feverish, jealous imaginings. Shakespeare rather makes us feel an undercurrent of troubling possibility or one of potentially rewarding complexity. Either surely requires adjustments for us while we respond to the unfolding action. But for both the action of the play and its implications on our own selves, anything even approaching a full resonance must wait for the continuing dialogue with the work that we rethink and refeel long after the final curtain has come down.

To deny the possibility of such appeals in Shakespeare's plays is to submit timidly to a pseudo-historical interpretation, one which may distort in as severely anachronistic a way as do those who ignore the vital distinctions between theatrical and psychological conventions in his day and in ours.

English Players "Beyond the Seas": Staging Problems

JERZY LIMON

When Fynes Moryson, the well known Elizabethan traveller, visited Frankfort during the annual fair in September 1592, he saw a public performance given by a company of English players. In his "Itinerary" he left us his account of the performance, which in fact is one of the earliest and most authoritative pieces of written evidence for the activity of English actors on the Continent. This is how he recalls the event:

> Germany hath some fewe wandering Comeydians, more deseruing pity then prayse, for the serious parts are dully penned, and worse acted, and the mirth they make is ridiculous, and nothing lesse then witty.... So as I remember that when some of our cast despised Stage players came out of England into Germany, and played at Franckford in the tyme of the Mart, hauing nether a complete number of Actours, nor any good Apparell, nor any ornament of the Stage, yet the Germans, not vnderstanding a worde they sayde, both men and women, flocked wonderfully to see theire gesture and Action, rather than heare them, speaking English which they vnderstand not....[1]

Several points need particular attention here. First, Moryson labels the players "wandering Comeydians" and "our cast despised Stage players," which indicates that already by 1592 there were English strolling companies active on the Continent, and that they were composed of actors who found no employment at home. Secondly, the company described had neither a "complete number of Actours, nor any good Apparell, nor any ornament of the Stage," all of which

1. *Shakespeare's Europe: Unpublished Chapters of Fynes Moryson's Itinerary. Being a Survey of the Conditions of Europe at the End of the 16th Century*, (London, 1903), p. 304.

186

contributed to the poor quality of the performance. And thirdly, the language used on stage was English, and although the spectators could not understand a word they "flocked wonderfully"—to Moryson's surprise—"to see their gesture and Action," which implies that the non-verbal acting devices used by the English were interesting enough to attract the attention of the audience.

Perhaps with some reservations all the three points may be treated as true or even characteristic of the English dramatic companies that started to tour Europe at the close of the sixteenth century, particularly in the early, or "reconaissance," phase of their activity there. The extant evidence leaves no doubt that the first companies to arrive on the Continent were small indeed, poorly equipped with costumes and stage properties, and that the language they used was English. However, this can certainly not have been true of the companies that flooded Europe later on, in the first half of the seventeenth century. The last of the famous strollers, George Jolly, in one of his supplications to the Council of Basle, dated 1654, offered to delight all who love plays "with his well-practised company, not only by means of good instructive stories, but also with repeated changes of expensive costumes, and a theatre decorated in the Italian manner, with beautiful English music and skilful women,"[2] and of course the performances were given in German. These quoted sources mark the hardships of the early years and the prosperous close of the period of English theatrical impact on the Continent, and illustrate clearly the line of development that the English companies had undergone.

Already in the mid-1580s there were English professional companies on the Continent. In 1586 the Earl of Leicester's men visited and acted at the court of the King of Denmark at Elsinore, whence they travelled as far south as Dresden.[3] The same company may have visited Gdansk in the following year.[4] Several other companies are recorded in various countries before 1592. However, Fynes Moryson is slightly mistaken when he labels the actors "cast despised Stage players," and when he calls them, in another place, "stragling broken Companyes." Although the frequent failure of the contemporary records to note the names of individual actors makes the identification

2. Quoted from Leslie Hotson, *The Restoration and Commonwealth Stage*, (New York, 1962), p. 171.
3. See A. Cohn, *Shakespeare in Germany in the Sixteenth and the Seventeenth Centuries: An Account of English Actors in Germany and the Netherlands and of the Plays Performed by Them During the Same Period*, (London and Berlin, 1865), pp. xxiv-xxx.
4. Johannes Bolte, *Das Danziger Theater im 16. und 17. Jahrhundert* (Hamburg und Leipzig, 1895), pp. 22, 25.

of these companies and tracing their precise tours extremely difficult, a sufficient amount of documentary evidence has been gathered to support the opinion that many of these actors were members of notable London companies, who, for various reasons, were forced to seek their fortunes "beyond the seas." Thus, of the numerous names extant of actors who were active on the Continent even in the reconnaissance phase of their regular visits, many may be found in London records. The names of Robert Browne, Richard Jones, William Kempe, Thomas Pope and Thomas Sackville may serve as examples.

This of course is not surprising in view of the fact that at times acting in London was uprofitable or even impossible, and, without the resource of going into the country or abroad, even the best of the city companies could hardly have survived. The conditions that forced the London actors to travel are well known; the three usually mentioned are the Puritan opposition, the ravages of the plague, which led to temporary inhibitions of acting, and the growing competition among the companies in London. However, not all of these factors contributed equally to the exodus of actors from England, and it was the last of them, i.e. the competition among the city companies, that seems to have played a dominant role in this unprecedented pheno-menon. This is particularly clear after the reopening of London theatres in 1594, following a two-year inhibition caused by the plague. Out of the numerous companies active in London in the preceding period, two only, the Lord Chamberlain's and the Lord Admiral's, now dominated the city's theatrical life. A sort of monopoly was established, which is confirmed by a letter from the Privy Council to the Master of the Revels, dated 19 February, 1598:

> Whereas licence hath bin graunted unto two companies of stage players retayned unto us, the Lord Admyral and Lord Chamberlain, to use and practise stage playes ... and whereas there is also a third company who of late ... have by waie of intrusion used likewise to play... Wee have therefore thought good to require you ... to take order that the aforesaid third company may be suppressed and none suffered heereafter to plaie but those two formerlie named belonging to us.[5]

Even if the contemporary account mentioning two hundred actors living in London is exaggerated,[6] there is little doubt that shortly

---

5. Quoted from E. K. Chambers, *The Elizabethan Stage* (Oxford, 1923), IV, 325.
6. Ibid., 303-4.

after 1594 a number of players found themselves unemployed, facing not only poverty, but also severe punishment under the force of law. It should not be forgotten that by the statutes of 1572 and 1598 unlicensed players were threatened with branding as "rogues, vagabonds and sturdy beggers."[7] The misery and hopelessness of their situation is additionally confirmed by contemporary evidence, along with the actors' significant statement: "We can be bankrupts (say the players) on this side and gentlemen of a company beyond the sea...."[8] In consequence, the sporadic tours of small companies on the Continent before 1594, reconnaissance in character, were followed by regular visits which would eventually turn into a permanent activity of English players until well after the Restoration.

Of course, the situation at home was only the stimulus, the driving force which made the actors seek fortune abroad, and the fact that their expectations of financial gain were, in most cases, fulfilled on the Continent was entirely dependent on other factors, the most important being the patronage of continental nobility and the steadily improving quality of performances. In spite of the fact that the English actors active on the Continent are traditionally labeled "strolling," "wandering," or "travelling" players, one has to remember that most of the major companies found service at noblemen's, ducal, or even royal courts, where they stayed for many years, undertaking occasional travels or none at all. It should also be added that in most towns public performances were prohibited almost throughout the whole year, and the actors were given permission to play only on special occasions, local celebrations, during feasts and fairs. Finding service at court was a blessing and a guarantee of survival, because apart from a more or less permanent income, the players were granted patents and licences, which enabled them to travel safely as servants of a given nobleman.[9] In view of this it is necessary to make the distinction between continental court performances and public performances, which initially differed entirely one from another.

Already in 1586, the King of Denmark had an English company in his service for several months. The same company played at the Elector of Saxony's court. More conspicuous was the case of the

---

7. There is also the Statute of 1604. See ibid. 269-71, 324-25, 336-37.
8. Quoted from Cohn, *Shakespeare in Germany*, p. xcvi.
9. Several patents of this type have been preserved to our times. One of these, given in 1640 to Robert Reynold's company by the Elector of Brandenburg, was published by Bolte, *Danziger Theater*, p. 69.

English players who entered the service of the Landgrave Moritz of Hesse, who, incidentally, between 1604 and 1605 had a private theatre built in Kassel, named the Ottoneum, in which the English performed until 1613.[10] The Electors of Brandenburg had large companies of English actors and musicians in their service from 1603 onwards. Another characteristic example may be found at the Royal Court in Warsaw, where several English companies stayed for a number of years, beginning in 1617.[11] The vogue for keeping English players at one's court must have been ubiquitous among the continental aristocracy, since the Prince of Poland felt a capricious and costly need to bring a whole company directly from London to Warsaw in 1617. The vogue originated towards the close of the sixteenth century and was of primary importance for the future fortunes of the English players on the Continent and, indirectly, for the quality and variety of their staging of plays.

One of the first privileges deriving from a nobleman's patronage was the possibility of increasing the number of actors in a company. That the company Fynes Moryson saw at Frankfort in 1592 did not have a "complete number of Actours" is by no means surprising. The few companies recorded on the Continent around that period were small indeed, five or six players being the average strength. It seems natural that the managers of the travelling companies tried to limit expenses by keeping down the number of actors. The same tendency may be noticed in England whenever the London companies toured the country.[12] 'The growing number of both actors and companies is noticeable almost immediately after 1594, a year which seems to mark the beginning of their regular activity on the Continent, and becomes even more apparent after 1600. Thus, there were twelve actors in 1596 at Strasbourg, ten in 1597 at Tübingen, twelve in 1600 at Cologne, fifteen in 1602 at Nuremberg, fourteen in 1604 at Nördlingen, eighteen in 1605 at Frankfort, nineteen players accompanied by sixteen musicians at Königsberg in 1611, twenty-four in 1615 at Cologne, etc.[13] Thus, in the early seventeenth century these

10. A detailed study of the Ottoneum was presented by Graham C. Adams during the annual Shakespeare Association of America meeting in 1980 ("The Ottoneum: A Neglected Seventeenth Century Theatre").
11. See my article "Komedianci angielscy w Warszawie. Przegląd źródeł " ("English Comedians in Warsaw. A Survey of Evidence"), Pamiętnik Teatralny, 3-4 (1979), 469-77.
12. See Alwin Thaler, "Travelling Players in Shakspere's England," Modern Philology, XVII (1920), 501-502.
13. For further details see Charles Harris, "The English Comedians in Germany Before the Thirty Years' War: the Financial Side," PMLA, 22 (1907), 455; and also E. Herz, Englische Schauspieler und englisches Schauspiel zur Zeit Shakespeares in Deutschland (Hamburg und Leipzig, 1903).

troupes reached the size of a typical London company, which, in turn, enabled them to stage unabridged texts of plays.

The latter fact brings about a whole set of problems connected with the development of staging techniques as used by the English on the Continent. One has to remember that the companies in question were composed of highly skilled professional actors experienced in complex productions of plays which were the highest achievements of the Renaissance and the Baroque. Of the several obstacles which made it impossible for them to present all their talents and craft, one has already been mentioned: the incomplete cast of actors. Another was the language barrier. There is no doubt that the early continental performances were given in English, with the last instance of this practice recorded in 1606 at Loitz.[14] In the case of private, or court performances an interpreter was occasionally hired, who simply translated the text simultaneously. This practice was not possible at all in the case of outdoor public performances. Acting before an audience not understanding a word of what was being said on the stage naturally affected the staging of plays. Any presentation of a full-length play was an obvious risk in such circumstances, and it seems more likely that the stress was put on the non-verbal elements of the performance. Perhaps the favourite form was a jig, although contemporary continental accounts refer to the plays presented as histories, comedies and tragedies. Thus, in 1590 Robert Browne was paid 15 guilders at Leyden for "having acted and played divers comedies and histories, besides for having made divers leaps."[15] In the following year, the same actor was given a passport to go abroad to perform among other things "games of comedies, tragedies, and histories."[16] In 1597, at the court of the Landgrave Moritz of Hesse at Kassel the English were paid for presenting a "comedy."[17] On the other hand, it is generally acknowledged that the distinction between particular genres was not very precise in those times and the word "comedy" was probably used in the quoted sources in its every-day meaning to denote anything funny, including the vaulting of the clowns.

There is little doubt that before the dropping of English and the substitution of German for it, which took place at the turn of the century, the texts of the plays presented must have been abridged, and it was actually the music and clowns that constituted the chief

---

14. Harris, "English Comedians in Germany," 448.
15. Cohn, *Shakespeare in Germany*, p. xxxii.
16. Ibid., p. xxix.
17. Ibid., p. lviii.

attraction. A humorous German poem printed at Frankfort in 1597 gives us an account of an English clown's doings:

> For so distort his face he can,
> He looks no longer like a man.
> And many a clownish trick he knows,
> Wears shoes that don't much pinch his toes.
> His breeches would hold two or more,
> And have a monstrous flap before.
> His jacket makes him look a fool
> With all the blows he takes so cool.[18]

The clownish tricks and pranks often mentioned in various sources as commonly used by the English players, apart from evoking cheap applause[19] were frequently the cause of serious trouble from severe authorities. The English were often prohibited from further performances for the indecencies they showed or said on stage. "Heard you the English and other strangers sing? / Saw you their jolly dance, their lusty spring?" This passage from a contemporary Dutch drama expresses the frequently repeated opinion.[20] In the Frankfort poem of 1597 we find the following lines:

> The tumbler also did us please,
> He sprang high in the air with ease ...
> His hose they fitted him so tight,
> His codpiece was a lovely sight.
> Nubile maids and lecherous dames
> He kindled into lustful flames ...
> For, know that those who paid their fee
> To witness a bright comedy,
> Or hear the tunes of fine musicians,
> Were more entranced by the additions
> Of bawdy jests and comic strokes,
> Of antics and salacious jokes,
> And what, with his tight-fitting hose
> The well-bred tumbler did disclose.[21]

18. Quoted from ibid., pp. lix-lx.
19. An anonymous Frankfort poet wrote a satirical piece on the English players, in which we find the following lines:

> And yet these actors play such stuff,
> They must themselves oft laugh enough,
> To think a man his money brings
> To them, to see such foolish things.

The full text of this poem was published and translated by Cohn, pp. xc-xci.
20. Ibid.
21. Translated by Ernst Brennecke in his *Shakespeare in Germany 1590-1700* (Chicago, 1964), p. 8.

The abundance of bawdy elements in performances should not be surprising in view of the fact that the Puritan attacks against theatres in London usually stress the immoral and lascivious elements of staging, i.e. "such wanton gestures, such bawdie speaches ... such kissing and bussing, such clipping and culling, Suche winckinge and glancinge of wanton eyes" together with "lewde adulterous kisses and embracements ... whorish, lust inflaming sollicitations ... real lively representations of the act of venery which attend and set out stage playes."[22] It seems rather obvious that at least in the early phase of the English players' activity on the Continent bawdy elements played a considerable role in their staging practices. With an audience not understanding the language spoken on stage, this was the easiest device to attract the attention of spectators and cause laughter. As in London, the "immorality" of productions was deepened by the fact that women's parts were played by youths. I have not come across any continental records which would confirm the idea that in the first half of the seventeenth century there were actresses in English companies "beyond the seas." We know for certain that wives of actors did sometimes go along. Richard Jones was thus accompanied in Poland, and in 1620 his wife sent a letter from Gdansk to Edward Alleyn.[23] John Spencer's wife collected the entrance money at Rothenburg in 1613,[24] and Robert Reynolds' wife was given a pension by no other than the King of Poland, Vladislaus IV, after her husband died shortly after 1640.[25] And it is "Jungen" that are mentioned in various records.[26] The first recorded actresses in an English company on the Continent appear in 1654 in George Jolly's troupe, i.e., towards the close of English activity there.

Furthermore, the "Englische Komödianten" must have become inseparably associated with bawdry as early as the late 1590s, because the companies which were to follow, having in their repertory serious tragedies in German prose translations, were at pains to convince city or town authorities that, in spite of the fact that they were English, there was nothing immoral or irreligious in what they wanted to present. This of course does not mean that the bawdry disappeared from the English productions on the Continent, but that when the

22. Chambers, *Elizabethan Stage*, IV, 222-23.
23. Published by W. W. Greg in *Henslowe Papers* (London, 1907), pp. 94-95.
24. Harris, "English Comedians in Germany," 456.
25. An account of this was given in 1642 by an English traveller, Peter Munday; see his *The Travels in Europe and Asia* .. , Hakluyt Society, vol. VI (London, 1925), 181.
26. Harris (p. 456) mentions only "one scrap of positive evidence": "2 Jungen" who accompanied Browne at Strasbourg in 1618; but Robert Reynolds' company at Torgau in 1626 had "vier Jungen" in the cast of players (see Herz, *Englische Schauspieler*, p. 31).

players switched from English to German, they simply had more to offer even to less sophisticated audiences. Thus, an English company that visited Elbląg [Elbing] in August 1605 was prohibited from further performances for having shown "disgraceful things" in their comedy.[27] When in 1615 John Green applied for leave to play to the City Council in Gdansk, he was answered that a permit would be granted after the councillors had seen the rehearsal of the plays to be shown.[28] In numerous instances consent was given to the English to play on condition that nothing indecent would be presented, which indicates that the reputation of the English companies was, justly or not, rather tarnished. Even as late as 1658, George Jolly's performances shocked the Viennese, who complained that his company's comedies were "spiced with the most scandalous obscenities."[29]

Interestingly enough, the frivolous actions on stage led to a peculiar theatrical custom which seems to have developed early in the seventeenth century. It became almost a rule that whenever the English players arrived at a continental town to give public performances, they invited, first of all, the local authorities, with families and friends, for a special show with admission free of charge. Very often, as was the case mentioned above with Green's company in Gdansk, this performance was of primary importance to the players, since it determined the councillors' decision as to whether they should be allowed to perform or not. This may also be interpreted as an early example of preventive theatre censorship on the Continent. The premiere of a new play was occasionally a similar pretext for a grand performance restricted to the elite only. Incidently, there seems to have developed yet another tradition: that of a farewell performance. In an application for leave to play, dated 30 August 1619, a company of English actors performing in Gdansk refers to this practice:

> Because we have had no opportunity to bid our spectators farewell, as we have not (contrary to our customs) given a farewell performance, it may be interpreted as mere tactlessness. Moreover, if this piece of news reaches our spectators in other places, it will be understood as an offence—as if we were banished for wrongdoing... Therefore, we humbly ask for permission to play on next Sunday and to present an interesting comedy to our spectators, so that we could leave with honour and a good name.[30]

27. E. A. Hagen, *Geschichte des Theaters in Preussen* . . . (Königsberg, 1854), p. 53.
28. Bolte, *Danziger Theater*, pp. 44-47.
29. Hotson, *Restoration and Commonwealth Stage*, p. 175.
30. All the supplications of this company were first published by Bolte, pp. 52-55.

Occasionally, a similar grand performance was given in honour of the town authorities, as was the case with an English company acting in Gdansk in August 1619: "Our company has noticed a common practise of expressing gratefulness for kindness and favour in the form of a particularly beautiful performance, which we would like to present in honour of the High Council."[31]

From what has been said above the conclusion may be drawn that in continental staging, as arranged by the English players, clowns and their bawdy jokes and pranks constituted the chief attraction, particularly in the early phase of their activity there. And, characteristically, clowns were the first to use German on stage, as we learn from a Münster chronicle of 1599. The same source leads us to yet another significant feature of continental staging, namely, music and dances, which seem to have played a far more important role there than they did in England, and therefore it is worth quoting in full:

> On the 26th of November 1599 there arrived here eleven Englishmen, all young and lively fellows, with the exception of one, a rather elderly man, who had everything under his management. They acted on five successive days five different comedies in their own English tongue. They carried with them various musical instruments, such as lutes, cithern, fiddles, fifes, and such like: they danced many new and foreign dances (not usual in this country) at the beginning and at the end of their comedies. They were accompanied by a clown, who, when a new act had to commence and when they had to change their costumes, made many antics and pranks in German during the performance, by which he amused the audience.[32]

It should be stressed once again that in the early years, as well as facing the language barrier, English players often performed before audiences not accustomed to theatre, and still less to the sophisticated staging techniques that had been developed in London. Therefore, many strolling companies labelled themselves "comedians and instrumentalists," and were most of them in fact composed of both actors and musicians (some of the latter highly praised in the history of English music: John Dowland may serve as an example). When required to do so, a dramatic company of this type could easily transform itself into an "orchestra," giving concerts accompanied by dances. In numerous continental accounts and descriptions of actual performances given by the English, it is frequently stressed that it was music and dances that attracted the attention of spectators and won their praise and admiration.

31. Ibid.
32. Quoted from Cohn, pp. cxxxiv-cxxxv.

Already in 1592 the same performance Fynes Moryson saw at Frankfort was described in different terms by a German. It was not the bad quality of acting and lack of apparel that struck him, but the "excellent music" and "perfect dances" such as he "had not seen or heard before."[33] As we learn from the Münster chronicle, music was played before and after the performance and, in addition, during the intermission between the acts of a play. This latter convention is confirmed by other sources, including an account given by Michael Praetorius, one of the major contemporary writers on music:

> So it is also done in comedies, where a sweet and lovely Musica instrumentalis is performed between the acts, with cornets, fiddles, and other similar instruments, varied sometimes with vocal music ... in order that the personatae personae might be enabled to change their costume, to prepare themselves for the next acts and to recreate themselves.[34]

This staging convention must have been developed in the nineties of the sixteenth century, and, interestingly enough, was not abandoned when the English players started using German on stage.

Thus in 1607 a company of English "comedians and musicians" performed at Königsberg and were paid 75 marks for the show, which among other things included music and dances.[35] In 1611 John Sigismund, the Elector of Brandenburg, left Berlin for Königsberg, for the purpose of receiving the investiture of the Duchy, and was accompanied by an English company of nineteen actors and sixteen musicians.[36] In 1613 a contemporary Nuremberg chronicle gives us the following account: "English comedians have acted and held beautiful comedies and tragedies ... and other such histories, besides graceful dancing, lovely music, and other entertainments ... in good German language."[37] One of the most famous English actors active on the Continent, John Green, in his application to the City Council in Gdansk, dated July 1615, recommends to the councillors not only the plays, but also "music and other interesting things," and makes it clear that the language used will be "pure German."[38] These "other interesting things" could mean leaping or perhaps pantomime. In 1608 the authorities of the city of Leyden allowed William Peadle,

33. This account is found in a letter, dated 13 September 1592, written by Balthazar Baumgartner the Younger to his wife. Quoted after J. G. Riewald, "New Light on the English Actors in the Netherlands, c. 1590-c. 1660," *English Studies*, XLI 1, 2 (1960), 66.
34. Quoted from Cohn, pp. cxxxv-cxxxvi.
35. Bolte, p. 34.
36. Cohn, pp. lxxxiv-lxxxv.
37. Ibid., pp. lxxxvii-lxxxviii.
38. Supplications of this company were first published by Bolte, pp. 44-47.

senior, an English dancer, acrobat and pantomimist, to give "various beautiful and chaste performances with his body, without using any words."[39] It should be added here that dumb-shows, such as that in Shakespeare's *Hamlet*, must have been another staging convention used by the English in the early period of their activity abroad; and the scraps of extant evidence seem to suggest that they served as a brief summary of what was to follow, which was particularly important when playing before an audience having no knowledge of English.

That music played an important role in staging until the end of the activity on the Continent is confirmed by later pieces of evidence. In 1617 a company of eight actors and musicians (including Valentine Flood) was brought by one George Vincent, "servant to the Prince of Poland," directly from London to Warsaw, where they stayed for a couple of years.[40] In 1619 John Spencer's company applied to the councillors in Gdansk, offering their "music and comedies."[41] A company visiting the same city in 1649, recommends a "decent and chaste" show, which would include "pleasant English music" and "fabulous ballet."[42] George Jolly, the last of the famous English strollers on the Continent, offered, apart from "good instructive stories," "beautiful English music" to the citizens of Basle.[43]

The available evidence seems to support Moryson's account of 1592 that the early performances on the Continent were given by small companies poorly equipped with costumes and stage properties. It is difficult to imagine that in this reconnaissance period the English players would take the risk and invest substantial means, if they had any, to buy expensive costumes and stage properties, not to mention carriages and horses, and to take them abroad without any guarantee of financial gain and personal safety. This is why the first tours were usually short, and the actors, having performed in one or two towns and in villages on the way, returned to London. It certainly took some time before they got acquainted with local customs and traditions and were able to plan their tours beforehand without taking the risk of finding the city's gates closed to them. Here, again, noble patronage was indispensable, with a permanent residence being an obvious advantage. Moreover, this patronage

39. Riewald, "English Actors in the Netherland," p. 76.
40. Ibid., pp. 89-90; see also Limon, "Komedianci angielsey w Warszawie, 471-72.
41. Bolte, p. 52.
42. The supplication of this company is in the collection of the State Archives in Gdansk, catalogue number: 300, 36/68, f. 71-74 and was first published in my article, "New Evidence for the Activity of the English Players in the Netherlands in the Second Quarter of the Seventeenth Century," *English Studies*, 62, 2 (1981), 116.
43. Hotson, p. 117.

enabled the players to acquire costumes and other items necessary for the production at little or no cost.

Already in 1586, the Elector of Saxony had costumes made for a company of English players that stayed at his court for several months.[44] In addition, the actors were promised one coat a year and a free table at court.[45] In 1597 in the list of expenses of the court of the Landgrave Moritz of Hesse, we find items like: "white clothes for the clown" and "a pair of shoes for the fool," and "six ells of white woolen cloth" which are necessary for the English to present their "comedy."[46] Thomas Sackville was given in 1608 three pieces of flesh-colour and three pieces of blue silk ribbon, as payment for performances at Brunswick.[47] The often-quoted undated letter which Richard Jones, who went to the Continent in the troupe of 1592 and may have therefore been at Frankfort at the time of Moryson's visit, wrote to Edward Alleyn shows what must have been the common condition of the actors going abroad:

> I am to go over beyond the seas w^t Mr Browne and the company . . . now, good Sir, as you have ever byne my worthie frend, so helpe me nowe. I have a sute of clothes and a cloke at pane fo^r three pound, and if it shall pleas you to lend me so much to release them, I shall be bound to pray fo^r you so longe as I leve; for if I go over, and have no clothes, I shall not be esteemed of. . . . .[48]

In view of this, entering service at a nobleman's court was a blessing, and a guarantee of survival. When the English players had established themselves on the Continent permanently, it was their rich costumes that were often admired and described. For instance, one of the well-known writers of the period, John Sommer, reflected on the luxury of his contemporaries, comparing them with the English: "Their collars must be set with pearls, and such a display of finery is indulged in, that they strut along like the English Comedians in the theatre."[49] It is worth mentioning that one of the original costumes used by the English players on the Continent, now lost, had been kept in the collection of the "Prussia" Society at Königsberg and was shown in a theatre exhibition in Vienna in 1882.[50]

44. We learn about this from his letter to the Steward, dated 25 October 1586, first published by Cohn, p. xxv.
45. Ibid., p. xxiv.
46. Ibid., p. lviii.
47. Ibid., p. xxxiv.
48. *Henslowe Papers*, p. 33.
49. Cohn, p. cxxxvi.
50. See K. Massner, *Die Kostümausstellung im K. K. Österreicheschen Museum 1891* (Wien, 1892-1893). This neglected source is noticed by Prof. Zbigniew Raszewski in his article "Jeszcze o teatrze zawodowym w dawnej Polsce," *Pamiętnik Teatralny*, 2 (1955), where he reproduces the photograph of the costume on page 155.

All of this, with the concomitant replacement of English by German, contributed to the high quality and splendour of staging in both temporary and permanent court theatres, and consequently increased the quality of public performances as well. Even the temporary court arrangements for production were akin to those of the English stage.[51] An example of such an arrangement may be found at Königsberg, where in the autumn of 1611 an English company of nineteen actors and sixteen musicians gave a memorable performance on the occasion of the investiture in the Duchy of John Sigismund, the new Elector of Brandenburg. A "theatrum" was arranged ad hoc, and at high cost, in the "old grand saloon" which was covered with red cloth, and the city of Constantinople was erected for the actors who presented *The Turkish Triumph-Comedy*.[52] The costumes were rich and costly, as were the stage properties. The scenery even included painted clouds, and in the list of expenses we find the following items: blue, red, and white cloth, fringes, gold border, 70 ells of red silk, 50 ells of red cord, Monks' dresses, 18 large and 17 long plumes, a sword with a gilt hilt, a wooden shield, four death's heads, carved work, and turned work.[53] There is little doubt that in such ideal conditions, and before sophisticated audiences, the staging of plays, given in German, must have been similar to that of the London productions.

Similarly, the repertory of the English players on the Continent included, in so far as German titles have been possible to identify, plays staged previously in the London theatres. One of the earliest repertory lists of John Green's company, dated 1607, included among others *The Proud Woman of Antwerp*, *The Jew*, *Doctor Faustus*, *Fortunatus*, and *The Turkish Mahomet and Hiren the Fair Greek*, all of which were in the repertory of the Lord Admiral's comapny.[54] The first anthology of English drama in German prose translations was published as early as 1620, followed by an enlarged edition in 1626.[55] Altogether about thirty English plays were published in that time, including eight plays by Shakespeare, and several by other major dramatists such as Marlowe, Dekker, Greene, and Kyd.[56] Naturally, in later periods, more plays were added to the English repertory. Without going into details, it has to be stressed that the very selection

---

51. See Hermann Grimm, *Essays*, (Hanover, 1859), pp. 159-60.
52. This may have been George Peele's play entitled *The Turkish Mahomet and Hiren the Fair Greek*.
53. Hagen, *Theaters in Preussen*, pp. 53-58.
54. Chambers, II, 281-82.
55. Ibid.; and also 285.
56. A full list of these plays is given by Chambers, II, 285-86.

of plays imposed technical constraints upon the actors, who were at pains to suit their staging to the demands of the dramatic text.

This was particularly difficult in the case of public performances, which, until the first public theatres were built on the Continent, were in most instances held in rather primitive conditions. The multiplicity of physical stage conditions obviously led to a variety of staging techniques, and the same play performed by the same company would be something entirely different when staged in a village inn, or in a town market place, or in a rich merchant's house, or in a public theatre equipped with a large stage, trap-doors, and machinery. It is therefore difficult, if not impossible, to formulate a consistent staging theory for public performances on the Continent. However, there seems to have been a general tendency among the English companies to improve the quality of their performances to the level of both court productions and those back in London. Partly they were supported by their rich patrons, who provided the actors with costumes, with some of their stage properties, and occasionally even with means of transportation;[57] and partly they tried to manage on their own. In the numerous supplications to town authorities that have been preserved in continental archives, it is the high costs of production that the English players mention most frequently in their appeals to prolong the time given them to play.

Thus in July 1615 the Elector of Brandenburg's company complained to the City Council in Gdansk that their "theatre had suffered much from rain and storm."[58] Surely, in this case the word "theatre" means scenery, elements of which were apparently left on stage overnight and had been damaged by rain and wind. In the same application rehearsals and "other preparations" that lasted for four days are mentioned. This implies that, in addition to rehearsing before the first performance, the actors had been busy ordering, buying and arranging various items necessary for the production. Several years earlier, in 1611, when John Spencer's company visited Gdansk, in their application the actors mention the "silk merchants" and "other craftsmen" to whom they owe money, and ask the City Council to grant them a permit for additional performances so that they can leave the city without any debt.[59] Similarly, John Green's company paid in 1615 in Gdansk 100 marks to have "galleries, benches, and other

---

57. As was the case in 1586, when the actors were given a "carriage-wagon" by the Elector of Saxony; see Cohn, p. xxvi.
58. Bolte, pp. 42-43.
59. Quoted from a supplication published in ibid., pp. 38-40.

things" made by local craftsmen.[60] This, indeed, was a large sum of money, equivalent perhaps to twenty English pounds,[61] and may serve as evidence of the actors' efforts to prepare a superb production, or at least the best they could afford. At the Frankfort fair at Easter 1605, English actors paid 10 florins for erecting and as much for taking down their "scaffolding"—that is, the stage.[62] John Spencer paid 135 florins for his stage at Regensburg in October 1613.[63] All these pieces of evidence lead us to the ultimate conclusion that whenever possible, or perhaps profitable, the English players tried to add splendour to their production and did not hesitate to invest money both in costumes and stage design. The splendour they achieved depended, of course, largely on their hopes of financial gain, the conditions on which they were permitted to play, and the number of performances. The latter, in the case of public performances, varied from a couple of days to two months of daily shows, as was the case of an English company of 1643 in Gdansk.[64]

In larger towns public performances by the English were usually announced by printed bills, of which several have been preserved.[65] In most cases performances were held outdoors and during the day, although several instances are known when parts of municipal buildings were turned into temporary theatres where artificial lighting was used. It is difficult to establish the length of a typical show, but two or three hours may have been the average. The author of a German satirical poem, dated 1615, is obviously exaggerating when he claims that:

> Folk like to see the English play,
> Far more than hear the parson pray:
> Four hours rather stand and hear
> The play, than one in church appear.[66]

---

60. Ibid., pp. 44-47.
61. For the financial side of the English players' activity on the Continent see Harris, 446-64.
62. Ibid., 462-3.
63. Ibid.
64. One of the supplications of this company, yet unpublished, is in the collection of the State Archives in Gdansk: 300, 36/68, f. 49-52; another, now lost, is cited by Bolte, p. 70. For other details connected with the number of performances given by various companies see Harris, 454-5.
65. One of these bills was reproduced by Cohn who dated it 1628, and by G. Könnecke, in *Bilderatlas zur Geschichte der deutschen Nationallitteratur* (Marburg, 1895), p. 171, who dated it 1650. Another bill, dated 1656, was reproduced by Hotson, p. 175.
66. Quoted from Cohn, p. xc.

In the first half of the seventeenth century, two permanent public theatres were erected on the Continent, both of which seem to have been architectural echoes of the theatres in London. The first of these, built around 1610 in Gdansk,[67] is undoubtedly reminiscent of London's Fortune and the available evidence seems to suggest that some of the English players may have been involved in the whole enterprise by bringing the idea and architectural details of an Elizabethan-style theatre to Gdanks. A public theatre erected in 1628 in Nuremburg,[68] seems to have been a derivative version of the Gdansk theatre. It is worth noting that both of these theatres were multi-functional. Apart from theatrical performances, other entertainments were held there: fencing tournaments, acrobatic feats, and animal-baiting, as was the practice in some of the London playhouses, such as the Hope. No pictorial evidence has been preserved for the physical stage conditions in either of these theatres. However, in the case of the Gdansk playhouse, other sources, including stage directions in plays written by local dramatists for that particular stage, indicate that the stage was rather large, equal perhaps to that of the Fortune; it was equipped with trap-doors, a place for concealment, and an upper acting area; and later, in the 1640s, complicated machinery was installed for opera productions. In such conditions as these, which were by no means typical for the Continent, the actors were enabled to present all their talents and craft; and the staging of plays by English companies must have been very similar to that back in London, which was the artistic goal of the players, for the extant evidence proves that their drive for financial gain, although important and basic, was accompanied by constant efforts to improve the quality of productions.

It therefore appears possible to distinguish certain trends and phases in the development of staging on the Continent. First was the reconnaissance phase, which lasted for about ten years starting from the mid-eighties of the sixteenth century and characterized by sporadic tours by small companies, poorly equipped with costumes and stage properties. Performances were given in English, the dramatic texts were abridged, and the leading role in staging was played by the

---

67. See my article "Pictorial Evidence for a Possible Replica of the London Fortune Theatre in Gdansk," *Shakespeare Survey* 32 (1979), 189-99; for a general study of the "English" stage on the Continent, see R. Pascal, "The Stage of the "Englische Komödianten" — Three Problems," *Modern Language Review*, XXXV, 3 (1940), 367-76.
68. See F. E. Hysel, *Das Theater in Nürnberg von 1612 bis 1863 nebst einem Anhange über das Theater in Fürth* (Nürnberg, 1863).

clowns, and by various non-verbal devices such as music and dancing. Next was the period before the Thirty Years' War, characterized by the increasing number of large companies protected and supported by noble patrons. Owing to this patronage, the activity of English companies became permanent. After the replacement of English by German, and with a sufficient number of actors, these well-equipped companies performed full-length plays; and in appropriate conditions their staging must have been similar to that in the London theatres. Then comes the final phase, which covers approximately the fifteen years before and the fifteen years after the middle of the seventeenth century. Only several major companies, led by veteran actors, remain active on the Continent, temporarily supported by a fresh supply of players from England, as the result of the closing of the theatres in London. In the last years, as was the case with George Jolly's company, the staging of plays was evidently influenced by new theatre trends coming from Italy. And one has to agree with Leslie Hotson that Jolly "knew that the popular taste was turning toward music, decorations, and machines of the Italian opera, and he had made up his mind to meet and even anticipate the demand," and that "for English theatrical history Jolly is even more important, since his development of music, scenery, and the use of actresses preceded Davenant's opera by several years. Jolly is in reality the first English producer to use the modern stage."[69]

Bearing in mind all the obstacles, dangers, and difficulties the English players had to face on the Continent, one is surely surprised at the scale and scope of their indefatigable travels after 1594. Apart from the frequently unfavourable conditions in London, several factors contributed to this phenomenon. It is beyond dispute that the popularity and fame of the English players originated in the high quality of their staging. One has to keep in mind that these actors were highly skilled professionals, whose art and talents surpassed the continental average. Given noble patronage and support they formed large, well-equipped companies, and after having shifted from English into German they acquainted their audiences not only with the greatest dramatic works of the times, but also with a standard of staging which in itself became a goal for their continental successors. The name "Englische Komödianten," at first associated with frivolity, later came to denote actors of high quality, and was even used by some German and Dutch companies long after the true English players had ceased their activity on the Continent. Moreover, the stage names

69. Hotson, p. 171.

of some of the actors, such as Hans Stockfish and Pickleherring, have been incorporated into the history of continental theatre. The most significant and characteristic feature of the English companies was undoubtedly their incredible ability to adjust to any staging conditions and to any type of audience, and this flexibility is in itself a proof of their high standard.

Finally, it has to be stressed that the English players were responsible for the dissemination of theatre art in countries with little theatrical tradition, and their activity on the Continent gave rise to professional theatre north of the Alps. With all this in mind, it may be said that they were, indeed, "the abstracts and brief chronicles of the time."

The Recovery of the Elizabethan Stage

JILL L. LEVENSON

I

During the years 1642 to 1660, the dismantled Elizabethan public theatre entered a long period of thorough reconstruction. By the time Nicholas Rowe published his edition of Shakespeare in 1709, the building had been transformed into a concept. Although features of the Elizabethan stage persisted through the age of Garrick, early theatre historians and drama critics ignored this physical presence. They wrote about Elizabethan stage conditions in generally abstract terms, sometimes idealizing them, more often patronizing them, but very rarely saying anything specific about the building, its accoutrements, or the companies who acted on its stage. Towards the end of the eighteenth century this process showed tentative signs of reversal. The editors of Shakespeare, sometimes contradicting views of the stage expressed in their prefaces, began to cite Elizabethan theatrical conventions in their notes and so to imagine the original staging of individual passages; and Edmond Malone produced his history of the English stage based on documentary evidence.

From that period until the present day, efforts intensified—at first, sporadically—to re-create the Elizabethan public theatre in concrete form. Ludwig Tieck's enterprises during the first half of the nine-teenth century introduced a phenomenon which would recur at irregular intervals until the 1950s: in England, on the Continent, and later in the United States, assorted intelligentsia or members of the theatrical avant-garde contrived the remodelling of existing theatres according to their notions of Elizabethan standards. Often they documented their experiments in various publications, and in addition, especially since the discovery of the Swan drawing in 1888, scholarship has contributed noticeably to such experiments. With the advent of Sir Tyrone Guthrie's Stratford Festival stage in 1953, another important trend originated:[1] in English-speaking countries, theatre people, scholars and entrepreneurs, frequently working together, have promoted the construction of new buildings which incorporate modified Elizabethan stages. The latest development arose during the past decade, which brought forth at least three plans—in England, the United States, and Canada—to reconstruct the Globe Playhouse in a milieu more or less simulating its original environment.

On the whole, then, theatre history offers a relatively organized account of the fortunes of the Elizabethan public playhouse over the past three and a half centuries. In the paper which follows, I shall explore segments of that account in some detail and, with the last segment, consider briefly why our own era seems determined to replicate the Elizabethan theatre.

II

The fate of the Elizabethan stage after the Civil War followed logically from the conditions which had forced the theatres to close. In its initial denatured phase, the playhouse hardly served as a model for contemporary practice. Its stage, architecture, scenic conventions, and other customs had been modified for use in the Restoration theatre, but the principles behind these features received very little attention, and their continuity none at all. The Elizabethan theatre served rather as a focus (or lack of focus) for moral and aesthetic judgments about drama in general and contemporary theatre in particular.

In two short treatises, for example, facts about the Elizabethan stage and its acting conventions—rare commodities then and now—substantiate the authors' criticism of late seventeenth-century theatre in England. According to Richard Flecknoe, in A Short Discourse of the English Stage (1664), drama in the Elizabethan age was compatible with religion, and theatre with the church [p. 3].[2] The theatre engaged

1. For helping me gather material on developments during and since the creation of the Stratford Festival Theatre in Ontario, I am grateful to Mr. Dan Ladell, archivist for the Festival.
2. Citations of both treatises come from Historia histrionica: an historical account of the English stage by James Wright (1699) / A short discourse of the English stage by Richard Flecknoe (1664), introd. Peter Davison (New York and London, 1972). Since Wright's Preface and Flecknoe's treatise are not paginated in this reprint edition, I have given them page numbers in square brackets in my text.

in delightful pedagogy: "It was the happiness of the Actors of those Times to have such Poets . . . to instruct them, and write for them; . . ." [p. 6]. Flecknoe praises the scenic plainness of the Elizabethan theatre in order to explain its moral impact, an effect much diminished by the "Magnificence" of the Restoration stage [p. 8]. In his words, one hears simultaneously the voices of the theatre historian and the moralist:

> . . . that which makes our Stage the better, makes our Playes the worse perhaps, they striving now to make them more for sight, then hearing; whence that solid joy of the interior is lost, and that benefit which men formerly receiv'd from Playes, from which they seldom or never went away, but far better and wiser then they came [p. 8].

At the very end of the seventeenth century, James Wright makes a similar case for responsible theatre in his *Historia histrionica* (1699). He peppers his treatise with defences for having written it and with descriptions of the old theatre which clearly put the new to shame. In his Preface, he insists that early drama has historical value and that "*the Profession of Players is not . . . totally scandalous, nor all of them . . . reprobate, . . .*" [p. iii]. The speakers in the dialogue which follows recall the theatre before the Civil War; they maintain that contemporary plays are "as much inferior to those of former Times as the Actors now in being . . . are, . . ." (p. 2), and one stresses that the many acting companies then "All . . . got Money, and Liv'd in Reputation," able to support themselves "meerly from their own Merit; the weight of the Matter, and goodness of the Action, without Scenes and Machines: . . ." (pp. 5-6).

The treatises of Flecknoe and Wright confirm the opinion of Arthur Colby Sprague that "There were persons in Betterton's time who found, indeed, that acting was on the decline, that the 'new Scenes, and Decorations of the Stage,' which were introduced soon after the Restoration, had been 'the Destruction of good Playing.' "[3] But the critics who measured the new stage by the old were outnumbered by those, like Dryden, who ignored both their houses, concentrating on "Dramatick Poesie" rather than performance. As M. C. Bradbrook points out in her important book on *Elizabethan Stage Conditions*: ". . . their anxiety to dissociate themselves from what appeared to be a more barbarous age would not allow them to recognise it [i.e., the Elizabethan stage]. . . . Since the earlier stage was generally condemned, its traditions were soon forgotten; . . ."[4]

3. Sprague is quoting from Charles Gildon's biography of Thomas Betterton (London, 1710) in his *Shakespearian Players and Performances* (Cambridge, Mass., 1953), p. 17.
4. M. C. Bradbrook, *Elizabethan Stage Conditions: A Study of Their Place in the Interpretation of Shakespeare's Plays* (Cambridge, 1968), p. 7.

Consequently, references to the Elizabethan theatre in the first eighteenth-century editions of Shakespeare—the primary source of such references at this time—lack any sense of concreteness, any sharply defined conception of the playhouse in which Shakespeare worked. Rowe, who superimposed contemporary act and scene divisions on Shakespeare's plays, offers his edition to the Duke of Somerset as "the best Present of *English* Poetry I am capable of making Your Grace."[5] In his forty-page account of Shakespeare's life, he makes one brief reference to the theatre—a description of Shakespeare's "first Acquaintance in the Play-house" so vague that it names neither company nor theatre (p. vi). His inquiries in this context have revealed only "that the top of his Performance was the Ghost in his own *Hamlet*," a disappointment because Rowe ". . . should have been much more pleas'd, to have learn'd from some certain Authority, which was the first Play he wrote; . . . what was the first Essay of a Fancy like *Shakespeare*'s" (p. vi). In a supplement to Rowe's edition (1710), Charles Gildon writes a sixty-seven-page "Essay on the Art, Rise and Progress of the Stage in *Greece*, *Rome* and *England*," which says nothing about Greek, Roman, or English theatres.[6] Like Rowe, he conceives drama as poetry; and he evinces suspicion of people associated with the theatre—actors, managers, playwrights, spectators—because they hamper the poetic muses.

This notion of the theatre as an obstruction to dramatic art grows more elaborate in the work of Alexander Pope, Lewis Theobald, and William Warburton. Pope goes on at greatest length about the players, those dreadful people who hobbled Shakespeare's genius and mutilated his text. For Pope and many of his contemporaries, the word "player," when it designated the Elizabethan actor, indicated perversity of every possible hue. Because of Shakespeare's association with "players," he lapsed in taste and judgment, and did not observe Aristotle's principles. As for Shakespeare's text, "the ignorance of the Players, both as his actors, and as his editors" has so filled it with "almost innumerable Errors," that "When the nature and kinds of these are enumerated and considered, I dare to say that not *Shakespear* only, but *Aristotle* or *Cicero*, had their works undergone the same fate, might have appear'd to want sense as well as learning."[7] Pope's

5. Dedication to *The Works of Mr. William Shakespear; in Six Volumes.* . . . , ed. N. Rowe (London, 1709), I, A2ᵛ. The account of Shakespeare's life occupies pp. i-xl of this volume.

6. The essay appears in *The Works of Mr. William Shakespear. Volume the Seventh.* . . . (London, 1710), pp. i-lxvii.

7. Preface to *The Works of Shakespear. In Six Volumes.* . . . ed. Mr. Pope (London, 1725), I, xiv-xv.

contempt for professional theatre in Shakespeare's age seems to have freed him from all scholarly compunctions; when he needs theatre history, as Gerald Eades Bentley points out,[8] he makes it up. In the notes, "A Table *of* Greenfield's" for *King Henry V*, II. iii. qualifies as the longest and most well-known example (Vol. III, p. 422). In the Preface, one meets this famous invention:

> Having been forced to say so much of the Players, I think I ought in justice to remark, that the Judgment, as well as Condition, of that class of people was then far inferior to what it is in our days. As then the best Playhouses were Inns and Taverns (the *Globe*, the *Hope*, the *Red Bull*, the *Fortune*, & c.) so the top of the profession were then meer Players, not Gentlemen of the stage: They were led into the Buttery by the Steward, not plac'd at the Lord's table, or Lady's toilette: and consequently were intirely depriv'd of those advantages they now enjoy, . . . (Vol. I, p. xix)

Theobald finds previous editions of Shakespeare unsatisfactory, but reflects the attitudes of Rowe, Gildon, and Pope in his own work. The little he says about Elizabethan theatrical conditions reveals that he views them as interfering with the progress of drama—in particular, with the transmission of Shakespeare's text. A few annotations indicate that Pope's inventiveness prompted Theobald to some reasonable (and some unreasonable) conclusions about theatrical conventions; others show that Theobald followed the current editorial practice of blaming textual anomalies on the "players."[9] For Warburton, Shakespeare's text did not escape the players soon enough. His editorial notes attribute to the actors "impious nonsense," "stupidity," "innumerable absurdities," and worst of all, "infamous, senseless ribaldry," delinquencies forcing him to "cashier" passages and risk "a castrated edition."[10]

By the mid-eighteenth century, then, Elizabethan theatre had totally dematerialized into a vague concept synonymous with irresponsibility—moral, aesthetic, and a combination of both, textual. Editors and actors who presented Shakespeare's plays showed no interest in the original contexts of performance. In their minds and on their stages,

---

8. In the Introduction to *The Seventeenth-Century Stage: A Collection of Critical Essays*, ed. and introd. Gerald Eades Bentley (Toronto, 1968), pp. ix-x.

9. For examples, see *The Works of Shakespeare: In Seven Volumes*. . . . ed. Mr. Theobald (London, 1733), I, 18 (note to the first act of *The Tempest*); IV, 30-31 (note to the second act of *King Henry V*); V, 219 (note to the fifth act of *King Lear*); and VII, 313 (note to the third act of *Hamlet*).

10. See *The Works of Shakespear*. . . . [ed. William Warburton] (London, 1747), II, 18 (note to *Much Ado about Nothing*, II. i.); IV, 110 (note to *The First Part of King Henry IV*, I. iv.); V, 329 (note to *King Richard III*, V. v.); and III, 287 (note to *The Winter's Tale*, I. ii.).

they neither saw nor heard Elizabethan drama in Elizabethan terms. More than time, changing critical and dramatic conventions distanced the eighteenth century from the English Renaissance playhouse. Contemporary productions grew more and more pictorial and literary; they became increasingly theatrical and, paradoxically, less dramatic. Large indoor theatres fostered not only spectacle but also a rhetorical acting style which enhanced the static moment: the set speech, the description—those passages which like arias could be isolated and savoured for their neoclassical qualities. Moreover, as R. D. Stock explains,

> . . . the art of acting was commonly depreciated in the first half of the eighteenth century, and it was also generally assumed that readers only were the proper judges of dramatic merit. . . . At least throughout the first two-thirds of the century, reviewers normally approached plays as books rather than as staged productions.[11]

All in all, the Elizabethan stage, its conventions and its plays, must have been inconceivable to the early eighteenth-century imagination.

Yet even before mid-century, signs of a new attitude appeared. Sir Richard Steele's Preface to *The Conscious Lovers* (1723) replaces all drama in its native dynamic tradition: "It must be remember'd, a Play is to be seen, and is made to be Represented with the Advantage of Action, nor can appear but with half the Spirit, without it; . . ."[12] By the 1750s theoretical essays in England and France emphasize the vital difference between reading a play and seeing it performed. Further, the theatrics of David Garrick drew attention to dramatic performance, as the author of *The Adventures of a Rake* (1759) illustrates:

> When the Skill of the Player is added to that of the Poet, and the one gives Utterance to the other's Conceptions, it is not the Actor or the Poet that we hear, 'tis the Character of the Drama that speaks to us. . . . *Shakespear's Macbeth* is scarcely intelligible to the Learned; Garrick's *Macbeth* lives, and is intelligible to the Vulgar. This proves to an evident Demonstration, that acting any Piece is preferable to reading it.[13]

This quotation reveals a subtle transition. As soon as drama is conceived as performance, its theatrical context assumes, if not respectability, at least a state of objective reality. When theatre courted drama in late eighteenth-century dramatic criticism and

11. R. D. Stock, *Samuel Johnson and Neoclassical Dramatic Theory: The Intellectual Context of the Preface to Shakespeare* (Lincoln, Nebr., 1973), p. 209.
12. Quoted in Stock, p. 210.
13. Ibid.

editions, the playhouse, the actors, and their customs functioned not as an unstable fulcrum of moral discourse, but as concrete means for illuminating dramatic texts. Writers imagined the physical conditions of production in order to interpret plays and resolve textual anomalies.

The profound imagination of Samuel Johnson initiated the process of restoring Shakespearean drama to the Elizabethan playhouse. Johnson's Preface makes no reference to the application of theatrical facts to theatrical texts; on the contrary, its emphasis on the reading of plays promises another conventional edition. Yet the Preface also testifies to Johnson's departure from his predecessors, because in it he does not flog the players in customary fashion, and when he discusses the reasons for textual corruption, he shifts responsibility to Shakespeare's style, the transcribers, the copiers, and the printing house.[14] What the Preface implies, the annotations substantiate. In particular, notes to several plays which themselves discuss or involve theatrical production—*The Taming of the Shrew*, *A Midsummer Night's Dream*, *King Henry v*, *Hamlet*—show how Johnson repeatedly tries to conjure the text as performance in a specific period of theatrical history:

Shrew, Induction. iii. asterisked note to 2nd Player, ". . . accept our duty": "It was in those times the custom of players to travel in companies, and offer their service at great houses." (Vol. III, p. 7)

Dream, I. iv. note 5 to the scene itself: "In this Scene *Shakespear* takes advantage of his knowledge of the theatre, to ridicule the prejudices and competitions of the Players." (Vol. I, p. 100)

Dream, I. iv. note 7 to Quince's advice about using a mask and speaking "small": "This passage shews how the want of women on the old Stage was supplied." (Vol. I, p. 102)

Dream, III. i. asterisked note to the scene itself: "In the time of *Shakespear* there were many companies of players, . . . Of these some were undoubtedly very unskilful and very poor, and it is probable that the design of this Scene was to ridicule their ignorance, and the odd expedients to which they might be driven by the want of proper decorations." (Vol. I, p. 126)

Henry v, Prologue. note 7 to "*And make imaginary puissance*": "This passage shews that *Shakespeare* was fully sensible of the absurdity of shewing battles on the theatre, . . . Nothing can be represented to the eye but by something like it, and *within a wooden* O nothing very like a battle can be exhibited." (Vol. IV, p. 362)

14. Preface of *The Plays of William Shakespeare, in Eight Volumes*, . . . ed. Sam. Johnson (London, 1765), I, xlvi. My citations of Johnson's notes come from this edition.

> *Hamlet*, III. iii. note 6 to *"the groundlings"*: "The meaner people then seem to
> have sat below, as they now sit in the upper gallery, . . ." (Vol. VIII, p. 213)

Of the editors who immediately followed Johnson, George
Steevens and Malone provided the most extensive dramaturgical
notes. By this time, the practice of quoting previous editors served not
as an opportunity to vent precious spleen, but as a technique for
setting out exhaustive scholarship on the text. A great deal of that
scholarship treats the Elizabethan theatre and its conventions. In
addition, Malone's notes refer to his *Historical Account of the Rise and
Progress of the English Stage*, . . . , the indispensable collection of
theatrical evidence which accompanies his edition. This *Account* may
accomplish all the abstract philosophical purposes which Edmund
Burke attributes to such antiquarian pursuits,[15] but its historical value
resides in the detailed impression it creates of the Elizabethan
theatrical milieu. The 1821 James Boswell edition of Malone, which
includes the final edition of *An Historical Account* and variorum notes,
continually brings the plays to life on their own stage, a stage imaged
in many of its particulars. The few samples I shall quote come from
the same plays cited for Johnson in order to illustrate the kinds of
detail and documentation which had become available since 1765:

> *Shrew*, Induction. i. note 6 to 2nd Player, ". . . accept our duty": quotes
> Johnson's note, then adds: "In the fifth Earl of Northumberland's House-
> hold Book, . . . the following article occurs. The book was begun in the year
> 1512:
>
> 'Rewards to Players.
>
> 'Item, to be payd to the said Richard Gowge and Thomas Percy for
> rewards to players for playes playd in Chrystinmas by strangers in my
> house after xxd. every play by estimacion somme xxxiijs. iiijd. Which ys
> appoynted to be paid to the said Richard Gowge and Thomas Percy at the
> said Christynmas in full contentacion of the said rewardys xxxiijs. iiijd.'
> STEEVENS." (Vol. V, p. 367)

> *Dream*, IV. ii. note 1 to Flute's phrase "sixpence a-day, . . .": "Shakspeare has
> already ridiculed the title-page of Cambyses, by Thomas Preston; and here
> he seems to allude to him, or some other person who, like him, had been
> pensioned for his dramatic abilities. Preston acted a part in John Ritwise's
> play of Dido before Queen Elizabeth at Cambridge, in 1564; and the Queen
> was so well pleased, that she bestowed on him a pension of *twenty* pounds a
> year, which is little more than *a shilling a day*. STEEVENS." (Vol. V, p. 307)

15. Edmund Burke's letter on this subject appears in James Boswell's version of *The
Plays and Poems of William Shakespeare*, . . . ed. Edmond Malone (London, 1821), III,
3-4. My citations of Malone come from this edition.

Henry V, Prologue. note 5 to "Within this wooden O": quotes Johnson, M. Mason, Henley, then adds:

"This theatre, like all our ancient ones, was denominated from its sign, viz. *The Globe*, and not from its shape. . . .

Shakspeare, meaning to degrade the stage he was describing, may call it a *cock-pit*, because a *cock-pit* was the most diminutive enclosure present to his mind; or, perhaps, because there was a playhouse called *The Cock-pit*, at which King Henry V. might first have been acted. N.B. From Mr. Henley's own drawing of *The Globe*, the outside of it, at least, appears to have been octagonal. STEEVENS.

"Mr. Steevens's first explanation was the right one. The playhouse called the *Cock-pit* was not built till several years after the appearance of Henry V. See the History of the English Stage, vol. iii. MALONE." (Vol. XVII, pp. 254-255)

Hamlet, III. ii. note 2 to Horatio's phrase "Half a SHARE" and Hamlet's response:

"The actors in our author's time had not annual salaries as at present. The whole receipts of each theatre were divided into shares, of which the proprietors of the theatre, or *house-keepers*, as they were called, had some; and each actor had one or more shares, or part of a share, according to his merit. See The Account of the Ancient Theatres, vol. iii. MALONE." (Vol. VII, p. 365)

III

By the end of the eighteenth century, then, scholarship in England had produced a fairly recognizable sketch of the Elizabethan playhouse, a sketch which would be in divers ways augmented, refined, muddled, and focused over the next two centuries, but never again completely lost. At the same time, contemporary theatrical conditions in England had continued to grow increasingly elaborate, and no one had yet contemplated the actual reconstruction of an Elizabethan stage for the performance of classical plays. That light seems to have dawned first in Germany at the close of the eighteenth century, and for two hundred years thereafter it illumined productions generally scattered in time and place, some of them clustered at the middle and end of the nineteenth century, and around the world wars in the twentieth.

In England, Romantic criticism of Shakespeare consistently adopted the kind of neoclassical attitude expressed by Charles Lamb's well-known statement "that the plays of Shakspeare are less calculated for performance on a stage, than those of almost any other dramatist whatever."[16] As Bradbrook explains, ". . . the main position [of these writers] is the dislike of a representational stage, and the inability to conceive of any other."[17] In Germany, however, the early Romanticists—Adam Müller, August Wilhelm Schlegel, Tieck— conceptualized standards of production for Shakespeare which had no analogues in current German dramaturgy. A movement had begun here, as in England, to restore to the stage Shakespeare's original text uncut and otherwise unmodified. But the German Romanticists, Schlegel in particular, sought authenticity not only of text but also of production. Later, Goethe would pronounce views similar to those of Lamb, Samuel Taylor Coleridge, and William Hazlitt, and the enthusiasm of Friedrich Schelling and of Friedrich Schlegel for Shakespeare would ebb, but by then Tieck had undertaken investigations of the Elizabethan stage which he would carry out in productions of Shakespeare's plays.[18]

Like an unnoticed colossus—and like William Poel at the end of the century—Tieck bestrode fifty years of theatre history. What he lacked in immediate influence, he compensated, through sheer tenacity, in long-range effect: late nineteenth-century German theatre would benefit from his experiments. Early in his multifaceted career "as a champion of culture and education,"[19] Tieck worked out the design of an Elizabethan stage which remained fundamental to his theories and practice throughout. Based on inadequate evidence and certain features of the modern playhouse, this design nevertheless broke with the scenic stage (*Illusionsbühne*) by providing a geometric front stage (*Raumbühne*) with an open rear stage, three tiers, a permanent architectural setting, and as little movable scenery as possible. To realize this plan, Tieck had to remodel existing theatres. The most accomplished of these transformations, Tieck's production of *A Midsummer Night's Dream* at the Neues Palais in Potsdàm (1843), proved successful, soon travelled to Berlin, and served as a model for performances in other German cities. For this production he merged the stage and auditorium, arranged the stage in two tiers with a gallery on top, employed a drop to indicate the single interior, and used no movable

16. "On the Tragedies of Shakespeare, considered with reference to their fitness for Stage Representation," in *Shakespeare Criticism: A Selection, 1623-1840*, introd. D. Nichol Smith (London, 1964), p. 193.
17. Bradbrook, p. 13.
18. My information about the German Romanticists' attitudes towards Shakespeare comes primarily from R. Pascal, *Shakespeare in Germany, 1740-1815* (Cambridge, 1937), pp. 20-36.
19. Edwin H. Zeydel, *Ludwig Tieck, the German Romanticist: A Critical Study* (Princeton, N.J., 1935), p. 247.

scenery. Each tier comprised three square sections for the performance of different scenes.[20]

Ludwig Tieck's reconstruction of the Fortune, 1836. (Pen and ink sketch by the author, from a reproduction of the original in the Munich Theater-museum.)

Tieck's concept of theatre history and his principles, stated as early as the first draft of his never-completed *Buch über Shakespeare* (1794), sound remarkably modern: "Indeed, ever since we tore down the old stage and built a completely unsuitable new one—where we display reality instead of art and fleeting deceptions instead of poetic illusion—we have produced a contradiction which the old dramatists could not have imagined."[21] But his work had little impact in his own time. As one of his biographers explains, Tieck unfairly suffered "the fate of the man of letters who rashly interferes in the business of the theater."[22] Like the academic Romanticist clique from which he emerged, Tieck attracted a small audience and few imitators.

20. Ibid., pp. 266-67, 327-29.
21. Quoted by Rudolph Genée in "Ueber die scenischen Formen Shakespeare's in ihrem Verhältniss zur Bühne seiner Zeit," *SJ*, 26 (1891), 143 (my translation). For another modern statement by Tieck, see Robert Speaight, *Shakespeare on the Stage: An illustrated history of Shakespearian performance* (London, 1973), p. 107.
22. Zeydel, p. 261.

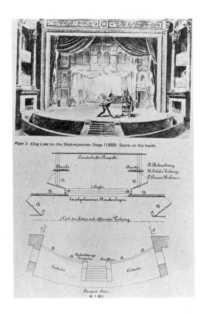

Karl Immermann, a poet, dramatist and producer, belonged to both select groups. A friend of Tieck's, he attempted to carry out the philosophy of theatrical *Echtheit* in some of his own productions which ranged from a relatively unadorned *As You Like It* played in a hall[23] to a *Twelfth Night* performed "in a specially constructed set which, although it professedly aimed at a reproduction of the Shakespearian stage, was strongly reminiscent of the classical-type proscenium of the sixteenth-century Teatro Olimpico at Vincenza—with a long narrow open platform enclosed by a façade broken by four entrance doors and a kind of inner-stage at the rear."[24] Contemporaneously, in London Benjamin Webster presented *The Taming of the Shrew* at the Haymarket (1844) in a production agreeable enough for revival two years later. This performance brought the complete text to the stage for the first time in more than two centuries, "as acted divers times at the Globe and Blackfriars Playhouses, 1606"—that is, as Webster and J. R. Planché understood certain Elizabethan stage conventions, with screens and curtains replacing scenery and spectacle.[25] *The Times* critic made a connection with Tieck:

23. See Richard Fellner, " 'Was Ihr wollt' auf einer neuen Shakespeare-Bühne," *SJ*, 32 (1896), 290-91.
24. Allardyce Nicoll, "Studies in the Elizabethan Stage since 1900," *Shakespeare Survey* I (1948), 2.
25. George C.D. Odell, *Shakespeare from Betterton to Irving* (New York, 1966), II, 267.

It was a suggestion of Tieck's that the plays of Shakspeare should be acted on the sort of stage which existed in the time of Elizabeth and James I, and although the revival at the Haymarket does not exactly follow this suggestion, still it is in the same spirit, and allows the audience to judge of the effect of a play unaided by scenery.[26]

But unlike Tieck, Webster showed little concern for authenticity: "Shakespeare's stagecraft remained a secondary consideration—if it was considered at all."[27]

At the end of the century, a flurry of activity among men of letters and theatre people produced an Elizabethan revival with more stamina than Tieck's in England, Germany, and France. Scholarship has not yet emphasized how all of these projects interconnected. In Germany, Munich hosted an active stage reform movement which purposed to determine and construct a theatre suitable for the performance of classical plays.[28] Behind the Munich stage reform lay Tieck's idea of an

26. 18 March 1844, quoted in ibid., 313.
27. J. L. Styan, *The Shakespeare Revolution: Criticism and Performance in the Twentieth Century* (Cambridge, New York, Melbourne, 1977), p. 20.
28. The Munich reform and its stage are discussed in *Shakespeare Jahrbuch* throughout the 1890s; see especially Eugen Kilian, "Die Münchener Shakespeare-Bühne," *SJ*, 32 (1896), 109-32, and Alfred Frhrn. Mensi v. Klarbach, "Theaterschau. Die Shakespeare-Bühne im Jahre 1893. Zur Geschichte und Kritik der Münchener Bühnenreform," *SJ*, 35 (1899), 362-75.

unadorned stage; an acting space unencumbered by scenery would liberate the spectators' imaginations and allow them to concentrate on drama's most important feature, the spoken word. In 1889 these notions materialized in the Munich Shakespeare stage, erected in the Hoftheater under the supervision of its manager, Karl von Perfall, its director, Jocza Savits, and the design technician, Karl Lautenschläger. Günter Schöne gives a lucid account of the stage's appearance:

> This stage . . . was divided into three parts: an apron, the stage, and the backstage. The orchestra pit was partly covered, and from this bare apron a stairway was built which led from the center into the orchestra pit and below. The actual stage was divided horizontally into two parts by means of a palatial backdrop. This backdrop had a large opening in the center which could be covered with a curtain, and on the right and left were two doors. In the upper part of the drop was a row of arches which could serve as the upper stage. The opening in the center led by means of three steps to the backstage which was surrounded by painted back-cloths.[29]

This well-known experiment, clearly the product of compromise between the Elizabethan stage and modern theatrical conventions, maintained strong academic ties throughout its existence. Initiated by scholars, it provoked debate among them through the turn of the century, especially in *Shakespeare Jahrbuch*. The experiment ended by 1906, but it influenced others: for example, the Kunstlertheater in Munich (1908) and Fritz Schumacher's production of *Hamlet* in Dresden (1909).[30] More important, it influenced Poel, who had seen Savits' production of *King Lear* in 1890 and found it "the best cast and the most stimulating performance of the tragedy I have ever seen."[31] Afterwards, Poel corresponded with Savits and met with him twice.[32] According to Edward M. Moore,

> . . . this production apparently gave Poel much of his impetus. . . . Heretofore he had only directed readings of the plays and the 1603 *Hamlet* twelve years previously. He now determined a serious attempt to revolutionize staging of Shakespeare in England. Thus *Measure for Measure* began his career; for out of this production came the founding of the Elizabethan Stage Society the following year.[33]

29. Günter Schöne, "Karl Lautenschläger: Reformer of Stage Scenery," in *Innovations in Stage and Theatre Design: Papers of the Sixth Congress International Federation for Theatre Research*, ed. Francis Hodge (New York, 1972), p. 64.
30. Ibid., p. 66. For additional imitations, see Klarbach, 367.
31. Quoted from *Monthly Letters* (London and New York, 1929), in Speaight, p. 108.
32. According to Robert Speaight, *William Poel and the Elizabethan Revival* (Melbourne, London, Toronto, 1954), p. 219.
33. Edward M. Moore, "Willaim Poel," *SQ*, 23 (1972), 27.

Poel's well-documented philosophy and methods had been crystal-lizing since the end of the 1870s. Regarded by Guthrie "as the founder of modern Shakespearean production,"[34] Poel identified his role more precisely in an interview for *The Daily Chronicle* (3 September 1913):

> Some people have called me an archaeologist, but I am not. I am really a modernist. My original aim was just to find out some means of acting Shakespeare naturally and appealingly from the full text as in a modern drama. I found that for this the platform stage was necessary and also some suggestion of the spirit and manners of the time.[35]

During his long career—among other things, he produced a play every year between 1887 and 1914[36]—many reviewers called Poel an archaeologist, a singular irony because his work signalled both the search of twentieth-century theatre for a purer, simpler, more fluid stage and the more specialized quest of scholars for the authentic Shakespearean text by means of its theatrical context. As Harcourt Williams writes, "Poel never abandoned his original conception of Shakespeare as a consummate craftsman of the practical theatre"[37]—a conception radical for its era. Poel aimed to recover the plays by recovering their original conditions of performance: "Actors must endeavour, by a careful and searching study of the text, in its first published form, to originate a method of presentation that shall be just to the poet's dramatic intentions, and conformable to the condi-tions for which the plays were written."[38] The modern playgoer must try to project his mind "within reach of those influences from which the Elizabethan playgoer undoubtedly obtained the greatest enjoy-ment, . . ."[39] Poel once explained: "I started the Elizabethan Stage Society in order to go straight to the Shakespearean text."[40]

Of the conventions which Poel tried to reproduce, the stage itself proved one of his most successful experiments. Designed from the dimensions of the old Fortune Theatre and from the De Witt drawing of the Swan, this stage was constructed in 1893, inaugurated by the

---

34. Tyrone Guthrie, *In Various Directions: A View of Theatre* (London, 1965), p. 64.
35. Quoted in Speaight, *William Poel*, p. 90.
36. M. St Clare Byrne, "Fifty Years of Shakespearian Production: 1898-1948," *Shakespeare Survey* 2 (1949), 4.
37. Quoted from *Theatre and Stage*, ed. Harold Downs (London, 1934), in Sprague, p. 149.
38. From a letter to *The Era*, 30 April 1881, quoted in Styan, p. 52.
39. From "Shakespeare on the Stage in the Elizabethan Manner," *The Times*, 2 June 1905, quoted in Sprague, p. 143.
40. From an interview in *The Observer*, 20 October 1929, quoted in Sprague, p. 148.

production of *Measure for Measure* at the Royalty Theatre, and used by the Elizabethan Stage Society until the Society's auction of its property in 1905. The sale catalogue contains a detailed description of this "UNIQUE MODEL OF THE OLD FORTUNE PLAYHOUSE, having a frontage of 30 feet with a depth of 24 feet. The entire height is 21 feet."[41] With other evidence, the description indicates that from 1893 and after the 1905 sale as well, Poel used a stage that extended beyond the proscenium—a stage that won the support of George Bernard Shaw and generally favourable response from the reviewers, who tended to carp about almost everything else.[42]

Enthoven Collection

MEASURE FOR MEASURE
at the Royalty Theatre, 1893

This illustration shows Poel's reconstruction of the Fortune stage within a proscenium arch

The production of *Measure for Measure* was but one notable event in a theatre history composed of striking innovations: the production of the First Quarto *Hamlet* at St. George's Hall on a raised platform with no scenery (1881); the performance of *Twelfth Night* at the Hall of the Middle Temple (1897); the revival of *The Two Gentlemen of Verona* at His Majesty's with an apron built over the orchestra pit and front lighting installed in the balconies (1910)—innovations retained for

41. Quoted in Arthur J. Harris, "William Poel's Elizabethan Stage: The First Experiment," *TN*, 17 (1963), 111-12.
42. See Harris, 114, and Styan, pp. 57-59.

Beerbohm Tree's *Henry VIII* two years later.[43] *The Times* review of the 1910 revival, appreciating the way Poel's setting enhanced the comedy's quality as a "fantasia" on love, indicates that by this time "it had become commonplace to recognize that Poel's Elizabethanism was no mere archaeological affectation, but of historical importance and answering a public demand."[44] Three years later, the first imitation of Poel's staging methods would appear in Martin Harvey's production of *The Taming of the Shrew* at the Prince of Wales. By 1927, the year of Poel's last experiment with an Elizabethan platform, Ivor Brown stated in *The Saturday Review* that "the better type of Shakespearean presentation to-day is simply Poel popularized without acknowledgments."[45] Later, Brown epitomized Poel's remarkable achievement:

> The Elizabethan platform was not only far larger than the average modern stage, but its triple division gave scope for swift alternations from one plane to another, both in structure and in temper. As soon as Mr Poel recreates his platform-stage he recreates the flow, the rhythm, and the energy of Elizabethan drama.[46]

Poel's influence in France became perceptible at about the same time that English productions began to use his techniques. However, Aurélien Lugné-Poe, having met Poel during a visit to London, imported "Shakespeare sans décors" to France in an article for the *Nouvelle Revue* (1897):

> I wanted to be among the first to bring into France an echo of these entertainments . . . Mr. William Poel and Mr. Arthur Dillon, the two founders of the [Elizabethan Stage] Society, deserve the gratitude of those who love the bare and simple work of art, and I thank them here in the name of all those who admire Shakespeare for having taught a Frenchman wanting to follow in the footsteps of the Elizabethan Stage Society.[47]

Lugné-Poe applied this lesson in a production of *Measure for Measure* (1898) which received lukewarm reviews and faded from view with the notions it embodied. It took fifteen years before these ideas

---

43. For concentrated summaries of these highlights, see Moore, 21-36; Speaight, *Shakespeare on the Stage*, pp. 132-39; and Styan's chapter "Mr Poel's 'Hamlet,'" pp. 47-63.
44. Styan, p. 62.
45. My chronology derives from Speaight, *William Poel*, p. 246. The comment by Brown is from "Salute to William Poel," *The Saturday Review*, 16 July 1927, quoted in Styan, p. 62.
46. Quoted from *The Saturday Review*, 18 February 1928, in ibid., p. 63.
47. Quoted in Robert Davril, "Les Pionniers," *EA*, 13 (1960), 167 (my translation).

reappeared, taking root in the theories of Jacques Copeau (*N.R.F.,* September 1913, "Un Essai de Rénovation dramatique").[48] However, other developments in France and England at the end of the nineteenth century anticipated uses of the Elizabethan stage current today. For the Elizabethan theatre, another period of transition had begun.

IV

Like the rest of this history, the most recent part illustrates a commonplace well stated by Guthrie: ". . . Shakespearean production does not operate in a vacuum. All the time it is being influenced by the general prevailing cultural climate and by the particular trends and fashions of theatrical productions."[49] Until the turn of the century that climate, those trends and fashions, rarely accommodated the staging of plays by means of Elizabethan conventions. Tieck, the early Poel, Lugné-Poe, and the Munich stage reform movement countered a dramaturgical tide of spectacle and realism; they emphasized rhythm, movement, and sound in a theatre grown statically pictorial. From its inception, however, the twentieth century has frequently reacted against theatrical verisimilitude and the proscenium arch. Modern taste, influenced for better or worse by cinematic practices and other technological features of the contemporary world,[50] no longer demands realism from the stage. Modern theatre, thus freed to enter an "anti-illusion phase,"[51] can now stress its own theatricality, and with various devices remind the audience that they attend a work of art. During the course of these changes, stagecraft has grown increasingly self-conscious and philosophical. Playwrights and directors write about their purposes, and repeatedly they describe their search for pure theatre, a symbolic mode which depends upon gestures and words, simple décor, fluid action and space, and contiguity with the audience. Clearly, pure theatre embraces the essential qualities of Elizabethan dramatic performance.

Not surprisingly, therefore, many well-known reformers of the modern stage have looked to Elizabethan theatre for a model. Some of these reformers, especially in France, justify their choice of standard by recounting the historical, psychological, and aesthetic affinities

48. Ibid., 167-68.
49. Guthrie, p. 65.
50. For a summary of some of the latter, see John Russell Brown, *Free Shakespeare* (London, 1974), p. 28.
51. Richard Southern, *The Seven Ages of the Theatre* (New York, 1961), p. 275.

they perceive between the English Renaissance and the present moment.[52] Whatever the rationale, they borrow lineaments and conventions of the Elizabethan playhouse in creating their own theatrical events. As early as 1896, in a revolutionary production, Alfred Jarry and Lugné-Poe purposely incorporated Elizabethan elements into the stagecraft of *Ubu Roi*: a single, unlocalized *mise en scène* and movable props which would allow "each spectator to see in the décor the scene which accords with his own perception."[53] Antonin Artaud's "notions of the theater derive[d] to some extent from his study of the Elizabethans, and he . . . [dreamed] of reviving them as part of his projected reform of the stage."[54] Other French reformers, from André Antoine to Copeau and the Cartel to Jean Vilar, have discovered through performances of Shakespeare and other Elizabethans a simplified *mise en scène* and continuity of action. As one critic writes: "One asks oneself, actually, what would have happened to the development of the French stage if Shakespeare and the discovery of Elizabethan stage conditions had not inspired men like Lugné-Poe."[55] Interestingly, Copeau's work, influenced by Harley Granville Barker's Savoy productions of *The Winter's Tale* and *A Midsummer Night's Dream* (1912 and 1914),[56] received extensive review by Barker in 1921[57]—an exchange representative of the cross-fertilization of ideas which distinguishes the modern theatre. Peter Brook epitomizes not only this process, but also the twentieth-century disposition to conceptualize stagecraft in Elizabethan terms; typically he advises: "One must be very prudent so that in putting walls around a theatre, one does not create illusion and artifice. In the Elizabethan theatre, there is a wall, but it is like the wall of a courtyard, a wall so natural that life appears more concentrated but not denatured."[58]

52. See, for example, Paul Blanchart, "Le Théâtre contemporain et les Élisabéthains," *EA*, 13 (1960), 145-58. In England and the United States, the critics tend to make this connection: see, for example, Bradbrook, pp. 114-15; Nicoll, 16; and Jonas A. Barish, "The New Theater and the Old: Reversions and Rejuvenations," in *Reinterpretations of Elizabethan Drama*, ed. Norman Rabkin (New York and London, 1969), pp. 30-31.
53. Quoted from Jarry's "De l'inutilité du théâtre au théâtre" (in *Tout Ubu*, ed. Maurice Saillet [Paris, 1962]) in K. S. Beaumont, "The Making of Ubu: Jarry as Producer and Theorist," *ThR*, 12 (1972), 149 (my translation).
54. Barish, p. 1.
55. Davril, 171 (my translation).
56. See Helena Robin Slaughter, "Jacques Copeau: metteur en scène de Shakespeare et des Élisabéthains," *EA*, 13 (1960), 180.
57. Speaight, *Shakespeare on the Stage*, pp. 186-89.
58. From an interview with Peter Brook prepared by Isidoro Romero and Richard Marienstras for l'Institut National de l'Audio-visuel (1974-1975), quoted in Richard Marienstras, "La représentation et l'interprétation du texte," in *Les voies de la création théâtrale*, edd. Denis Bablet and Jean Jacquot (Paris, 1977), v, 17 (my translation).

The evolution of this brave new world provided the ideal atmosphere for what J. L. Styan calls "the Shakespeare revolution," that is, "The search . . . for the theatrical effect and experience of the original performance, . . ."[59] Both the theatre and scholarship sought this particular kind of authenticity,[60] but they usually followed Tieck and Poel with a difference, in a less academic exercise. Although influenced by Poel, therefore, Barker modified the earlier, more antiquarian approach and conceived a well-known fundamental principle which would govern many twentieth-century productions of Shakespeare: ". . . Gain Shakespeare's effects by Shakespeare's means when you can; for, plainly, this will be the better way. But gain Shakespeare's effects; and it is your business to discern them."[61] In his own productions at the Savoy—*The Winter's Tale, Twelfth Night, A Midsummer Night's Dream*—Barker used basic conventions of the Elizabethan playhouse; the simple, fluid setting and the stage projecting into the auditorium helped him to achieve his aim of transferring illusion "to the subliminal region of the actors' interpretation of the play."[62]

After his *Dream*, a series of famous disciples carried out Barker's principles: Barry Jackson at the Birmingham Repertory Theatre; W. Bridges-Adams at the Stratford-upon-Avon Shakespeare Festival; Lewis Casson, with his wife Sybil Thorndike; Robert Atkins at the Old Vic; Harcourt Williams at the Old Vic.[63] The objects of their quest remained constant: ". . . simple settings, speedy playing, continuity of action, reliance on teamwork, and unabridged texts. . . ."[64] Simultaneously, a few directors followed Poel, attempting to reproduce with some exactness the *ambiance* and structure of the Elizabethan playhouse: for instance, Atkins extended the forestage of the Old Vic over the orchestra pit; later, Guthrie emphasized the thrust even more by adding curved steps from the pit to the apron; Michel Saint-Denis made other adjustments to this forestage; and Nugent Monck remodelled an old Georgian building in Norwich into the Maddermarket Theatre, a very small playhouse, Elizabethan in style, with a stage based on that of the old Fortune.[65] But according

59. Styan, p. 9.
60. For modern trends in theatre and scholarship, see Bradbrook's third chapter, "Shakespearean Criticism—Twentieth Century," pp. 19-28; Werner Habicht, "Shakespeare im Buch und auf der Bühne," *Anglia*, 96 (1978), 349-70; and Styan, *passim.*
61. Harley Granville-Barker, *Prefaces to Shakespeare* (Princeton, N.J., 1978), I, 23.
62. Harley Granville-Barker, *The Exemplary Theatre* (London, 1922), p. 211.
63. Styan, pp. 105-106.
64. Byrne, 10.
65. Styan, pp. 123-24.

to Styan, "These developments were straws in the wind."[66] The more important productions, such as those of Nigel Playfair at the Lyric Theatre, Hammersmith, and of Jackson at the Birmingham Repertory Theatre, did not employ reconstructions of the Elizabethan theatre; rather, they adapted those features of the English Renaissance play-house which would most clearly reveal Elizabethan texts to modern audiences.[67]

Representing the latter development, Guthrie's career began in the 1920s, a period which belonged to the continuum when experiments with the open staging of Shakespeare grew increasingly widespread and varied. Terence Gray's Cambridge Festival Theatre, the Ashland Festival, the San Diego summer productions, Atkins' adaptation of a Blackfriars boxing stadium, and the Harrow School annual productions—all of these animated this era of prolific innovation which spanned over two decades.[68] Guthrie's first celebrated experiments—*Hamlet* in the ballroom of a Danish hotel (1937) and Sir David Lindsay's *Ane Pleasant Satyre of the Thrie Estaites* in the adapted Kirk Assembly Hall at the Edinburgh Festival (1948)—have become familiar theatre history. In their own time, they strengthened Guthrie's developing conviction "that no radical advance in the production of Shakespeare would be possible until we could create a stage which resembled, far more nearly than the Old Vic or any other proscenium theatre, the sort of stage for which the plays were written."[69] As a result, they contributed to the creation of the Stratford Festival stage in Ontario (1953).

When Tanya Moiseiwitsch designed this stage in the early 1950s, experimentation with open stages poised at the edge of frenzy. Walter Kerr, the prominent theatre critic who covered New York at that point, noticed the "restless, half-understood drive toward another kind of theatrical experience" reflected in the generation of off-Broadway performances on improvised platforms that allowed a new, close relationship with audiences: he reviewed one such production in 1951, forty-six in 1957; he could have reviewed eighty or more in 1959.[70] On Broadway, he reported, directors improvised aprons and

66. Ibid., p. 125.
67. Ibid., pp. 125 ff.
68. Ibid., pp. 185-87.
69. Guthrie, p. 66.
70. Walter Kerr, "The Theater Breaks Out of Belasco's Box," *Horizon*, I (1959), 42. On the revival of interest in the Elizabethan stage in the 1950s, see also Richard Southern, *The Open Stage and the Modern Theatre in Research and Practice* (London, 1953), p. 25.

Jill L. Levenson

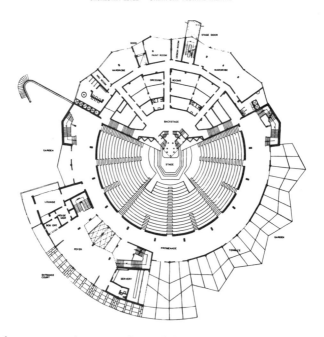

raked stages, "so determined . . . [did they] seem to dump the players —and the play—into our laps."[71] Guthrie's new stage not only met his own standards for the production of Shakespeare, but also fulfilled the obvious craving for open stagecraft and intimacy between actors and audience. Addressing the Shakespeare Stage Society in 1952, he argued: *"There will be no drastic improvement in staging Shakespeare until there is a return to certain basic conditions of the Shakespeare stage. There is no need for an exact replica of the Globe Theatre, but it is essential to make the contact between players and audience as intimate as possible."*[72] He therefore proposed a structure "embodying the functional but not the decorative features of an Elizabethan Theatre,"[73] a playhouse allowing fluidity of staging and involvement of the audience in the experience of the play; and Moiseiwitsch realized his proposal in a modified Elizabethan stage—a permanent structure with balcony, trapdoors, seven acting levels and nine major entrances—finally set within a steeply sloped Greek-inspired amphitheatre which surrounds it on

71. Kerr, 42-44.
72. Quoted in James R. Aikens, *"This Unworthy Scaffold"*: *The Story of the Festival Stage* (Stratford, Ont., 1972), [p. 3]. (This brochure is an unpaginated insert in the 1972 souvenir program for the Festival.)
73. Quoted in ibid., [p. 3].

three sides with a 220-degree sweep and which places all 2,300 spectators within a 65-foot radius from the stage.[74] With this structure, Kerr declared, "We were, all of us, players and playgoers alike, at last in the same building. The actors were doing most of the work, as usual, but we were engaged in a communal and reciprocal experience, . . ."[75]

As Stratford Festival programs show, Guthrie's theatre worked not only for classical productions but also for modern, not only for drama but also for music, ballet, and mime. In addition to clear-cut economic advantages, it enjoyed the aesthetic benefits of improved acoustics and sight-lines. Its manifold success quickly inspired imitation in the English-speaking world "with its particular heritage of plays based on Speech"[76]: Chichester, the Delacorte in New York, the Guthrie in Minneapolis, the Vivian Beaumont at Lincoln Center, the Mark Taper Forum in Los Angeles, and the Crucible in Sheffield all followed the lead of the Festival Theatre, experimenting with its design and stagecraft.[77] The promotional literature and programs of these theatres, some of which include multi-purpose stages, tend to echo Guthrie's principles; from Ottawa to Eastern Australia, they promise scenic simplicity, fluid staging, and intimacy.

While the Stratford Festival Theatre continues to serve as an important model, the 1970s brought forth a new kind of experiment in Elizabethan stagecraft: reconstructions of the Globe Theatre based as precisely as possible upon what is known of the original. Like Guthrie's innovations, these have existed only in the English-speaking world. Of the three originally in progress, the project in Detroit, Michigan, reached the most advanced state, it acquired architects' diagrams, a budget, and a plan of implementation. In Victoria, British Columbia, an investment consortium known as the Lord Chamberlain Players Society negotiated for a site on which to build a replica of the Globe within a replica of an Elizabethan village. This project had a budget, but no precise schedule. Finally, Sam Wanamaker, the American actor and director, has undertaken at least since the early 1970s "To construct a third Globe Playhouse on or near its original site within a comprehensive development concept appropriate for the area";[78] among other things, he expects to produce

---

74. *Stratford Festival Story* (Stratford, Ont., 1980), p. 4.
75. Kerr, 45.
76. Southern, *Seven Ages of the Theatre*, p. 287.
77. Styan, p. 201.
78. From "What it's all about: Declaration of purpose," *The Bankside Globe*, 1 (1973), 5.

the plays of Shakespeare and his contemporaries in this theatre. Various difficulties, most of them economic, forced this idea into seclusion mid-decade, but Wanamaker has recently begun again to promote his plan, raising money and gathering academic support. The spokesmen for these three projects have all described their plans as the realization of a dream, a conception which goes back to Tieck. Of the three schemes, Detroit and Southwark rely on the advice of scholars and trace their origins to a proposal made in the 1971 World Shakespeare Congress in Vancouver; Victoria, less academic, depended upon the researches of Mr. Barry Morse, an actor belonging to its consortium, and the suggestions of architects. None of the three has emphasized the part actors will play in their theatrical ventures.

Like Guthrie's theatre, the reproductions stimulate some fundamental theatrical questions. In the 1950s, his adapted Elizabethan playhouse provoked consideration of important principles and those features of theatrical architecture which "recur most often, most spontaneously, and most profitably"; it suggested that one shape might be better than another, producing both "better relations between actors and audiences . . . [and] also better plays."[79] At the present moment, the reconstructions immediately raise more urgent and practical questions. Can this antiquarian dream materialize in inflationary times when building such a theatre costs in excess of $13 million, when touring a company like the Stratford Festival's requires more than $70,000 per week, and when North American and British cities face bankruptcy and severe cutbacks in subsidies to the arts? Can any city now justify the expense of a playhouse whose theatrical purposes are singular and limited? What will a replica accomplish that the modified playhouses have not already achieved? Moreover, can an Elizabethan structure with its rectangular stage, few entrances, poor sight-lines, and crowded conditions work for modern actors and audiences? To what extent can twentieth-century amenities be introduced before the replica turns into an adaptation?

Those who promote the replicas have various motives: the Victoria consortium envisaged profitable investment in a scheme analogous to Canada's Wonderland; the Detroit and Southwark planners stress more scholarly ideals. And in the end, the restorations signify a dream more scholarly and philosophic than theatrical or down-to-earth. Since the eighteenth century, critics and editors have sought access to Shakespeare's texts, and experimenting in a replica of Shakespeare's

---

79. Kerr, 45. I want to thank Mr. Nicholas Pennell of the Stratford Festival company for suggesting to me the key questions that arise about the reconstructions.

theatre promises a degree of enlightenment not yet attained. As well, a reconstructed Globe would objectify in a historically validated form lessons in theatrical architecture which the twentieth century has learned to value. And perhaps the Elizabethan playhouse has grown during our era into a symbol of the "communal and reciprocal experience" which theatre can offer—has offered in the past—and which fails to distinguish most other aspects of modern life. The people who think about these texts, these values, and these expe-iences—scholars and critics like John Russell Brown—long to make the symbol concrete, to see revived the "marvelous reality, tangibility, *touchability*" of Shakespeare's theatre.[80] Our century may be witness-ing the transformation of the Elizabethan playhouse from a concept to an icon.

---

80. *The Third Globe*, ed. C. Walter Hodges, S. Schoenbaum, and Leonard Leone (Detroit, 1981), p. 28.

The Contributors

RANDOM CLOUD (RANDALL McLEOD), Associate Professor of English, University of Toronto. Author of 'Gon. No more, the text is foolish.' in *The Division of the Kingdoms*, and other articles.

ALAN C. DESSEN, Professor of English, University of North Carolina at Chapel Hill. Author of *Elizabethan Stage Conventions and Modern Interpreters*, and other books and articles.

RONALD HUEBERT, Associate Professor of English, Dalhousie University. Author of *John Ford: Baroque English Dramatist*, and various articles.

T. J. KING, Professor of English, City College of the City University of New York. Author of *Shakespearean Staging, 1599-1642*, and other studies.

JILL L. LEVENSON, Professor of English, University of Toronto. Editor of *Modern Drama*, and author of various articles.

JERZY LIMON, Lecturer in English Literature, University of Gdansk. Author of 'Pictorial Evidence for a Possible Replica of the London Fortune Theatre in Gdansk', and other articles.

BARBARA A. MOWAT, Director of Academic Programs, Folger Shakespeare Library, and Editor, *Shakespeare Quarterly*. Author of *The Dramaturgy of Shakespeare's Romances*, and various articles.

D. F. ROWAN, Professor of English, University of New Brunswick. Author of 'The Cockpit-in-Court', and other articles.

HERBERT WEIL, Professor of English, University of Manitoba. Author of 'The Options of the Audiences: Theory and Practice in Peter Brook's "Measure for Measure"', and other articles.

Index

231